ISBN 978-1-5278-9569-0
PIBN 10927026

English
Français
Deutsche
Italiano
Español
Português

www.forgottenbooks.com

Mythology Photography **Fiction**
Fishing Christianity **Art** Cooking
Essays Buddhism Freemasonry
Medicine **Biology** Music **Ancient
Egypt** Evolution Carpentry Physics
Dance Geology **Mathematics** Fitness
Shakespeare **Folklore** Yoga Marketing
Confidence Immortality Biographies
Poetry **Psychology** Witchcraft
Electronics Chemistry History **Law**
Accounting **Philosophy** Anthropology
Alchemy Drama Quantum Mechanics
Atheism Sexual Health **Ancient History**
Entrepreneurship Languages Sport
Paleontology Needlework Islam
Metaphysics Investment Archaeology
Parenting Statistics Criminology
Motivational

THE
MISSES O'CONNOR'S SCHOOL
FOR GIRLS.

(ESTABLISHED TWENTY YEARS.)

DUPORTH, OXLEY.

This School offers all the comforts of a refined Country Home together with the advantage of the best Teaching procurable in Brisbane.

The object of the School is to train Girls to be cultivated, capable Gentlewomen.

The House is situated on a hill eight miles south of Brisbane. Though open to sea breezes, it is protected by trees from westerly winds. The Grounds are extensive and well laid out, including Tennis Courts, Playground, Flower and Vegetable Gardens, Orchard, Poultry Yard, and Paddocks.

Certificated Teachers reside in the House, and Teachers from Brisbane attend daily to give lessons in Languages, Music, &c.

TERMS ON APPLICATION.

GUIDE

TO

QUEENSLAND.

Compiled from Official and Private Records, with the recognition of

THE HON. SIR HORACE TOZER, K.C.M.G.,

AGENT-GENERAL FOR QUEENSLAND,

BY

CHARLES SCHAEFER RUTLIDGE, F.R.G.S., F R.C.I.

LONDON:
DEAN & SON, LIMITED, 160a, FLEET STREET, E.C.

Right Hon. LORD LAMINGTON, K.C.M.G., F.R.G.S., &c.,
Governor and Commander-in-Chief of the Colony of Queensland.

(Reproduced by kind permission of the proprietors of the *British Australasian.*)

DEDICATED

BY SPECIAL PERMISSION

TO THE

RT. HON. LORD LAMINGTON, K.C.M.G., F.R.G.S., &c.,

GOVERNOR OF QUEENSLAND.

PREFACE.

THE opening of an extensive display of minerals from the Colony of Queensland, together with a collection of agricultural and industrial products, in the Queensland Court, Greater Britain Exhibition, Earl's Court, London, has been considered a favourable opportunity for the publication of the following pages, which embrace a careful revision of the earlier edition and the addition of much matter which has been considered essential to the character of a "Guide." A special feature in this connection is the fairly copious index which has been prepared, by which the value of the information has been much enhanced.

The limits of the work having precluded any attempt to produce an exhaustive guide to the Colony, the endeavours of the writer have rather been directed towards presenting to the inquirer such information respecting the climatic, social, and industrial conditions of the country, the resources and prospects of agricultural and mineral production, and the most recent legislation regarding mining and land, as will be of service to the investor on this side, or to those who intend to make their home in the Colony.

Wherever possible, the figures have been brought up to the close of 1898; the acknowledged difficulty of obtaining official figures at so early a date has prevented this being done as fully as could have been desired.

The author desires to express, as before, his warmest thanks to the various Heads of Departments and other Government officials who by their courtesy have lightened the work of production, and to the numerous authorities quoted.

The Queensland National Bank,
LIMITED.

Incorporated under " The Companies Act, 1863," of the
Legislature of Queensland.

BANKERS TO THE QUEENSLAND GOVERNMENT.

Subscribed Capital, £800,000.   Paid-up Capital, £412,433.

Interminable Inscribed Deposit Stock, £3,116,619.

Under Government Audit.

All new Business since 1893 protected under Clause 9 of the Scheme of Arrangement.

COLONIAL BOARD.	LONDON BOARD.
JAMES MUNRO, Esq., Chairman.	CHARLES EDWARD BARNETT, Esq.
A. J. CALLAN, Esq., M.L.A.	SIR EDWYN SANDYS DAWES, K.C.M.G.
JOHN CAMERON, Esq.	HON. VICARY GIBBS, M.P.
JAMES MILNE, Esq.	ROBERT MUTER STEWART, Esq.
G. S. MURPHY, Esq.	REGINALD HOPE SPENS, Esq.

HEAD OFFICE, BRISBANE.
General Manager—WALTER VARDON RALSTON.

LONDON OFFICE, 8, PRINCES STREET, E.C.
Manager—J. W. DICKINSON.

BANKERS.
BANK OF ENGLAND, LLOYD'S BANK, LIMITED.
Auditors—MESSRS. JACKSON, PIXLEY, BROWNING HUSEY & CO.

BRANCHES.
SYDNEY, NEW SOUTH WALES. QUEENSLAND.

ALBION.	DALBY.	MUTTABURRA.
ALLORA.	FORTITUDE VALLEY.	NORMANTON.
BARCALDINE.	GERALDTON.	PITTSWORTH.
BLACKALL.	GYMPIE.	PORT DOUGLAS.
BOONAH.	HALIFAX.	RAVENSWOOD.
BUNDABERG.	HERBERTON.	ROCKHAMPTON.
BURKETOWN.	HUGHENDEN.	ROMA.
CAIRNS.	INGHAM.	SANDGATE.
CHARLEVILLE.	IPSWICH.	SOUTH BRISBANE.
CHARTERS TOWERS.	ISISFORD.	THARGOMINDAH.
CLIFTON.	LAIDLEY.	THURSDAY ISLAND.
CLONCURRY.	LONGREACH.	TOOWOOMBA.
COOKTOWN.	MACKAY.	TOWNSVILLE.
CROYDON.	MARYBOROUGH.	WARWICK.
CUNNAMULLA.	MOUNT MORGAN.	WINTON.

AGENCIES.

VICTORIA—National Bank of Australasia.	SAN FRANCISCO—Bank of California.
SOUTH AUSTRALIA—National Bank of Australasia.	SCOTLAND—Royal Bank of Scotland.
	„ British Linen Company Bank.
WESTERN AUSTRALIA—National Bank of Australasia.	IRELAND—Ulster Bank, Limited.
NEW ZEALAND—Bank of New Zealand.	INDIA AND CHINA — Hongkong and Shanghai Banking Corporation.
TASMANIA—Bank of Australasia.	„ Chartered Bank of India, Australia, and China.
NEW YORK—Messrs. Laidlaw & Co.	
BERLIN—Deutsche Bank.	„ Mercantile Bank of India, Limited.
COPENHAGEN—Landmandsbank.	

AGENTS IN SCOTLAND AND IRELAND :—EDINBURGH—Messrs. Torrie, Brodie &
Maclagan, 25A, St. Andrew Square. GLASGOW—Messrs. Wm. Ewing & Co.,
45, Renfield Street. DUNDEE—Messrs. Andrew Hendry & Sons, 85, Murraygate.
DUBLIN—Messrs. Guinness, Mahon & Co., 17, College Green.

The Bank grants DRAFTS on all the above Branches and Agencies, also TELE-
GRAPHIC TRANSFERS, and transacts every description of Banking Business in
connection with Queensland and other Australian Colonies on the most favourable
terms.

The London Office receives Deposits for fixed periods at rates which can be
ascertained on application.

CONTENTS.

QUEENSLAND.

GOVERNMENT LAND

Has recently been thrown open to Selection in all parts of
the Colony, in—

AGRICULTURAL HOMESTEADS.

The area to be selected varies with the quality of the land, from
160, 320, to 640 acres, at 2s. 6d. per acre, payment extending over
10 years.

AGRICULTURAL FARMS.

Area up to 1,280 acres, at 10s. per acre upwards, payment extending
over 20 years.

GRAZING SELECTIONS.

Farms and Homesteads in areas up to 20,000 acres, on 14, 21, and
28 years' lease, at annual rent of ½d. per acre upwards.

SCRUB SELECTIONS.

These are divided into four classes (according to quantity of timber
on land to be cleared), area of each up to 10,000 acres, lease for
30 years; no rent for first 5, 10, 15, or 20 years, according to class,
remaining periods ½d. and 1d. per annum per acre.

UNCONDITIONAL SELECTIONS.

Up to 1,280 acres, the purchase of the freehold being from 13s. 4d.
per acre upward, payable in 20 annual instalments.

AGRICULTURAL LANDS PURCHASE ACT.

Large Freehold Estates of choice agricultural land are also being
bought by the Government, surveyed into Farms ranging from
40 to 640 acres, in various favoured localities, for the purpose of
bringing about close settlement. These lands are sold on an
extended payment of 20 years, and become the freehold by payment practically of £7 19s. a year for every £100 of the purchasing
price. Should the purchaser desire to secure his freehold earlier,
he can do so by paying the remaining instalments of principal,
together with ¼ per cent. for interest.

Free Passages to Queensland are now granted to Farm Labourers
and Female Domestic Servants who have always been engaged as such,
from seventeen to thirty-five years for Single and to forty-five years for
Married Persons. Applicants must be seen by an authorized agent, and
must pay £1 for ship-kits.

RATES OF PASSAGE BY QUEENSLAND LINE
OF STEAMERS.

Agents: Messrs. GRAY, DAWES & CO., 23, Great Winchester Street, London, E.C.

Open Berths, each, including Ship-kits	£13 13	0
Closed Cabins, four Berths, each	16 16	0
Closed Cabins, two Berths, each	17 17	0

STEAMERS LEAVE LONDON FORTNIGHTLY FOR QUEENSLAND.

For Pamphlets and all other information apply—
AGENT-GENERAL, 1, VICTORIA STREET, LONDON, S.W.

LIST OF ILLUSTRATIONS.

— THE —
UNION BANK OF AUSTRALIA,
LIMITED.

ESTABLISHED 1837.   INCORPORATED 1880.

Paid-up Capital, £1,500,000 Reserve Funds, £750,000 ·· Together	£2,250,000
Reserve Liability of Proprietors ·· ··· ·· ·· ·· ··	3,000,000
Total Capital and Reserves ·· ·· ·· ·· ·· ·· ··	£5,250,000

HEAD OFFICE—71, CORNHILL, LONDON, E.C.

BRANCHES IN QUEENSLAND.

BRISBANE.   BUNDABERG.   CHARTERS TOWERS.

GYMPIE.   MACKAY.   MARYBOROUGH.

PITTSWORTH.   ROCKHAMPTON.

TOOWOOMBA.   TOWNSVILLE.

The Bank has also Branches throughout the principal Cities
and Towns of Australia and New Zealand.

Letters of Credit and **Bills of Exchange** upon the Branches are
issued by the Head Office, and may also be obtained from the Bank's
Agents throughout England, Scotland, and Ireland.

Telegraphic Remittances are made to the Colonies.

Bills on the Colonies are purchased or sent for collection.

Deposits are received at Head Office at rates of interest, and for
periods, which may be ascertained on application.

W. R. MEWBURN, *Manager.*

OCTOBER, 1898.

PART I.

Progress, and Range of Natural Resources.

IN the Statistics of Queensland is found matter for deep reflection and much encouragement, as evincing the past productiveness and *enormous* possibilities of our Natural Resources.

When it is seen that in less than fifty years we have increased our exports from £72,000 odd—the product of the then outlying settlement of Moreton Bay — to £10,079,000; that since the separation of Queensland from New South Wales in 1859 (when the population of the former was about 25,000) we have increased nearly nineteen fold; that amongst Australasian Colonies we lead in sugar production, are second in pastoral matters and weight of gold produced, whilst third in point of size; when to all this is added the fact that ours was the last one of the group which was made a separate colony, the mind can but vaguely conjecture the enormous possibilities which lie before us. Next to Western Australia this colony has the most extensive coast line of any of the divisions of Australasia, it being some 2,200 to 2,500 miles in extent, thus affording unlimited facilities for international commerce in the varied products of the interior.

Whilst more generally explored than the larger colonies of Western Australia and South Australia, Queensland possesses in the far interior potentialities for wealth which are unknown to the average colonist— certainly undreamed of by the rest of the world.

Artesian bores—upon a modest estimate yielding a total daily flow of 200,000,000 gallons — have already changed the aspect of life in the western country, and will prove an important factor in the close settlement of some of the most fertile of our land, of which the chief drawback has hitherto been an irregular water supply.

The total area of the colony is 427,838,080 acres, of which barely one-thirtieth part (viz., 14,626,876 acres) is alienated, or in course of alienation, besides 254,787,200 acres which are held under pastoral lease, constituting an effective area of 269,414,076 acres, which shows an unappropriated area of 158,424,004 acres for pastoral and agricultural occupa-

B

tions. Geographically considered, Queensland extends from S. lat. 28° 8′ to lat. 10° 30′, and from E. long. 153° 30′ to 138°, and is thus about equally divided on the map by the tropic of Capricorn. Outside the tropical line the most perfect climatic conditions may be met with, whilst practically the whole of the colony. may be said to be healthy and eminently adapted for a white population, as shown by the vital statistics of the year 1896, which give a death-rate of only 12·01 per 1,000 (taking the fourth lowest place in Australia), *far lower* than that of the United Kingdom of Great Britain and Ireland, which stands at something like 21·00 per 1,000 persons, or that of Europe generally, the mean average of which is much higher still. In this connection may be mentioned the very high birth-rate as compared with that of the adjacent colonies, being 30·1 per 1,000 (1896) against 28·5 per 1,000 in South Australia—the next in order of precedence—and 22·7 per 1,000 in Western Australia.

These are mighty factors in the prosperity of any State, a prosperity which in the case of Queensland is largely evinced by the high marriage rate for the same year, viz., 6·05 (couples) per 1,000. By comparison with the rates of the other six Australasian colonies for a period of thirty years it will be seen that we take first place, the mean average for Queensland being about 8·61, whilst that for New South Wales and New Zealand was respectively 7·91 and 7·63. When it is remembered that the second colony has now been established 111 years, or three times as long as our own, inducing a stability largely tending to an entrance into the marriage state (although she no longer holds the premier position in that respect, as in 1893–4), it must be conceded that Queensland can hold her own with any country in the world—age being taken into consideration. We find that the area of the Colony is equal to something under one and a half square miles per head of population, whilst New South Wales has one inhabitant to each quarter of a square mile, and Victoria has rather more than thirteen inhabitants per square mile. Assuming, therefore, that in point of productiveness (as is shown by intercolonial statistics) we are not far behind these last-mentioned colonies, there is room and to spare for from three million to eight million new-comers !

Stupendous as has been the progress of some of the older colonies, our 1896 returns show that amongst the colonies we take third place in the matter of exports. In relation to population this amounts to £19 13s. per head, a figure considerably over those for Victoria, Western Australia, and New Zealand ; indeed, with the single exception of South Australia (including Northern Territory), we are admittedly the largest exporters

B 2

'Red Letter' Day with the Blacks: Waiting for the Distribution of Blankets.

per head of population, and only need an increased population to out-distance all the other colonies. Speaking of South Australia, a glance at the figures, discloses the fact that in 1896 the exports exceeded imports by £433,284, whereas, in the case of Queensland, the excess of exports over imports in 1896 reached the substantial sum of £3,730,455 (the imports per head being £11 13s.), which somewhat discounts the position held by South Australia as heading the list of exports per cap.! Our own *imports per cap.* for the same year were all but the lowest of the group, thus proving conclusively our superior ability to support a large population. In 1898 the excess of exports over imports was £4,199,000.

Apart from figures, however, a trip through Queensland is sufficient to convince the most sceptical of her vast resources and climatic advantages over many a field for emigration which at present is at the zenith of public favour. The colony extends northward from the boundary of New South Wales 1,300 miles (exclusive of the possession of British New Guinea, towards the maintenance of which Queensland is a contributing colony), and westward from Point Danger (at S.E. extremity) some 950 miles to the South Australian border, and embraces every variety of tropical, sub-tropical, and temperate climatic conditions. The dangers to life from wild beasts which are common in many parts of the United States, Canada, South Africa, &c., are here unknown—the reptiles alone being at all troublesome, and that over a small extent of country. With very few exceptions, life and property are as secure as in Great Britain, and the few remaining blacks (aboriginal) are so outnumbered by the white population, whilst most of them have become reconciled to their altered conditions, that they do not afford the slightest menace to the public safety. Wool, gold, and meat export have been the main industries of the past, but the production of sugar is increasing at a marked rate—there being an enormous quantity of land adapted to the growth of his crop; and dairy farming, combined with mixed farming, promises to play an important part in the not distant future.

Queensland has been styled the "lazy man's paradise"; we prefer to state that it is a poor man's—as well as a rich man's—country. With capital and labour going hand in hand, there is no country in the world which would respond more readily to the energy of man; and we have the proof of the assertion in what has been accomplished in the short space of thirty-nine years' independence! I have shown that our exports now total over £10,000,000 per annum, and it is worthy of note that in 1898 £9,120,095 were contributed by the four leading products, as against £7,649,482 in 1896 :—

	1896.	1898.
Wool	£2,984,210	£3,018,098
Gold	2,115,685	2,855,780
Meat and allied products	1,686,507	1,920,057
Sugar	863,080	1,329,876

On the other hand, the local production of many articles—for which the conditions of soil, climate, &c., have been *proved* to be admirably suited—has fallen far short of the demand, necessitating a large import. This condition of things is, in a measure, due to want of agricultural and industrial enterprise, and partly to lack of population to support some of the larger industries; such as paper mills, iron works, powder mills, oil mills, and perfumeries; in very few cases is it due to the want of the raw material. It will thus readily be seen that Queensland offers the *widest* scope for capitalist and agricultural labourer, the following being some of the more important items in the imports during the year 1896 :—

Manufactures of metals (including machinery, hardware, &c.)	£835,517
Soft and fancy goods	1,185,128
Bags, sacks, woolpacks, twine, &c.	96,198
Chemical products	149,904
Paper, books, printing materials	152,569
Tobacco, in all forms	74,572
Hops and malt	62,861
Dried fruits, fish, confectionery, &c.	344,607
Vegetable oils	32,788
Rice	42,633
Flour and cereals	616,247
Green fruit, seeds, plants, and vegetables	181,132

The proportion of the above which might be produced in this colony can be safely valued at £2,000,000, and their production would not only afford the means of living to a further population of 100,000, at the least, but would in turn largely stimulate existing industries, by the accession of persons to the colony.

Speaking generally, the reward of labour is greater than in the older countries of the world, for whilst a period of universal depression has temporarily affected wages, it has also effected a reduction in the cost of necessaries; increasingly liberal land laws, improved agricultural methods, and a genial climate, combining to make the struggle for life less hard here than elsewhere—especially to those who are engaged in the pursuit of agriculture. As instancing the way in which these advantages are becoming recognized, the official returns recently placed the area under cultivation at 336,775 acres—an increase of 84,700 acres, or over one-third upon that of 1893.

But what a small area is this when compared with the vast area of agricultural land still unappropriated! The total agricultural and grazing farm land open to selection at the close of 1895 amounted to 10,289,683 acres (of which 455,103 acres were made available in the same year—strictly for agricultural occupation), and in 1896 over 3,018,769 acres of the finest land in the colony—well watered, in close proximity to markets, and with the best of railway facilities—were thrown open to selection upon the most liberal terms. Land of this class is always obtainable.

It has been seen that home consumption will, in some directions, absorb a considerably greater output than we can at present claim, but it is as an exporting colony that we shall eventually take the lead; and we are already turning our attention in that direction—as previously shown. Our strength does not lie so much in our size as in the wonderful fertility of soil, range of climate, and antipodeal relation to the big markets of the world. The size is beyond the grasp of the average visitor—being about twice that of Canada, five and a half times that of Great Britain, twelve times the size of England and Wales together, and one hundred and ten times that of the largest county in England, viz., Yorkshire.

As regards fertility of soil, enough cannot be said; the mean *average* return per acre for some of our crops being as follows:—

Wheat, 15·89 bushels as compared with New York State yield of 14·86—average for a quarter of a century.

Barley, 18·72 bushels as against New York mean average of 22·38.

Maize, 24·85 bushels as against New York mean average of 30·73.

Rice, 36·45 bushels as against average in India of some 26 bushels.

Rye, 20·73 bushels as against New York mean average of 13·67.

Potatoes, 2·37 tons as against New York mean average of about 2 tons.

Cotton, 181 lbs. of clean cotton per acre—same as in United States, America.

Sugar, 1·69 tons per acre of cane (about 1·50 tons in New South Wales).

Tobacco, 8·77 cwt. of dried leaf per acre, as against United States mean average of 6½ cwt.

Hay, 1·93 tons as against New York mean average of 1·19.

Without here quoting the yield obtained from other crops, sufficient variety has been shown to demonstrate both the fertility of our farms and the wide range of products which result.

Seeing that we can show a *better return per acre* of wheat, rye, potatoes, tobacco, and hay than obtains in the United States (where the use of fertilizers is largely practised), a higher yield of rice than in India, as well as a heavier crushing of sugar than in New South Wales, and a very close approximation in other crops to average yields of the world, we think our confidence in our Natural Resources is not misplaced.

Whilst on the subject of export, it may be of interest to examine the following list of British imports during 1895, supplied by the courtesy of the Under-Secretary for Agriculture, as showing the very large opening there is in Great Britain for some of the above products, and many more which may be profitably produced here :—

IMPORTED INTO GREAT BRITAIN FREE OF DUTY.

Article.	Value.
Bacon	£7,925,979
Hams	2,898,018
Butter	14,245,230
Caoutchouc	3,760,178
Cheese	4,675,130
Maize	7,808,860
Cotton, raw	30,429,428
Eggs	4,003,446
Farinaceous substances	1,140,390
Flax	2,998,778
Almonds	340,409
Lemons	365,320
Oranges	2,111,190
Guttapercha	389,258
Honey	41,302
Nuts for oil, &c.	768,783
Cocoanuts	321,550
Olive oil	522,811
Palm oil	1,320,690
Poultry and game	605,160
Rice	1,982,460
Silk, raw	1,002,206
Cinnamon	48,001
Ginger	167,101
Pepper	299,468
Unenumerated spices	336,069
Sugar (excluding beetroot)	31,058,923
Wax	194,047
Wood—furniture, hardwoods, and veneers	900,214

Subject to duty :—

Cocoa	1,296,190
Cocoa, husks and shells	467
Cocoa, prepared	307,057
Coffee, raw	3,777,423
Currants	773,069
Figs	178,325
Raisins	888,769
Tobacco, unmanufactured . . .	2,079,603
Tobacco, manufactured (except cigars) .	208,254
Wine, in casks	3,073,819

And here I would like to refer to the peculiar advantages enjoyed by Australia in general, and Queensland in particular, owing to the fact that our winter (not very severe at any time) occurs at the same time of year as the European summer, and *vice versâ*, a circumstance of the greatest moment to exporters, producers, and the population generally. Thereby we are enabled to find a ready market abroad for surplus products at times when prices here are usually low, to relieve and steady the local market throughout the year, and by the betterment of the producer to effect an increase in wages generally. Perhaps the most promising industry, if this advantage in respect of seasons be availed of, is that of butter and cheese making. The local butter supply of Europe, North America, and—it may be said—a large portion of Asia is, at certain seasons of the year (owing to climatic drawbacks) very far short of the demand, and a practically limitless market is thus, at one season of the year or another, open to products of the best quality only. Indeed, in some countries—such as Japan—there is reason to believe that a *permanent* market may be secured. The high percentage of butter fat yielded by the milk of our *well-kept* herds; the immense area of dairying country which we have—as compared with New South Wales and Victoria; the extensive educational process which is going on under the direction of our Department of Agriculture; and the spread of the "factory system" —largely due to the encouragement afforded by the Government in the way of assistance to build factories for the manufacture of cheese and butter—should place us in a position to overtake our home consumption and make a name in the world's markets above that even of Victoria (which contributed, in 1894, a total of 9,519 tons 18 cwt. to the British market). Already a number of cold storage depôts have been erected by the enterprise of Government and others; refrigerating cars are used for the conveyance of perishable products on the railway, and a bonus of 1d. per lb. of butter on shipment was recently being paid by the Government. A trial shipment of 7½ tons was made under Government supervision in February, 1895, and realized a fair price in the London market. During 1897 and 1898 a few hundred tons were shipped with success to London, and an important trade is likely to ensue.

Eggs form another item which is of interest in relation to export. At a time when but 3d. to 6d. per dozen can be realized here, owing to the bountiful supply—say November to February—a ready market is available in Great Britain for a few million dozen at 9d. to 1s. per dozen.

Shipping facilities are now offered by the British India direct line of steamers between Queensland and Great Britain—specially fitted with cold storage, the climate is eminently adapted to the raising of poultry for laying and for the table, and enterprise and moderate capital are alone needed to establish a most profitable industry.

Maize, honey, a variety of fruits, &c., would find a good market in Europe if exported under favourable conditions ; indeed, the prices realized on trial shipments have been sufficient to justify the conclusion that the study of requirements of those markets as regards quality and time of shipment will lead to a large trade between this colony and the home markets.

Take, for example, the encouraging results attained by the neighbouring colony of Victoria in shipments of fruit. These arrived mostly in first-class condition, and the growers were rewarded by a gross return in the London market of 10s. to 14s. per case of apples, and 7s. or 8s. for pears. Wet and over-ripe lots fetched 4s. to 8s. 6d. per case.

In addition to the above, the consignors received a bonus of 2s. per case from the Victorian Government, which may be taken as covering cost of packing, freight, and selling charges.

No bulk shipments of green fruit appear to have been made as yet to the European market from our colony, principally from the fact that our surplus at present finds a profitable market in the adjoining colonies—to which we consigned, in 1896, 1,053,257 packages of the value of £67,000, besides a few experimental shipments of preserved pineapples—value about £100. Of the latter a few cases were sent to the United Kingdom. With the advent of Mr. Benson—fruit expert to the Department of Agriculture—fresh interest and energy have been infused into the realization of this valuable national asset, and Queensland may look forward to shortly receiving a very substantial increase to her revenue from this source.

Bird's-eye View of the City of Brisbane, showing Wharfage.

Before, however, this can be the case, there is ample scope for the fruitgrower in the supply of local requirements, dried and preserved goods to the value of about £30,000 having been imported in 1896. And the *sole* reason for the loss of this sum to our colony is *the want of fruit-growers*. The quality and variety of fruits which we have been and are now producing cannot be excelled in Australia, yet recent returns give our fruit-growing area as being only about 10,294 acres, besides 3,308 acres of gardens and orchards, a mere fraction of that of the Southern Colonies. Experimental shipments of Queensland honey have been made to London, and expert opinion goes to show that, when initial prejudices have been overcome on the other side, and our shippers have realized the high standard of excellence and the *uniformity* of quality exacted by the home markets, a grand opening exists here for hundreds of tons per annum. In bountiful harvests the price of maize (corn) has occasionally fallen very low, and upon one of these occasions a trial shipment was made to Great Britain. Although not financially a great success, this departure was by no means a failure. The good condition of the grain upon arrival demonstrated the fact that—with the introduction of better agricultural appliances, improvements in shipping methods, and lower freights—all our surplus might be profitably disposed of in Great Britain alone (of which the annual import is something like *one and three-quarter million tons*) and that, by relieving the market here, a good return might be secured to the grower all the year round.

Onions, similarly, have been shipped from Melbourne (Victoria) as *general cargo*, reaching London in good condition, although, owing to the shipment leaving at the wrong time of year, a glutted market had to be encountered, and the consignment was not as profitable as would have been the case under more favourable conditions. This item offers the widest of fields for the Queensland farmer, as not only is a way being opened up for future export by the enterprise of our neighbours, but, first and foremost, the present production is some 2,660 tons below our annual consumption, and the local grower is supported by an import duty of 20s. per ton. The quality of onions grown here leaves nothing to be desired; in fact, the writer has seen specimens of several varieties raised in the vicinity of Brisbane by European growers which will bear comparison with those of any land. Before leaving the subject of export, we may mention that the sale of South Australian wines is now being pushed in London, and there seems to be no reason why our own Colony, which has produced some excellent vintages, should not follow suit in this matter. Not only is the consumption of imported *wine* in the United Kingdom very large, being of the value of £3,000,000 to £4,000,000 per annum, but dried fruit in the shape of *currants* and *raisins* were imported by that country to the aggregate value of £1,660,000 in 1895 alone, and it is most satisfactory to note that a move is being made in our own Colony towards what should eventually prove a most important export industry. Grapes, apricots, apples, peaches, figs, plums, &c., are prolific growers in Queensland, and fairly large quantities are already produced in the Southern and Western districts, which would often yield a better return in the dried state than when fresh. *Single* shipments of dried fruits from over-sea countries to Australia have reached the high figure of 4,000 tons —valued at £120,000—of which the bulk might have been grown and dried here. The neighbouring Colony of Tasmania is already engaged in the industry, and South Australian enterprise has also taken up this matter; it now rests with ourselves to show that we will not take the back place in a trade for which our climatic and topographical conditions are so well suited. In the Huon district of Tasmania a Mr. Robt. Harvey has at work four evaporating machines of a capacity of 50 bushels of dried fruits per day; whilst at the establishment of Messrs. Hardy & Sons, Limited, of McLaren Vale, near Adelaide (S.A.), *sixty tons* of currant grapes were prepared during the 1896 vintage, and 1,700 tons of grapes were converted into wine. Compared with the last-mentioned production from *a single establishment*, our own 1896 crop of about 2,286 tons of grapes seems to leave plenty of room for extension. As with all industries for which support is sought in the great markets of Europe, &c., it is, however, necessary that only the primest qualities should be sent out of the Colony. Experimental processes should be discarded as far as possible and the highest quality aimed at, as only such will command attention at the hands of large "home" buyers. It is encouraging to record that both by precept and example—together with the granting of prizes for excellence in fruit and vegetable growing—the Department of Agriculture are doing their utmost to foster this and allied industries, and in this way openings are being made not only for those who at present are engaged in developing our agricultural resources, but for the immense army of workers which our land is destined to see and is capable of supporting in comfort, if not in affluence. Before dealing somewhat in detail with our crops, live stock, topography, minerals, industries, land laws, social institutions, &c., we think we cannot do better than quote a portion of a newspaper article by the Rev. John Lamond, B.D., of Skelmorlie, N.B., who recently visited Queensland, and whose remarks on his return to Scotland are particularly weighty as coming from a disinterested visitor.

He says, speaking of the Darling Downs :—" I have never seen, and I never expect to see again, such beautiful pasture lands. . . . What impressed me most were the vast openings for industry throughout Queensland and the whole of Australia. . . . In our little island, which we can conveniently cross at some points in three or four hours, it is difficult to realize the vastness of these Australian plains. It almost appeared to me that the surplus population of the world could be poured into them, and even then Australia would be comparatively empty."

Further on he says :—" What is needed above all in Queensland is that people should settle upon the land. I have sometimes wondered that our crofters and ploughmen do not emigrate in larger numbers. They have a practical knowledge of agriculture, and have been trained in habits of industry. In Queensland, as in other parts of Australia, they would find land at a small initial cost, and there is no reason why after twenty or thirty years of honest labour they should not be in comfortable circumstances."

And again :—" I ought to state that the Queensland Government are giving agriculturists every inducement to emigrate, and that there is a special demand in the colony for men born north of the Tweed. I met several of ' our boys,' full of hope for the future, going north to Cairns, Mackay, and other settlements. The advantage of going to the colonies is that there are more openings there than at home. At the same time, life has not that rich background of interest which we are familiar with in the old land."

WATER SUPPLY.

Of paramount importance to all, we believe we may say—certainly of as great importance to the agriculturist as quality of soil—is the question of water supply. Without it the best of land and the most favourable temperature are useless to man and beast; with its aid the very desert may be made to blossom as a rose. Whilst the mean average rainfall of Queensland is high it is somewhat irregular, and, although many portions of the colony are rarely, if ever, visited by drought, in others it is almost an annual occurrence. One of the highest rainfall records was that of 241·448 inches at Goondi for the year 1894; and the lowest, that of 2·48 inches, at Kallidawarry, *viâ* Windorah (some 700 miles west of Brisbane), in 1892.* Over a large extent of country the careful conser-

* The heaviest rainfall for twenty-four hours known to the Government Hydraulic Engineer took place on or about February 3, 1893, at Crowhamhurst—distant some fifty miles in a direct line from Brisbane, on the Brisbane River drainage area—when 35·76 inches were registered. On February 21, 1887, 18·31 inches of rain fell in Brisbane during the twenty-four hours.

vation of rain and surface water is alone needed to permit of judicious
irrigation of crops. This practice is being increasingly adopted in many
places with marked success. In 1896 an area of 8,368 acres was treated
in this manner, and a gain was secured varying from 10 to 100 per cent.
in the case of lucerne, sugar cane, maize, and pumpkins. In the district
of Ayr, comprising the rich alluvial lands of the Burdekin delta, over
5,000 acres under sugar cane, potatoes, &c., were irrigated. In *dry*
seasons, and with many crops at any time, the practice is an invaluable
one, and every farmer should be in a position in this colony to fall back
upon artificially stored water. Cane, cereals, fodder plants, and fruit
trees all pay handsome returns for the outlay, and it is only a matter of
time when a good water reserve will be considered as necessary as a
plough. In many districts, especially in the Western and North-Western
country, the rainfall is so irregular that the conservation of water could
not be attempted if such were the only source of supply, and for many
years not only did the more severe droughts occasion endless loss amongst
cattle and sheep, but many of the townships were threatened with extinction for want of water. About thirteen years ago a private bore was
successful in raising some 80,000 gallons per diem, and in 1895 the matter
was taken up in a spirited manner by the Government. Search was made
for geological formations which would be likely to yield artesian supplies,
and a bore was put down at Blackall, from which 178,000 gallons were
obtained (since increased to 300,000 gallons) per diem. This was followed
by others, until now we have some 463 bores (mostly in the Western
districts), of which over 300 have been successful, and are yielding
a supply which is computed at 150,000,000 to 200,000,000 gallons
per diem. The former would equal over 50,000,000,000 gallons per
annum—an enormous body of water. By the kindness of Mr. J. B.
Henderson, Member of the Institute of C.E., &c., Government Hydraulic
Engineer, I am enabled to make comparisons of the volume of
our artesian supply with that of some of the best-known Australian
and British reservoirs. In round numbers the above-mentioned annual
discharge is more than seventy times the capacity of the Enoggera
Reservoir (from which source Brisbane until recently obtained its sole
supply); over twenty-one times that of the Malmsbury Coliban (supplying
the three important Victorian towns of Castlemaine, Sandhurst, and
Carlton); eleven times that of the Yan Yean (supplying Melbourne);
and six times that of the Prospect (supplying Sydney). The figures
relating to the British reservoirs are even more interesting, particularly
when viewed in the light of the population they supply. Lake Vyrnwy

(in the vicinity of the city of Liverpool), Lake Thirlmere (near Manchester), and Loch Katrine (near Glasgow), each support over 500,000 persons, or more than the population of all Queensland, and their ascertainable contents are respectively about one-fifth, one-eighth, and one-twelfth the capacity of our bore water. Compared with Lough Vartry, from which the city of Dublin is supplied, the annual discharge of Queensland artesian water is twenty-nine times as great. The population dependent upon the water of the Lough amounts to between 300,000 and 400,000. The last example we will mention is the Lough Island Reavy Reservoir (County Down, Ireland), near Castlewilliam and the River Muddock (a tributary of the River Bann) of which the capacity is 1,793,750,000 gallons, or about 1-39th part of our annual artesian supply. The following are the capacities of the reservoirs quoted above :—

	Contents in Gallons.
Enoggera	1,000,000,000
Malmsbury Coliban	3,255,000,000
Yan Yean	6,400,000,000
Prospect	10,812,313,000
Lake Vyrnwy—capacity above cill of dam	12,131,000,000
Lake Thirlmere—capacity above cill of dam when risen	8,130,686,000
Loch Katrine—contents of upper 7ft., including 4ft. which Loch has been raised	5,687,500,000
Lough Vartry	2,400,000,000

Amongst bores sunk by Government, the largest yield is obtained at Charleville, viz., 3,000,000 gallons per diem. The temperature of the water as delivered is 106° Fahrenheit, and as it possesses valuable mineral properties it is much used by residents and visitors for bathing purposes. The flow is generally under control by means of a valve, but the static pressure at the surface is such (100 lbs. per square inch) that a magnificent jet of water some 120 feet in height can be thrown up at will. The above has been sold to the Charleville Municipal Council for the sum of £1,500. Of private bores some fifty-three overflow to the extent of 1,000,000 gallons per diem and upwards ; fifteen of these yield 2,000,000 to 3,000,000 gallons ; and five have an output of 3,000,000 to 4,000,000 gallons. Temperatures vary from 70° in the case of Back Creek on the Central Railway (depth 180 feet) to 196° at Dagworth bore (depth 3,335 feet), and 173° at Winton, about eighty miles to the south-east, where the depth of the bore reaches 4,010 feet. At Winton ladies have been known to make excellent tea with the water as it issues from the bore; it is also utilized by travellers for cooking meat and eggs. Besides the varied suitability to irrigation, watering of stock, and cure of certain forms of disease, the high temperature and great pressure at which much of this water is delivered will be found of immense value commercially and mechanically, and water from the last-named and other bores is already being utilized for mechanical purposes. At Thargomindah the pressure exceeds 230 lbs. per square inch. It will be seen from the few preceding remarks that much has been done in a short space of time towards the development of our resources in the interior, but much remains to be done before close settlement can take place in the Western districts. It was estimated in 1896 by our Government Hydraulic Engineer that water-bearing strata occur over at least 106,000 square miles. Besides this enormous area—which has been already proved to be more or less satisfactory from an artesian point of view—there still remain some 132,000 square miles of country of the geological formation in which these water supplies occur, viz., the Lower Cretaceous or rolling Downs Formation, which have not been touched by the driller, and steps are being taken to ascertain whether this South-Western country will respond as readily when tapped as has been the case with that already explored. It is a remarkable fact that owing to the nature of the soil, &c., the Western country—although deprived of a large portion of the rainfall by the ranges which intercept the vapour-laden clouds from the Coast — produces grasses of better quality than other portions of the Colony, so that with the advent of water the stock-carrying capacity of pastoral properties will be largely increased. Nor should we forget the possibilities for agricultural settlement which have been opened up in this manner and are being already availed of. At Barcaldine and at Cunnamulla artesian water has been used on a small scale for the irrigation of cereals and vegetables, and the results will probably lead to an extension in this direction. The reticulation of these two and other townships with means for the conveyance of bore water to the residents has been effected, and doubtless the practice will be followed wherever artesian supplies can be secured. A noticeable feature in the greater number of artesian bores is that, although there is usually a very marked falling off in the supply immediately the "first flow" has been tapped, the general tendency is towards increase of flow as time goes on, an unmistakable evidence of the practically illimitable extent of the sources of supply. Many hypotheses have been put forward as regards the location of the "head" from which these take their rise, but we cannot discuss them here. For further information we would refer the reader

A River Frontage.

to an interesting paper on the subject by Mr. Robert L. Jack, F.G.S., F.R.G.S., Government Geologist, and other publications of our own and the New South Wales geological departments.

From the 1896 report of the Government Hydraulic Engineer I learn that the estimated value of our artesian bores up to the end of the financial year was some £900,000, and the total length of boring effected in search of water up to 30th June, 1897, is set down at 111 miles, a steady increase on previous figures. The average depth of the Western bores is 1,084 feet, but some excellent yields have been obtained at a much less depth; as at No. 12 bore, Richmond Downs, where a yield of 1,000,000 gallons per diem has been secured at 560 feet; at No. 2 "Coreena," 1,500,000 gallons at 904 feet; and at No. 2 "Tinnenburra," 1,948,780 gallons at a depth of 992 feet. The location of these bores can be ascertained by consulting the report and appendices. On the other hand, many bores have had to be carried to a depth of 4,000 to 6,000 feet, generally resulting in a water supply of hundreds of millions of gallons per annum. Exclusive of the casings, which are usually left in the successful wells, the cost of boring ranges from 17s. per foot to as much as 55s. per foot in the case of those of great depth; in fact, the owner of one private bore, some 4,000 feet in depth, is reported to have spent about £13,000 on the same, casing included. The altitude of the various bores in the Colony is very varied, and so far as at present known this does not appear to be a factor in determining the flow of water. The bore of which the mouth seems to be at the greatest altitude is that at Tambo—1,325 feet above sea level—yielding 200,000 gallons per diem. At Burketown, where the surface ground is only 12 feet above sea-level, a flow of 155,560 gallons per diem is attained; and at Northampton Downs the magnificent output of 1,500,000 gallons per diem has been secured at an altitude of 1,090 feet above sea level. In other instances the positions are reversed, the Muckadilla bore, at 1,169 feet above sea level, yielding but 23,000 gallons, whilst that at Yarmouth—703 feet above the sea—gives 2,709,990 gallons per diem.

The *natural* supply of water in the Colony generally is not, however, nearly so scanty as has been popularly supposed. In addition to the noble streams which traverse many of the pastoral properties, there are numbers of lakes—some more or less salt—which will become generally known and utilized as close settlement takes the place of unwieldy and oftentimes unprofitable cattle runs. Whilst nowhere approaching the size of Lakes Eyre, Torrens, Gardiner, and Frome (of South Australia), our own are sufficiently large to command some notice. In the South-

West we have Lakes Wyara, Numalla, Bullawarra, Bulloo, Pender, Yumberarra, Kingie, Tharlinda, Barolka, and Mackillop (or Yamma Yamma); in the West we have the Diamantina Lakes, and Lakes Machatti, Spring, Phillipi, and Amaroo; whilst Lake Nash is situated on the border of the northern territory of South Australia. Not many miles from the township of Boulia are a number of natural artesian springs known as Elizabeth Springs. At Angy, some fifty miles to the north of these, and within twenty-eight miles of Boulia township, twenty or thirty strong springs give an abundant supply of water. According to reports quoted by Mr. R. L. Jack in 'Geology and Palæontology of Queensland,' the temperature of the water is not above normal heat, but so far as is known no analysis of the same has been made.

In Central Queensland there are two large lakes, each several square miles in extent, which are comparatively unknown, viz., Lake Buchanan and Lake Galilee (or Jochmus). Both of these handsome sheets of water are close on twenty miles in length and four or five across their widest part; the latter is only some fifty miles distant from the town of Aramac, and can be reached by coach and saddle-horse from Barcaldine on the Central line of railway. About seventy miles from Springsure is another very beautiful piece of water named Lake Salvator. Numerous springs of cool, clear water find their way into this lake, where fish, fowl, and platypus abound. Further north are found Lake Elphinstone, a fresh-water lake six miles long and two broad; the less important Lake Powlathanga, near Charters Towers; and Lake Lucy, at the head of the Burdekin, about 130 miles distant as the crow flies, in a north-westerly direction. Among the "beauty spots" of the Colony are Lake Eacham ("Yeetcham" of the blacks), Barrang, and Boonoobagolamee, on the tableland in the vicinity of Cairns. The first named measures about a mile and a half in length by one mile in breadth, and is remarkable for the luxuriance of tropical growth by which it is surrounded. The water of all is fresh and of excellent quality. During medium seasons many beautiful stretches of fresh water adorn our cattle stations, but as these are intermittent I will just mention Lake Idamea, at Glenormiston, which is two miles in length, a quarter of a mile wide, and thirty feet deep in a good season. Scattered throughout the colony are numbers of springs, providing the clearest of health-giving water; many of them, such as that at Spring Bluff—on the main range, just below Toowoomba—as well as the Spa waters of Helidon, in the same neighbourhood, being noted for their perennial coolness.

The latter have given rise to a most important bottling industry, the main spring—owned by the Helidon Spa Water Company, of Brisbane, Queensland—enjoying the great distinction of containing more lithia than the water of any of the European Spa waters, the Marquelle at Baden-Baden being excepted. The water is used over the length and breadth of the Colony, and is experiencing an increasing demand in other lands on account of its therapeutic and palatable qualities.* Besides the various groups of hot springs in the neighbourhood of Boulia and Warenda, there are those of Enniskillen, between Tambo and Blackall, in the Central Districts. Some have a high temperature and most valuable medicinal properties. Of these the Innot Hot Springs, situated two miles and three-quarters north-west of Woodleigh Station, near Herberton, at an elevation of 1,900 feet, afford a notable example; the water from these is used either as a hot bath, the natural temperature being 189° Fahr., or bottled for drinking purposes, and according to analytical report is equal to many of the renowned European mineral waters for the cure of certain forms of disease.† In the Etheridge district also are extensive hot springs, having valuable medicinal properties; these are about forty-five miles distant from Georgetown, and bear the name of the Einasleigh Hot Springs. They consist of five distinct springs of the most beautifully clear blue water, of a high temperature (the exact heat has not been ascertained). An analysis of a sample from " B " Springs gave the following weight of solids per gallon :

				Grs.
Carbonates of calcium and magnesium	.	.	.	6·25
,, ,, sodium and potassium	.	.	.	15·94
Chloride of sodium and potassium .	.	.	.	32·61
Total fixed salts .	.	.	. . .	54·80
Volatile matter	.	.	. . .	2·80
				57·60
Sulphuric acid	.	. . . . .	.	a trace
Sulphuretted hydrogen .	.	. . .	.	2·19 per gal.

* The composition of " Helidon Spa Water " is as follows :—Total solids, upwards of 228 grs. per gallon, of which the principal are :—

Carbonate of Sodium .	.	. .	.	212·14 grains.
,, ,, Lithium .	.	. .	.	2·68 ,,
,, ,, Calcium .	.	. .	.	7·35 ,,
,, ,, Magnesium	.	. .	.	3·39 ,,
Chloride of Sodium	.	. .	.	2·99 ,,
Silica . . .	.	. .	.	·29 ,,
				228·84

With traces of alumina, iron, and rubidium.
Specific gravity :—1·0076.

† Innot Spa Water contains the carbonates of soda, lime, and magnesia ; chloride of sodium ; sulphate of lime ; silica, alumina, and iron ; and a trace of lithia besides the usual small percentage of organic matter.

The above is a chlorinated sulphuretted water, of similar medicinal qualities to that at Harrogate (England), but the relative strength is only as seven to one. Few, if any, of these springs can boast of picturesque surroundings or beauty of colour, such as the "Pink Terraces" of New Zealand (now destroyed by volcanic action), but in point of symmetry the calcareous basins of many of them are in no way inferior to those of our sister isles.

On the Mulligan River, in the extreme west of the Colony, and on the Saxby River, a tributary of the Flinders, which empties itself into the Gulf, are found hot mud springs, of which the efflorescence usually surrounding this class of spring consists mainly of a sesquicarbonate of soda (native "Trona"), and is used largely as a baking soda and for other purposes. The following is an analysis of a sample of this incrustation, by Dr. Flight :—

Water	27·793
Silica	0·600
Chlorine	3·369
Sodium	2·183
Carbonic acid	33·735
Soda	31·690
	99·370

The incrustation formed by the Mitchell River Mud Springs, about ten miles north of Gamboola on the outskirts of the Palmer Goldfield, has been submitted to analysis by the late Government Analyst, with the following result :—

Soda	37·54
Lime	2·8
Oxide of Iron	2·19
Sand	31·72

Further up the coast on the York Peninsula are a group of heavily mineralized springs, known as the Soda Springs. These are situated a short distance inland from Princess Charlotte Bay, and are near the route from the Musgrave to the Coen township. The South-Eastern and the whole of the Western portion of the Peninsula are abundantly watered by rivers of exceptional length, many of those on the Western watershed being navigable for craft drawing about five feet of water, for a distance of thirty miles from their mouth. Immense tracts of moderately fertile land are still unoccupied on the western side, and seeing that the climate, although tropical, is by no means severely so, and the rainfall is far more regular whilst little heavier, if any, than that of Brisbane, great inducement offers to the settlement of this portion of the Peninsula. In what is known as the Gulf country, viz., that which is washed by the waters of the Gulf of Carpentaria, the rivers—many of considerable size—form a perfect network with which the excellent land could be readily irrigated and turned into a veritable garden. The temperature here is also pleasant during the greater part of the year; the rainfall, though rather irregular, is ample. On the Gregory River and its branches fruit of varied description grows most prolifically. Oranges, lemons, and bananas may be seen on the cattle stations, which, if grown in quantity, would find a ready market in the towns of Normanton, Burketown, Croydon, &c. Grapes are grown to perfection, and most kinds of vegetables, so that it will be seen that this locality is greatly favoured by nature as regards water supply, and should commend itself to agriculturists generally.

I have alluded to the rainfall of this Western watershed as being similar to that of Brisbane, and may add that that of the North-Western portion of the Colony is about equal to that of the far-famed Darling Downs. It is, however, as previously inferred, on the coast that the rainfall is greatest, and that there is the least need to resort to artificially raised supplies. The district of Geraldton enjoys the unique distinction of having the highest record both for annual mean rainfall and mean number of wet days in Queensland. From the map of Mr. J. B. Henderson showing the rainfall to the end of 1896, it is seen that the former stands at 153·69 (inches) and the latter at 155 (days), approximately. The actual rainfall in 1894 was 155·50 inches, the number of wet days 159. It is interesting to note in this connection that the maximum rainfall in England is 145 inches, whilst London has about 24 inches; Nottingham, 23·9 inches; Paris, 22·9 inches; New York, 43 inches; and Melbourne, 25·44 inches per annum. The ports of Cairns (101·45 inches), Cardwell (89·77 inches), Port Douglas (87·63 inches), Cooktown (73·15 inches), Mackay (72·38 inches), and others within the tropics enjoy heavy rainfalls, and here sugar, coffee, bananas, mangoes, and rice produce heavy yields.

The heaviest rainfall south of the tropic of Capricorn is at Nerang (70·44 inches), followed closely by Brisbane (51·32 inches), Gympie (49·89 inches), Bundaberg (49·67 inches), Maryborough (49·26 inches), and Toowoomba (44·25 inches).

In common with the South-Western, Central, and Northern divisions, the coastal districts in the south-east of Queensland possess various

stretches of inland water, not all of them well known as yet. In alluding
to lakes in the rest of the Colony I have only mentioned the principal
ones, and of those in the Port Curtis electorate I will just mention Lake
Graham, lying towards the head of Alligator Creek; Lake Learmonth,
in the vicinity of the Morinish Goldfields; Lake Murray, a few miles out
from the city of Rockhampton; and Lake Victoria.

Undoubtedly the finest sheets of water near our coast are the chain
of lakes in the Wide Bay electorate known as the Noosa Lakes, and
comprising Lakes Weyba, Dunella, Cootharaba, Cooroybah, Nibra, Como,
and Cooloolah. Although in reality containing fresh water, these extensive and picturesque lakes become periodically more or less salt, owing
to tidal influence; forming a resort for millions of fish, endless in variety
and of the finest eating quality. Perhaps one of the commonest visitants
of the "finny tribe" is the "sea mullet" (*Mugil dobula*), which is not
believed to permanently inhabit these waters, although a small number
may do so. Speaking of edible fish, we believe the record weight was
obtained at Rockhampton (some 200 or 300 miles to the north of these
lakes), from a wharf of which city an enormous fish of the cod species
was secured at the close of 1896 by the combined efforts of two anglers,
not, however, until a number of hooks and portions of lines had ministered
to his voracious appetite. The weight recorded at the Corporation
weigh-bridge was 3 cwt. 7 lbs., and the length 6 ft. 3 in. As may be
imagined, a heavy line was required to land this monster, and the haul
was considered of such interest that a photograph was obtained, and is
now in the possession of a resident of Winton, Central Queensland.
Further particulars of our Queensland fishes will be given further on.

Inland from the Noosa Lakes, some sixty-five miles in a direct line,
and almost midway between Jondaryan on the Western Railway and
Kilkivan on the North Coast Railway, lies the district of Nanango, one
which is especially favoured in regard to water, soil, and temperature,
although not so much so in facilities of transport.

That which, however, concerns us more particularly just now are
the numerous large creeks (viz., Stuart, Barker's, Baramba, Boonara, and
Boyne) and almost innumerable smaller watercourses with which the
neighbourhood abounds. Deep and permanent lagoons are found on
many of the flats removed from the creeks, and the nature of the country
generally is such that water is readily stored by means of dams, where
not already found. Wells have been sunk in various places with a fair
amount of success. On the Stuart Range, about twenty miles from the
town of Nanango, is a splendid piece of fresh water, but owing to the

Water Scene in the Queen's Park, Brisbane.

Water Scene in the Queen's Park, Brisbane.

dense scrub by which it is surrounded its existence was for a long time unknown to the residents.

South-east of the above, on the northern side of the Southern and Western line of railway, is another of these beauty spots, known as Lake Clarendon. Although not shown on most maps, it is of large size and easy of access, being but a short ride from Gatton railway station. Wild fowl and game abound, and it is a favourite resort of residents, yet comparatively unknown outside of the district.

All the important towns of Queensland have an abundant supply of water for household and municipal purposes, obtained from river, reservoir, or bore. Perhaps the most abundant supply is to be found in the metropolis, which is not only served by the Enoggera Reservoir—having a capacity of 1,000,000,000 gallons—but to this have been added, of late years, the reservoirs at Gold Creek, Highgate Hill, and Mount Crosby, giving a flow per twenty-four hours of 9,000,000 gallons. In addition to these public sources of supply, tanks for the storage of rainwater are almost invariably attached to residences, so that ample water is secured for all purposes, and there is scarcely a cottage even but has its bathroom. On the southern side of the City, in the vicinity of Mount Gravatt, lie a chain of water-holes of great depth and containing the best of water, which could in addition be utilized in the public service. Amongst others could be mentioned the towns of Toowoomba and Warwick, supplied from reservoir and the Condamine River, respectively. The Warwick water supply deserves especial mention, as being practically inexhaustible and of excellent quality. At Gympie and at Charters Towers there are large sources of supply in the rivers of these two districts, viz., the Mary and the Burdekin. Lagoons of large extent supply the city of Rockhampton with the best of drinking water.

In many districts where the rainfall is deficient a compensating abundance of dew is met with; indeed, without this wise provision of nature the herbage in drought-stricken localities would speedily become exterminated and far more serious losses in stock occur than is the case. To travellers, also, the heavy dew-fall of Queensland has often been of incalculable value, it being not a very uncommon practice with them—when in the "back blocks" and short of water—to drag a blanket over the dew-laden ground, and to utilize the water obtained by wringing it out.

In concluding these few remarks I think I cannot do better than quote the following from a Western newspaper—*Winton Herald* of 25th November, 1896—as indicating the appreciation which has been shown for the liberality of our Government in the encouragement of artesian boring:

"An immense tract of our western country, which would be otherwise valueless for grazing purposes, owes its present utility to the benefit derived from the artesian bores with which this part of the colony abounds. Every year large sums are spent in these ventures, and in the majority of cases so successful have they proved that there are few pastoral holdings which have not one or more artesian supplies in addition to the improvements in the shape of tanks, &c. In our own district a large number of stations are now carrying on active boring operations, and others still further west have in many instances had their energy rewarded by striking a never-failing source of water supply. The Government deserve every credit for the assistance given to local bodies by the advance of money for boring purposes, though in our own case this is unnecessary now. What chiefly affects this district is the Government plan of sinking bores *for the purpose of encouraging settlement on the land*. The soil is second to none in Australia, and needs only regular rainfall or artificial water to make it produce almost any grain suitable to a tropical climate—veritably a land flowing with milk and honey. But *revenons à nos moutons*. Under the Central Boring scheme, the Government intend sinking artesian wells, rather centrally situated, in various districts of the colony, and we are credibly informed that this district is fortunate enough to be so favoured, though no particulars will be available for a short time."

We believe that definite proposals respecting Government assistance to pastoral tenants of the Crown in sinking artesian wells have been under consideration by the Honourable the Treasurer.

SOILS.

In local parlance these are divided into "scrub," "forest," and "plains"—though the terms to the new-comer are somewhat unmeaning. A more accurate division is that given by the Curator of the Brisbane Botanic Gardens* at the Agricultural and Pastoral Conference of 1889, as follows:—Argillaceous (or clayey), loamy, sandy, marly, calcareous, and humus soils, all of which are represented in the colony. Of the two first-mentioned classes is much of our far-famed Darling Downs and western country, as well as a proportion of forest land; whilst the last-named are invariably known as "scrub," comprising all those river flats and hillside slopes which have received a large amount of vegetable mould and other detritus from higher lands, and which are—or were originally

* Reports of the proceedings may be obtained on application at the offices of the Department of Agriculture, Brisbane.

—covered with an almost impenetrable jungle of trees and undergrowth. In the neighbourhood of Cardwell, a depth of thirty and forty feet of soil is not uncommon. The sandy soils are many of them most fertile, as at Roma, whilst others, such as have been utilized on our coasts for cocoa-nut, mango, and pineapple culture, have but a limited amount of fertility. Of the two remaining classes of soils, that which I have styled "cal-careous" (containing at least 20 per cent. of carbonate of lime) is the least commonly met with, a deficiency which we can afford to make up by artificial means, considering our wealth of almost inexhaustible humus soil. Inadvisable as the practice is, many—if not most—of our scrub farms have been unintermittently planted with the same crop for perhaps ten to twenty years; and whilst some of our farmers practise the rotation of crops, the "old country" system of letting the land lie fallow every four or five years, as well as that of applying fertilizers, is seldom adopted—nor indeed has the fertility of our alluvial soils and some of those of volcanic origin become even yet sufficiently exhausted to carry conviction to all. Much as we should reprehend some of the methods of the Chinese market gardeners in the Colony, a valuable object lesson is afforded by the assiduous artificial irrigation and application of fertilizers which they invariably practise, even on the naturally fertile flats and gullies where they locate their gardens. As instancing the unaided results obtained on "scrub" soils, it may be mentioned that in the Gympie Land Agent's district two crops of maize, each fifty bushels per acre, have been obtained in one year; also two crops of potatoes, aggre-gating 6 tons per acre; oaten-hay, 2 to 3 tons per acre; green lucerne, 4½ to 9 tons per acre (according to the number of times it was cut); sweet potatoes, 10 and even 20 tons per acre; and sugar cane, 40 to 60 tons, yielding from 22 cwt. to 30 cwt. of sugar per acre. With proofs such as these, are we not justified in stating that we have land of un-surpassable, if not unapproachable fertility?

Nor are the above mere isolated instances of phenomenal yields. In the Cairns and Douglas districts the *average* yields of maize for the five years ending 1890 were (according to the report of the Registrar-General for 1895) 40·75 bushels and 44·23 bushels per acre respectively, although, owing to the exceptionally unfavourable climatic conditions between 1890 and 1896, this average was not maintained. It will readily be seen that for a district to *average* (over the space of five years) anything like the above-quoted figures, some very high yields must have been obtained. In the district of Mackay during the year 1895 some 600 bushels of rice were obtained from the small area of 14 acres, being at the rate of

42·85 bushels per acre, and our *average yield* for the year 1890 was 32 bushels, as compared with the average obtained in India—one of the chief rice countries in the world—of *12 bushels*. As high as 68 bushels per acre has been obtained by Mr. McPherson in Brisbane, and in 1886 an average of 66·44 bushels was obtained.

Fertility is not, however, confined to "scrub" land. The red and chocolate coloured loams of our elevated table lands—often 30 to 40 feet deep; the clays of our south-western and western plains; the volcanic soil on which much of our heavy forest timber grows, and the sandy loams of Roma, Goondiwindi, &c., have each their special recommendations.

In the chocolate soil of the Stanthorpe district, 3 tons of grapes, 3 tons of oaten-hay, 3½ tons of potatoes, and 23 bushels of wheat to the acre have been frequently noted; whilst the red soil of Toowoomba and Highfields produced at the rate of 2½ tons of grapes per acre in the year 1896. The comparatively low average yield of maize in the Herberton district (29·35 bushels) as disclosed by the agricultural returns for 1895 would seem to favour the assumption that, either owing to climatic hindrances in that year, or careless cultivation, justice was not done to the crop. Previous to 1882 crops of 60 to 80 bushels of maize, and 2 tons of oaten hay per acre had been harvested, and considering the acknowledged fertility of the chocolate and scrub soil of this table-land, as evinced by the heavy forest timber, large scrub timber, and dense undergrowth of the district, we cannot accept these figures as by any means the best it can show. This is fully borne out by the average which is shown for 1896, viz., 40·53 bushels per acre. The special characteristic of our table-lands—or plateaus—is the cool temperature which they enjoy in comparison with land in the same latitude but at a less elevation from the sea-level. The temperature of Herberton, for instance, is five to seven degrees lower than that of the neighbouring towns of Cairns, Townsville, and Bowen (the latter two are coastal towns *further from* the Equator); whilst in the neighbourhood of Toowoomba the thermometer registers throughout the year a considerably lower temperature than is the case at Yandilla, Southport, Ipswich, Texas, Cunnamulla, and Thargomindah. This is the most marked in midsummer, when the difference ranges between 6° and 18° in favour of Toowoomba, as against 3° to 10° less in early summer and 3° to 7° less in mid-winter than the above-mentioned places, which are all in the same or a higher latitude.

Although not directly connected with the question of soil, this peculiarity of the table-lands has a most important bearing upon the agriculture engaged in, as we not only have in these lands all the requisites in the way of soil, but the climatic conditions are such that most—if not all—of the fruits and crops raised in the temperate zone of Europe and the United States may be grown here to perfection. I shall have occasion to refer to these later on.

So far we have only considered the humus or scrub soils (the term "scrub" being loosely applied, often to all land covered with heavy undergrowth, whether of alluvial or volcanic origin) and those found on our table-lands, not coming in the category of scrub soils.

Our forest lands are extensive, and of such varied character that to attempt to " bunch " them is absurd. A large proportion of forest timber grows on what may be called a " hungry " loam, on heavy clay, and sandy soils. Much of this soil, although not suited to all crops, may, with deep cultivation, drainage, and artificial feeding, be made to produce various field and fruit crops to perfection. There is, however, all over the colony a large amount of lightly timbered country (some of which goes by the name of " bastard scrub ") with great depth and fertility of soil, on which grain crops, fodder crops, and artificially sown pasture may be raised with excellent results. These loamy soils vary from black to red, and constitute the greater portion of the agricultural land still in the hands of the Crown, the scrub lands, owing to their paramount fertility, having nearly all been alienated—although there are always a large number of holders ready to re-sell at a moderate figure.

Clay soils are found throughout the greater portion of the colony, but are chiefly represented by the black and drab soils of the Darling Downs, the Maranoa, and western and central plains. When aided by a sufficient water supply these have proved of great cropping quality. They are fairly friable and sometimes of great depth, but in most cases require artificial irrigation and drainage to be of much agricultural value. In some few localities the rainfall and natural drainage are sufficient, and where this is the case many heavy crops have been secured. The great success attendant upon artesian bores to date is encouraging a very extensive testing of our resources in the direction of artificial water supply and conservation, and much has already been done to render these and other lands responsive to the labours of the agriculturist. It is conceded by all stockmen that the country at present being redeemed from drought by artesian water produces far better grasses than do our coast lands, an experience fully backed up by the observations of the Chairman of the Royal Commission upon Irrigation (Victoria, 1885) on his visit to the United States in the same year, upon which occasion he was accompanied by John L. Dow, Esq., M.P. (Vict.), and another special reporter. It

c

was remarked by these gentlemen that none of the districts visited (and they were many) were so productive nor were they so profitably cultivated as those in California, Colorado, Utah, and New Mexico (all of which are irrigated); and may we not infer that soils which—without irrigation— have in fair seasons produced such luxuriant pasturage as our western plains, will with its assistance rival and possibly outstrip those even of California? I mention this State for the reason that, of all the Union, California was alone considered by these gentlemen to approach in natural advantages those of their own colony, and we think we may lay claim to at least an equal place with our sister colony.

Calcareous and marly soils are not common. They are, however, to be found here and there, but, owing to their small area and the scattered districts in which they are situated, no general guide to their position can be given.

Last, but not least, are the sandy soils, of which the Roma district may be said to be typical. The suitability of these to the culture of the vine has been proved by the foremost position occupied by Roma in grape production, which, according to official returns,. reached in 1896 nearly one and a half million pounds weight, or, in exact figures, 3,306 lbs. per acre in full bearing. From the neighbouring district of Mitchell, on which sandy as well as loamy soil is found, a return of about one ton per acre was obtained, and about fifteen years ago as much as 10s. and 12s. per gallon was realized from wine made here.

The cultivation of wheat has also been very successful in the Roma and Mitchell districts, the average returns per acre being, in 1894, as high as 15·65 bushels and 14·99 bushels respectively. The above are in both instances higher than *a twenty-five years' average* for the State of New York, quoted in 1890 by the Director of the New York Agricultural Experiment Station. Our mean average between 1877 and 1895 was 12·29 bushels.

More might be said on this most important subject, and possibly opportunity may offer when referring to the various crops and districts in detail, but sufficient evidence, we think, has been adduced to demonstrate that, although much agricultural soil is at present given up to pastoral pursuits, or—even worse than that—to the undisturbed possession of kangaroo and dingo, there is ample land of the very best quality for agriculturist and pastoralist alike.

CLIMATE.

Speaking of Queensland from an agricultural point of view, the climate is exceptional. The vast area of territory, extent of coast-line, and geographical position induce climatic conditions under which almost any crop may be grown and any occupation followed. These may be classed as temperate—as experienced in the high lands of the south-eastern portion; sub-tropical—extending over the remaining portion of Queensland south of the tropic of Capricorn, and including the table-lands within the tropics; and tropical—found in the northern portion of the colony. Accurately speaking, the latter is about equally divided between the south temperate and the tropical zones.

It will have been seen that in point of productiveness our soil can vie with that of any of our neighbours, which may be partly accounted for by the fact that our genial climate often allows our farmers to harvest two or even three crops in the year, where the southern colonies can only harvest one, whilst our tropical products cannot—by reason of geographical position—be raised by any other Australian colonies except South and Western Australia. These two have not so far devoted any appreciable attention to agriculture, so that in this respect we should hold a far higher position than we do.

The summer extends from September to April (inclusive), and although within the tropics these months are, with few exceptions, decidedly hot, the temperature during the remainder of the year is pleasant, and well suited all over the Colony to the growth of temperate field and fruit crops and vegetables.

The summer season in the south-eastern portion of Queensland, on some of the more northern coast lands, and the elevated table-lands, resembles somewhat the winter season in the tropics, whilst the months of May, June, July, and August afford the most beautiful weather—a dry, healthy atmosphere, genial temperature, and cloudless sky—which if not "the joy of the agriculturist" in the past may, with proper attention to the conservation of water, become so in the future, and has always been the theme of unstinted praise by visitors from other climes. By many our climate is considered fully equal to that of Madeira, the Riviera, and the chief sanatoriums of the Old World. The rigours of winter—snow, ice, &c.—are not experienced here, and their appearance causes as much interest as would that of our "black swan" in Great Britain; the only objectionable features of winter being dry, cold winds, which come from inland, and are styled "westerly winds." The visitor finds these rather pleasant than otherwise, although by residents of long standing they are considered bitterly cold. One notable feature is the almost entire absence of the hot winds of the southern colonies and the "willy-nillies" of the north-west of Australia. Cyclones visit some of the northern towns (as is the case in all tropical countries), but only at long intervals, such disturbances on land and sea being fortunately but rare occurrences.

Compared with various towns throughout the world on the same parallel of latitude—and in many cases even further removed from the Equator—many of our towns, both without and within the tropics, can show a very much milder mean average temperature. It may suffice for our purpose to instance the city of Brisbane (about 68° Fahr.) as compared with New Orleans (69·1°) and Cairo (72·2°), Rockhampton (72°) as compared with Havana (79·1°), Townsville (75°) as compared with Bombay (81·3°). The 1891 lowest mean shade temperature for the Colony was found at Stanthorpe (58°), and the highest at Normanton (78°), from which it will be seen that although extremes of temperature may, and do, sometimes occur, Queensland, on the whole, is not subject to them. As the traveller goes west or north (speaking generally) the temperature rises, the south-eastern portion being in the matter of climate one of the most favoured spots on the earth, summer heat being almost invariably tempered by regular wind currents which set in from the sea; and in a lesser degree this applies to some of our northern seaports and table-lands. In no portion of this Colony is the temperature a bar to the residence of a white population, although, owing to the ease and small expenditure with which labourers from the adjoining South Sea Islands may be imported, most northern agriculturists (especially cane growers) prefer to employ this form of "coloured labour," and merely supervise the work of these so-called "boys." I think we may consider the fact that most Queensland trees are evergreen—compared with the great preponderance of deciduous trees in, say, Great Britain and the States—as in some measure supporting our plea for climatic advantages over the major part of the globe.

Although advisable in order to produce the very best results, the winter housing of live stock is neither necessary nor often practised. Immense flocks of the finest merinos, long woolled, and cross-bred sheep run on their pastures the year through; cattle reach their best during the winter season, running at large in a good "paddock"; horses likewise, when not engaged in heavy work, find all their needs in the open fields, winter as well as summer; and even dairy cattle have been habitually left during the winter months to browse on the open pastures.

In the North the rainy season may be considered as extending from December to April, and it is during these months that the agriculturist expects to see the main growth of all tropical crops. Following on these is a cool season of short duration, in which he can produce anything he

Interior of a Queensland Drawing-room.

may fancy in the way of vegetables, &c. The Southern rainy season is not so long nor so marked—indeed, in some years the rainfall has been spread over the whole year in such a manner as to entirely dispose of the "rainy season" for that year.

GRASSES.

The subject of grasses and grazing is of the greatest importance— and should be of the greatest interest—to all who, whether as pastoralists or farmers, have anything to do with the raising of stock. Our natural grasses possess a vitality—and in good seasons a luxuriance—which have contributed somewhat to apathy in the past. Thanks, however, to the praiseworthy efforts of our colonial botanist, F. M. Bailey, Esq., F.L.S., and our Department of Agriculture, who have supplied information respecting the relative value of our multitudinous grasses and have given practical assistance towards supplementing or substituting these by more suitable varieties where needed, an intelligent interest is awakening in the minds of many, and we may hope soon to see much larger areas of artificially sown indigenous and foreign grasses than we at present possess. Grass is the mainstay, and in the great majority of instances the only food, of our 6,000,000 cattle, 17,800,000 sheep, and 480,000 horses! As such it should command a large share of attention at the hands of practical men.

The testimony of all travellers goes to prove that some of our *natural* pastures (particularly in the western interior) possess the most valuable fattening and drought-resisting qualities, and when aided by artificial water supply they have still further improved. On many of our well-managed farms irrigation is practised with the best of results, some 275 acres in the neighbourhood of Toowoomba—largely prairie and natural grasses—having made rapid growth in the spring under this treatment. In one district 5,000 acres were in 1897 irrigated to great profit. Speaking of artificially sown pasture, the area returned under that heading fluctuates considerably, that for 1893 having been 18,000 acres odd, whilst that for 1897 was smaller. The splendid results which can be obtained from sheep, cattle, horses, and pigs by these methods being well known, the reason for this falling off must, it is thought by our Government Statistician, be ascribed to the cutting of a portion of the above area for hay. However this may be, it is certain that a series of good "dripping" seasons would have a tendency to discourage the laying down of *fresh* pasturage, although it is evident that this method of providing stock foods is gaining favour. The area required to support stock varies from one to four acres for sheep, and ten to twenty-five acres per head of cattle or horses. The long, rank pasturage of coastal and tropical Queensland affords excellent food for cattle and horses, and its growth is phenomenal to those unacquainted with climatic conditions such as we enjoy. Even on the western plains the grasses are sometimes sufficiently long to completely hide from view the sheep which they support, but within the tropics a height of twelve feet has been known to be attained, notably on the Morgan River, in the vicinity of Cooktown. The country on which this is found is locally called "Devil-devil," presumably from its furrow-like and swampy nature, which makes it almost impassable in wet weather. But whilst the grass of the interior is more scanty, its staying qualities are superior, and it is pre-eminently adapted to the feeding of sheep, which attain a greater weight of carcase here than in any other portion of the colony. In the Diamantina district, on Monkira Cattle Station (between the twenty-fourth and twenty-fifth parallel of latitude), a high-class herd of shorthorns, containing many pedigree beasts, is kept up solely on the native grasses, and the properties of these grasses are such that, although descended from cold climate stock, the cattle leave nothing to be desired as regards condition and hardiness. The same, indeed, may be said—perhaps with greater force—of the herds on the Georgina River, than which no better large herds of cattle have been raised in the colony.

With regard to the other Australian colonies (excepting Tasmania and Western Australia) our number of cattle per acre seems very small, but it will, I think, be readily conceded that this is rather due to our vast and perhaps somewhat unwieldy extent of country and to former want of water than to any inferiority of pasture, in view of the fact that large numbers of our pastoralists have come to us from these self-same colonies, and that our live stock are much more numerous in relation to the population than are those of any one of the group; for whilst Queensland had in 1896 some 189 per head of population (expressed in terms of sheep), the next colony in order of precedence (N.S.W.) had but fifty-seven, or about one-fourth as many per cap., which, of course, gives us a far greater exporting power. With closer settlement and the vastly improved pasturage which arises from it—of which many of our southern neighbours are to some extent already deriving the benefit—may we not reasonably expect not only a higher ratio per head of population, but per acre also?

Before passing on to the question of stock, with which the subject we have been considering is so intimately connected, I feel I cannot do better than to draw attention to a few extracts from a paper read before our Stockbreeders' Association in 1894 by F. Manson Bailey, Esq., F.L.S.; to some more recent information from the same high authority, published by the Department of Agriculture in pamphlet form; and to some very pertinent utterances of Professor Shelton, M.Sc. (late Queensland Instructor in Agriculture), which were delivered at one of our agricultural conferences, and subsequently printed. At the meeting of stockowners, Mr. Bailey said :—

" The indigenous grasses of Queensland number about 300 kinds, all of which perform some more or less important work in the economy of nature, and will, as they are better known, be found of advantage to the human race. In a pamphlet published by me a few years ago, about 160 sorts were brought under notice. In this paper I shall only draw attention to a few, which I would strongly recommend at once being experimented with :—

" Landsborough Grass (*Anthistiria membranacea*, Lindl.), also known as the 'Barcoo Grass' and 'Red Gulf Grass,' is an annual, and one of the first that should be brought under cultivation, especially for hay. Probably no grass, either indigenous or foreign, is so relished by stock. So fond, indeed, are they of it that after eating down the plant they will lick up every stray fragment that may be found lying upon the ground. If this grass has but the least chance it will produce good seed for the next season's crop. When under cultivation, it makes a dense intricate growth from one and a half to over two feet in height, and being very leafy and full of seed should make nutritious hay. It is the rule to cut grass for hay when in flower, but with a grass like the one described this rule cannot be strictly adhered to, for from an early period of its life it continues to flower and mature seed. When closely fed it bears good seed on stems only two or three inches high, and, although a tropical grass, has been found to thrive admirably in the Brisbane district.

" The Blue Grass (*Andropogon sericeus*, R. Br.). This is a general favourite with the Queensland pastoralists. It forms a good leafy bottom, and the stems are never very hard and 'cany,' so if cut at a proper time would form good hay; it seeds freely, so if it has anything of a show it is not likely to be lost. There are several forms of this grass; some of these are of quite a delicate growth, all of which would, besides being good pasture grasses, be suitable for hay. The tall Tassel Blue Grass, *Andropogon sericeus, var. polystachyus*, however, would not be suitable for this latter purpose.

" Of the genus *Panicum* our indigenous kinds number between fifty and sixty, out of which the following three might be selected for trial under cultivation :—

" *P. decompositum*, R. Br., which is very excellent grass, either for pasture or hay, especially that form most generally met with upon downs country. The seed of this grass is one of those used by the aborigines for food. In some parts this is known as 'Barley Grass.' I have also heard it called 'Mitchell Grass.' Mr. E. Palmer tells us that the native name at Cloncurry is 'Tindil.' This grass attains the height of from two to three feet, forms a good leafy bottom, the stems also are leafy, and the panicle large and spreading, bearing an abundant crop of seed ; in fact, it possesses all the requisites of good hay grass.

" *P. distachyum*, Linn. This is another excellent grass, and although it is what may be termed a tropical species, it has been found to thrive well near Brisbane, where some years ago I saw a small patch under cultivation, and at the time it occurred to me that it would be a very suitable kind to sow with the 'Landsborough,' for the purpose of hay.

" Of all Panicums it would be difficult to find one superior to the 'Warrego Summer Grass' (*P. flavidum*, Retz). In localities where this kind grows it has the name of being the best fattening grass known. It attains the height of from one and a half to two feet, is very leafy, and is a prolific seed-bearer. Both this and the last-named are also found in India.

" One species of *Setaria*, a genus closely allied to Panicum, may be selected for cultivation. The one I refer to is frequently to be met with in scrubs bordering Queensland rivers. I am not aware of its having received a local name, but to botanists it is known as *Setaria macrostachya*, H. B. and K. In the scrubs this grass has a somewhat straggling habit, but when sown in the open field it has been seen to greatly improve, and from what I have seen of it, I consider it fully equal, if not superior, to the *S. italica*, which is probably better known amongst farmers by its local name of 'panicum.'

" The Satin Top, in some localities also known as Blue Grass (*Andropogon erianthoides*, F. v. M.). This is one of the most remarkable of our grasses. Any one seeing it when in flower would be surprised if told that it was probably, for downs country, one of the very best that could be grown, yet nevertheless such is the case. The flowering stalks attain four or five feet in height and are very 'cany,' but its shortly creeping root-stock forms a very close leafy turf, before and even when the plant is in flower. It is considered to possess high fattening qualities, and when only two or three inches high has been known to keep sheep in better condition than any of our other grasses of double that height.

"*Astrebla* is an Australian genus, all the species of which are known as 'Mitchell grasses' and highly extolled for their vitality; they are usually met with in those parts of Australia subject to long droughts. They are coarse plants as a rule, but though their stems may appear dried up and without life, upon the fall of even a slight shower they seem to renew their life and burst out into growth at each knot of the tall hard stems. The above character applies to the species *A. pectinata* and its tall, coarse variety *triticoides*. The species *A. elymoides*, known in the Gulf country under the name of 'Curly Mitchell Grass,' is of a very different habit; instead of forming erect stout stems, its stems trail over the ground, often several feet in length; these are leafy, and a considerable part is occupied by the inflorescence. Under cultivation this sort would probably be found a useful hay grass, even in the Brisbane district. The first-mentioned kinds should be grown with the object of obtaining seeds for sowing in drier parts of our colony; they thrive well and have produced good seed near Brisbane. In appearance the seed resembles small grains of wheat, and in former times was largely used by the aborigines for food, and in fact might even be grown at the present time as a food grain.

"*Pollinia fulva*, Bentham—the *Saccharum fulvum* of Robt. Brown, and *Erianthus fulvus* of Kunth—has always been highly spoken of by pastoralists under one or other of the following local names:—'Brown Top,' 'Sugar Grass,' 'Red Grass,' and 'Bastard Mitchell Grass.' In my pamphlet on 'Queensland Grasses,' p. 25, I speak of it as 'usually being met with on wet land,' and such has been my experience, but lately in a packet of grass specimens received from a pastoralist on the Georgina River the following note was attached to the specimens of this grass:—'It is much more drought-resisting than the Mitchell Grass, and springs more quickly after rain.' It produces much sweet, nutritious herbage, and is much relished by stock, so that when met with it is generally found closely cropped. It, however, seeds freely, if only allowed the chance, which is probably the reason it has not long since been lost."

The following is extracted from the pamphlet referred to, and I need scarcely add is worthy of careful consideration by all those at present engaged in stock raising, or who intend to enter this industry. In the opening sentences of the remarks just quoted, Mr. Bailey refers to the cultivation of experimental areas of the native grasses, and I am glad to be in a position to record that his enthusiasm on this and kindred matters has in the present instance been at length rewarded, and that at date of writing several plots have been laid out in the gardens of the Acclimatisation Society, Bowen Park, Brisbane, and are in a thriving condition.

"Queensland is proverbially rich in the number and nutritive character of her indigenous grasses; but when one takes into account the great extent of territory and the fertility of the soil no wonder need be expressed at her grasses being numerous in species and abounding in nutrition. Our grasses have peculiarities also which have attracted the notice of persons from other parts of the world, and perhaps the most striking feature is the extraordinary tenacity of life which many of them possess. To fully understand this character, one must have been out on our western plains during a drought, and been a witness to the breaking up of the dry time, or a fall of rain for an hour or so, to fully believe in the magic-like change which comes over the country; the old dry, hard clumps or tufts of grass, which to all appearance before the fall of rain were dead, will be found in a few days' time covered with green leaf, affording abundant food for the famishing stock. All the grasses of these extensive plains are of a tufty character. Those of a creeping or spreading growth are found along the watercourses and around waterholes. This isolation of the plants has doubtless its advantages during the time of drought; each individual plant has more room for its roots, and during heavy continuous wet the plants are less likely to rot off than if crowded together; the small opening spaces also afford room for the many useful fodder herbs which spring up at their particular season of growth. It must not be inferred that, because in their native habitat a number of our grasses, both large and small, grow in detached tufts, this feature would be detrimental to the formation of a good permanent turf. Therefore, when any such are found recommended in this paper it is assumed that the tufty growth of these species in certain localities is due to surrounding circumstances. On the other hand, some of our most excellent kinds have a decided tussocky character, which if brought under cultivation would only be found suitable for rough, uneven, rocky land. Grasses from the colder climates of the globe do not, as a rule, take kindly to any part of Queensland, while those of our own tropical parts are found to thrive equally well in southern portions of the colony. It may also be well to bear in mind, when selecting kinds for experimenting with, that a grass in its natural habitat oftentimes gives but a poor idea of its real qualities; a poor, weak, and apparently worthless kind, which a person may meet with here and there in one of our dense scrubs, may, when it gets the chance of spreading by a clearance being made, so change character as to be by a partial observer unrecognizable, and therefore supposed to be an exotic accidentally brought to the colony with the seeds of some other plants.

"In very few localities or situations are grasses entirely wanting. Our dense scrubs have kinds peculiar to them which are only waiting the hand of man to bring them out into cultivation, and it is gratifying to know that in the few instances where this has been done success has crowned the experiment. Our tropical kinds thrive in the southern parts, and those of the great western and north-western downs or plains have been known to succeed when brought and planted both in and around Brisbane. This, unfortunately, is only known to the few.

"Our grasses are found to be in the greatest variety on the open coast lands and on the vast southern downs; here within a few paces one may gather from thirty to forty kinds. This would not be found the case on those extensive plains reaching from the Thompson to the Georgina rivers, where the number of kinds is limited to about ten or twelve in a similar radius. The pleasing feature is that the excellence of the kinds fully makes up for the paucity of the number—there is an almost total absence of troublesome or obnoxious kinds. Here I must be allowed to make a digression, to say that very few indeed are the purely obnoxious grasses of Queensland, and many of these at an early stage of growth furnish a great quantity of leafy herbage which is most nutritious. When seeding they are obnoxious to the sheep-farmer on account of the injury caused by the seeds getting into the wool. In the same way the tiller of the ground speaks of the couch grass as being an obnoxious, troublesome weed, when in its proper place no more valuable grass is known. Thus it will be observed that some of the so-called obnoxious grasses may prove of value to the dairyman.

"All persons having to do with stock will acknowledge that a necessity exists for variety in the food of cattle as well as man. This wise provision is forcibly brought home to the mind of one travelling during the present season across the extensive western plains which have before been alluded to; the season has been a favourable one, and the country retains much of its primeval appearance—that scourge the 'exotic weed' has not as yet overrun the indigenous plants. The stock from these parts fetch the highest price in the market. For an explanation of this problem we have not far to search. Besides the excellent grasses there is an admixture of wholesale and nutritious herbage. I have before observed that a peculiar feature of this pasture is that the grasses are in a manner isolated in tufts, and that while these tufts are at no great distance asunder, there still remains room for the growth of other plants between them. This space is usually occupied by plants which exist but a short time, and as one kind dies away, having gone through the course of its life by flowering and maturing its seed, another springs up to take its place, and goes through a similar course of existence. Thus it will be seen that the stock have a good variety of herbage to browse upon."

The following remarks of Professor Shelton on the subject of "Bush Hay," coming from a gentleman of such world-wide experience, will be of special interest to stock owners who desire to conduct their operations on scientific lines. Alluding to the above, he said :—

BUSH HAY.

"By this dubious cognomen the wild grasses of Australia when converted into hay are commonly known. Whether the hay is cut from the coast forest lands or the interior plains matters not ; all forms of hay made from the wild grasses receive, in Queensland at least, instantaneous popular condemnation as 'bush hay.' This general prejudice against hay made from the native grasses is somewhat difficult to explain, albeit it has doubtless, like most ideas widely held, a basis of experimental facts. It is not easy to understand why grasses of unsurpassed excellence when grazed should be comparatively worthless when dried into the condition of hay. It is a rule without exception, so far as I know, that, sour or otherwise, inferior grass makes an inferior hay, and *vice versâ*. Of course it is equally true that many of the best grasses cannot, from peculiarities of texture or habit of growth, profitably be made into hay. Not unlikely faulty methods of haymaking are the explanation of the prevailing dislike of hay made from the wild. grasses. Certainly I have seen both hay and ensilage exhibited at various agricultural conferences and elsewhere, made from wild grass, that to all appearances was the very perfection of fodder. The hay was beautifully coloured, aromatic as the best English hay, and of first-class texture. Hundreds of thousands of tons of grass easily susceptible of manipulation into this best of hay are annually, upon our grazing lands, converted into smoke and ashes, within sight of farmers who are striving by laborious ploughings and seeding to make crops of lucerne and oaten hay. I can think of few, even of the best English grasses, that surpass as a source of horse hay Kangaroo Grass (*Anthistiria ciliata*) or Oat Grass (*Anthistiria avenacea*), while Blue Grass (probably *Andropogon sericeus*) and Mitchell Grass (*Astrebla elymoides*) are the most promising of grasses for hay suited to sheep and cattle. This must be

Group of Outbuildings on a Cattle Station.

borne in mind—these wild grasses cannot be treated in haymaking as we treat bulky lucerne and oats. If these fine grasses are allowed to remain exposed to dews and scorching suns after having once become well dried, they deteriorate rapidly, losing colour, flavour, and quality, becoming soon as poor as ' bush hay ' well can be. The period of growth at which the wild grasses should be cut will vary with the different species. The coarser-growing sorts will need to be cut earlier than the finer and more leafy; but all should be cut somewhat early, say not much after the time of blossoming. During clear, hot weather, the crop will not bear exposure much longer than one day. The finer, lighter sorts that are cut in the morning should be raked in the afternoon, and the curing process finished in windrow and cock. By thus following the work up closely, allowing the least possible exposure to the weather, the colour of the hay with its other valuable qualities will be retained. This better class of bush hay ought to be available in quantity, and at a moderate price, to every householder in the Colony. Most likely the native meadows would be greatly improved, even for subsequent grazing, by mowing. The mowing would prevent offensive weeds from coming to seed and cause a thickening of the sod that could not but be advantageous. A great improvement in these wild meadows might doubtless be effected by going over the soil in the early spring time with the harrow or scarifier, thus loosening the indurated soil and facilitating the ingress of air, heat, and moisture to the soil beneath.''

LIVE STOCK AND MEAT EXPORT.

The pastoral industry is generally—and I think justly—looked upon as of the highest importance in all the Australasian Colonies, of which it has always been the pioneer industry. Queensland is no exception to this rule; indeed she is the pastoral colony *par excellence* of the group. Although not possessing so many sheep as New South Wales, nor quite so many horses as that colony, she far out-distances the other colonies in number of cattle, having somewhat over six million head—as many as all those of the other colonies together. Following the usual practice of reducing all live stock returns to terms of sheep (on the basis of one horse or one horned beast to ten sheep or ten pigs), the 1897 live stock returns show us to have the equivalent of 83,591,668 sheep—just upon one-third of the approximate grand total for the seven Australian colonies, which is equal to 253,530,647 sheep, whilst our area is just between a fourth and a fifth of Australia. In relation to our exports, this industry takes a very high place, as much as £5,000,000 odd being contributed by wool, meat, hides, and allied products in 1898, just about half the value of our total exports.

We have, however, by no means reached the full measure of our capabilities ; rather, we have but entered on the race with the great cattle-breeding countries for the markets of the world.

Victoria, New Zealand, and New South Wales are all more heavily stocked per square. mile than is our colony (presumably owing to their smaller area ; the smallest of the three being most heavily stocked, and so on—in direct ratio to their size). According to 1894 figures, the first-named colony had 406 head of live stock (terms of sheep) per square mile, exclusive of pigs, whilst we had in 1896 but 133·42 head per square mile on the same basis of calculation. There is little doubt but that, with our genial climate, we should be in a position to graze as many head per square mile as Victoria, and upon the above very *modest* estimate (equal to more than one and a half acres per sheep, or about sixteen acres per large beast) we might carry some 271,409,782 sheep—or other live stock in proportion. It should be remembered that all the colonies which exceed our ratio of stock to area not only have far larger areas under agricultural occupation than ourselves—thus relatively raising their stock ratio on purely pastoral lands—but are so much more densely populated that (as previously stated) our proportion of live stock to population is—even now—greater than any others of the group, and is some forty-two times as great as that of Europe. Upon the whole, as shown by figures given in Mr. Thornhill Weedon's ' Queensland, Past and Present '—the official year-book of the Queensland Government—our live stock have increased rapidly, notwithstanding some very severe checks, in the shape of bad seasons, commercial depressions, and occasional outbreaks of epidemic diseases, which are by no means as severe in these colonies as in other portions of the globe. The latest, and perhaps the most serious visitation our herds have experienced has been that of the "tick" (involving an outlay of £20,000 or more), but the stringent quarantine regulations which were put into force—whilst proving a temporary drawback to the industry—have proved so effective that in most districts the trouble has been overcome. It has been authoritatively stated that no advance of the scourge has taken place since July, 1896 ; indeed at time of writing the most encouraging reports continue to come in as to its noticeable abatement. The few—and comparatively mild—diseases with which our stock owners have made acquaintance are as follows : *Pleuro-pneumonia*. In the "sixties" much loss was occasioned by this disease, and on Jan. 29, 1862, the Pleuro-Pneumonia Act was put into force, from which time its ravages abated, and it is now scarcely known. (Inoculation of healthy cattle with lymph from a pleuro-pneumonia beast, as now practised, is a thoroughly reliable specific.) *Tuberculosis*—A disease which in human beings as well as in cattle is receiving much attention of late; it is confined to the moist coastal districts, and as inspectors possessing the highest medical qualifications examine all cattle killed at the various meat-works, and further preventive measures are being brought forward, there is no doubt that our Colony will soon be able to boast of comparative immunity from this disease also. *Anthrax* appears but seldom, and the sphere of its influence is small.

Blackleg, fluke, foot-rot, catarrhal fever, intestinal worms, and worm nests (spiropteric tumours) do not offer any serious menace to the pastoralist. Scab is unknown.

Viewed in the light of our very large number of live stock per inhabitant, it is scarcely a matter for surprise that our home consumption should be large. According to a careful calculation, based on the best figures available, the Registrar-General in his 1896 Report sets this down at 365 lbs. of beef, mutton, pork, and veal per head of population in the principal towns and their suburbs, &c. They consume three times as much per capita as do the inhabitants of the United States (of which the flesh consumption is 120 lbs.); nearly four times as much as Britishers, and nearly six times as much as Germans did some fifteen years ago. Facilities of transport have, however, largely increased of late, and these have tended both to lower our own meat consumption, by bringing a greater variety of foods to our door, and to raise that of small meat-eating countries through a consequent fall in values. The growing interest in agricultural pursuits, and consequently increased consumption of vegetable foods in Queensland, coupled with an anticipated expansion in our meat export to other countries, will tend to still further lessen this contrast. It is even stated that some nations which have hitherto been looked upon as almost exclusive vegetarians are adopting a meat diet; a statement which would seem to lend colour to my assumption as regards the tendency towards equalization of the world's meat supply.

The live stock of Queensland consist of horses, cattle, sheep, and a few thousand pigs, besides a number of goats, of which no official account seems to be taken—although these latter sometimes largely contribute to the sustenance of settlers in new or poorly grassed districts. Analyzed the proportion of stock to area in 1897 was: Horses, 0·72; cattle, 9·11; sheep, 26·62 per square mile; and the ratio per inhabitant was: Horses, 0·99; cattle, 12·56; sheep, 36·72; pigs, 0·23.

HORSES.

The exact number recorded at the close of 1897 was 479,280—an increase of 11·8 per cent. on the figures for 1894. Statistics prior to the separation of Queensland from New South Wales are somewhat unreliable, but as far as I can ascertain, the number of horses in 1844 was 650; these had increased by the year 1848 to something over 2,000 head, and it is roughly computed that at the close of 1859 the number had again risen to about 20,000 head. Six years later we have an authentic record that the number was 51,090, which would be equivalent to an increase during that time of more that 17 per cent. per annum, on the assumption that there were no losses—a moral impossibility. Few horses (and those "blood" stock) were imported, so that the suitability of the climate for horse breeding cannot be gainsaid.

For farm and all heavy draught classes, a number of sires and dams of the "Clydesdale," "Shire," and "Suffolk Punch" breeds have been from time to time imported—to use a stock phrase—"regardless of cost," so that as fine a stamp of draught horses are to be met with as "at home." Pure bred stock, of course, run into fancy prices, but good serviceable horses for plough or dray can be now bought for £5 to £10, although a few years ago they fetched double the present price.

Of light harness we have some excellent, as well as indifferent, examples. Sires of such breeds as the "Cleveland Bay," "Roadster," and "Norfolk Trotter" are to be found scattered over the Colony, and can generally be obtained for breeding purposes for a small fee, but frequently, owing to apathy, these advantages are not availed of, a loose system of letting inferior stallions run with the mares is followed, and bad stock results. In Coachers and Hunters growing interest is exhibited, and is being fostered by handsome prizes for excellence in these classes, given at the annual meetings of the National Agricultural and Industrial Association of Queensland, at Bowen Park, Brisbane.

Of coachers, both Yorkshires and Cleveland Bays are found here, and a really excellent class of stock is growing up.

Although we have a small number of Arab and other thoroughbreds, by far the most numerous class is the "hack." Here also is the widest range as regards quality and, consequently, price. Saddle horses—the progeny of full-blooded sires and sturdy mares—are worth £8 to £15, but it is a common occurrence to see a fairly staunch unbroken colt go for a couple of sovereigns in one of the numerous auction sale-yards. The hardiness of some of these "scrubbers" is, however, great; many of them being capable of carrying their riders fifty miles a day for a week at a stretch without sustaining any injury. In point of size this section of our horses equal the best to be found in the Old World, their height varying from 14½ to 17 hands—with breadth in proportion. In the less densely populated districts, mobs of unbranded horses—the descendants of a mixed lot, mostly those which have eluded station control—roam in a more or less wild state; these are occasionally caught and sent to auction, where they are dubbed "brumbies," and although a few turn out to be serviceable beasts, the unsophisticated often have bitter cause to bewail their purchase. Horse riding is so common a practice, and horse flesh is comparatively so cheap, that an astounding number of horses change hands at the sale-yards. It is in the breeding of racehorses that Australia, and Queensland as much as her neighbours, has made the greatest progress, and in which a never-dying and national interest is taken. It is a matter for regret that so noble a sight and inspiriting a sport as horse-racing should be made an occasion for the gambling spirit, which is so common an adjunct to the "turf," but great as the evil still is, legislative attention has been already directed to this matter with a measure of success, and I hope will at some no very distant date still further seek to wipe out in our Colony this world-wide stain on the grandest of sports. A few specimens of mules are to be met with, but owing probably to the absence—speaking generally—of rugged country, such as they are specially suited for, the breeding of this class of stock has not been engaged in, and I do not think it is likely to be.

As regards export, many attempts have been made to establish a regular trade in horses with other parts of the globe less favourably situated for breeding, and although some few shipments to India from this Colony (and to Great Britain from the adjacent Colony of New South Wales) have been successful, the percentage of returns—owing to losses, cost of feed, and attendance during the voyage—has so far prevented the trade being put on a sound footing. That a market exists for well-conditioned, staunch stock is evidenced by the fact that a shipment in November, 1896, from Sydney, per "Southern Cross," averaged £20 per head landed in London, and hacks, per "Gulf of Lions," brought £20 10s. to £27 14s. each. The second great obstacle to this outlet for our surplus lies in the great disfigurement entailed by our system of branding; but as this is a matter which is certainly remediable, we may look forward to its removal when our surplus really necessitates the finding of an outside market. At the present time the number of horses is not much in excess of the requirements for station and general use, and occasional inquiries for military purposes from India—and very recently from the seat of war in the Philippines—tending to reduce the above, no serious apprehensions regarding this matter need at present be entertained.

CATTLE.

Starting from the year 1844, when there were said to be some 13,000 head of cattle in what afterwards was to become Queensland, the number of these rapidly increased to 37,000 odd in 1847. By the end of 1859 (the date of separation) they reached 300,000 in number, in 1865 they amounted to 848,346, and at the close of the year 1897 had reached 6,089,013. That such an enormous growth of stock should necessitate an extensive market goes without saying, and whilst for the first few years this was found in local requirements and in shortages amongst the southern colonies, the increased attention paid in the latter to stock breeding has all but closed that market to any but their locally raised cattle and sheep, and Queensland has been obliged to look further afield.

Amongst cattle bred for beef, the chief are of Durham and Shorthorn origin; there are, however, a few Hereford and Devon crosses and Aberdeen Angus polled cattle to be met with. As showing the capabilities of the favourite Shorthorn, I quote the following from a paper by Mr. Peberdy, a stock owner of large experience, read at the Rockhampton Conference in May, 1891 : "In the old days, when there was no trucking of stock, it was a common thing for Durham oxen, descended from the best herds on the Bulloo and Cooper's Creek, to march from their homes to Melbourne—from 1,000 to 1,200 miles—and there compete with, and frequently beat, cattle raised on the best Victorian pasturage within 100 miles of the yards. Personally, I have known Durham cattle to travel *through Queensland to Melbourne*, the journey occupying over *forty weeks*, and then some of the draft carried in a greater weight of beef upon their frames than I ever saw upon the frame of a scion of one of the competing breeds that had been bred and fed at large upon Australian pasture. To particularize a few instances of extreme hardship I have known Durham cattle to suffer, I may mention that some years back several drafts of Western Queensland cattle had to make three consecutive *dry stages*, viz., *forty miles*, *thirty miles*, and *seventy miles*. Following these came a draft from one of the heaviest-fleshed Durham herds in Western Queensland. Before they reached the end of the seventy-mile stage the water had failed, and they had to make upwards of *100 miles without a drink*. All of these drafts accomplished the task et them without loss or damage, and were marketed, at the completion o a 1,000 mile journey, prime fat, the last draft averaging over £10 per head." The class of cattle found in dairy herds still leaves much to be desired, but great improvements are being effected amongst intelligent dairymen's stock by the introduction of imported and pedigree Jersey, Alderney, Brittany, and Ayrshire bulls. I may refer to this in dealing with the subject of Dairy Products.

The prices of cattle vary much according to breed and nature of the season. No idea of the values of pedigree beasts can be given, although Australian squatters have been known tò pay £1,500 or £2,000 for a bull; but the price of ordinary stores of from two to three years of age is at present 25s. to 35s., whilst fat cattle are worth on trucks at inland railway stations from 50s. to 60s., and cows 30s. to 40s. Cows in milk range from £3 10s. to £6. At the Enoggera yards, Brisbane, and in other centres, values are, of course, higher. On January 21, 1897, prime fat bullocks realized £3 12s. 6d. to £4 5s.; medium, £3 to £3 7s. 6d.; best cows (dry) fetched £2 7s. 6d. to £3; others from £1 17s. 6d. to £2 2s. 6d. For statistical purposes the Colony is divided into Southern, Central, and Northern divisions. The first-named carries by far the greatest number of cattle, whilst the Central district has the smallest number of the three (1897). Owing to inclement seasons, the large increases which seem to have obtained in early days (when only the pick of the country was occupied) have not been maintained, a year or two of high percentages being generally followed by a similar period of depression.

SHEEP.

The introduction of these, about the year 1840, formed the foundation of the great squatting interests of to-day; the term "squatter" (literally "one who sits down") having been first applied in 1842 to pastoralists generally, and since retained by them.

The total number of sheep in Mr. Leslie's pioneer flock was little more than 5,600, comprising about 4,000 ewes, 1,500 wethers, and 100 rams; by the year 1847 the number in the Colony was 536,580; by 1859 it was 2,000,000; by 1865, 6,594,996; and 1896 live-stock statistics show the number at the end of that year to have reached 19,593,696, or an increase of nearly two hundred per cent. on the 1865 figures! As in the case of cattle, this growth is in the face of the heavy "draws" made upon both classes of stock for home consumption (estimated for 1896 at 233,182 cattle and 932,728 sheep), by losses from bad seasons, and those killed for export, so that the natural increase must be set down at a much higher figure than is given above.

The principal breed is unquestionably the Merino, of which the clip has often commanded very great attention in the home markets. The early history of the establishment in the parent Colony of this breed is of great interest to Queenslanders, for it may be accepted as an undoubted fact that its adaptability to New South Wales conditions had much to do with the favour it found with our own pastoralists.

From a work by G. W. Griffin, Esq., United States Consul at Sydney in 1888, published by direction of the Colonial Treasurer of New South Wales, I gather that the first importation of Merinos was made by Capt. McArthur in 1797. These few Spanish Merinos were supplemented in 1804 by further purchases from the royal stud at Hampton Court, the prices paid ranging from £6 to £28 per head; the weight of fleece of the highest priced beast being 7 lbs. 12 ozs. at date of shearing previous to the sale.

French and American sheep of this breed—each having their own peculiar excellences—were in the first instance imported into Victoria about the date of our formation into a separate colony, and doubtless contributed to the high quality of Merino stock throughout the colonies. At a sale of Rambouillet or French Merino rams in 1861 by Messrs. R. Goldsborough & Co., an average price of £83 per head was obtained for fifty head. Of our own flocks probably the most notable is that of the Hon. Wm. Allan, M.L.C., of Braeside, Dalveen. In colour these sheep differ from the ordinary Merino, being almost exclusively black, and are hardier and more active than the white breed. The wool has now made itself a very high name in the colonial and home markets, and will probably lead to a spread of this strain of Merino.

Besides the above, a variety of coarse-woolled breeds, such as Lincolns, Leicesters, Cotswolds, Shropshire Downs, and South Downs, are in the Colony, besides crosses of the Merino.

A remarkable and beneficial change has during the past few years overtaken this branch of the pastoral industry, for whilst in the early days it was in the hands of a very small number of men, we find almost uniformly, on looking at the statistics of the past five years, that the number of owners has increased and the average size of flocks has decreased. The net number of sheep in the Colony, after home consumption, losses, and export had been met, were in 1893, 1894, 1895, and 1896 less than in the three preceding years, which were exceptionally good ones. As regards the distribution over the Colony, something may be said. Out of the 103 Petty Sessions districts and sub-districts, as shown in the Registrar-General's 1896 Report on Agriculture and Live Stock, only eleven are without sheep; in thirty-eight districts the number per district is under 1,000 ; in six districts the number is between 1,000,000 and 2,000,000,' and in one it is over 2,000,000, whilst the remaining forty-seven districts have anything between 1,000 and 1,000,000.' Very few are found in the northern portion of Queensland, 17,887,398 being in the southern and central. Over 11,000,000 sheep—or more than half the total number in the Colony—are found in the Petty Sessions districts of Cunnamulla, Hughenden, Longreach, Muttaburra, St. George, Winton, Blackall, and Barcaldine, so that there may be said to be unlimited *room* for the extension of the industry—provided, of course, that the market is first secured. Only a very superficial idea of the price at which stock will sell can be given in these pages ; breed, time from last shearing, and nature of the season affect values to an enormous extent. The following extract from the *Brisbane Courier* of January 29, 1897, will give a fair idea of prices in the principal Brisbane sale-yards :

" The weekly stock sales at the Enoggera yards yesterday afternoon opened to a small attendance of local buyers, and right throughout the market was exceedingly dull, with a consequent large fall in prices. About 4,160 sheep were penned. The Jondaryan sheep were the first offered, and all of the cross-breds were cleared at from 6s. 6d. to 7s., and at 8s. 6d. for one small pen, but only a few of the merino wethers were sold from 5s. to 5s. 9d., the balance being withdrawn. East Prairie merino wethers sold from 3s. to 3s. 6d., merino ewes at 3s., cross-bred wethers at 5s., and cross-bred ewes at 4s. 3d. Merino wethers from Ellington, a small draft, fetched 5s. 9d., and 4s. 6d. upwards was given for another lot of merino wethers from East Prairie. St. Helen's merino wethers were worth from 4s. to 5s. ; Jimbour cross-bred ewes made from 4s. 9d. to 5s. 6d. ; and a small pen of five reached 8s. 6d. ; while merino wethers from the same establishment found buyers at 3s. 9d. to 5s., some of the best of them being withdrawn. For cross-bred wethers from Darkie Flat, 5s. to 5s. 9d. was paid, and a picked pen realized 8s. 9d., and Eton Vale cross-bred wethers were placed at 4s. 9d. to 6s. 6d. From 5s. to 7s. 9d. was given for merino wethers from Kurrawah, and from 3s. 3d. to 4s. for merino wethers from Spring Meadows, while Logie Plains merino wethers were worth from 4s. 6d. to 4s. 9d., and Headington Hill merino wethers from 5s. to 5s. 9d. A fair indication of the low state of the market was afforded by the comparatively small values received for the Yandilla draft of merino wethers ; prime-conditioned sheep, which a month or two ago found ready purchasers at from 8s. to 10s. 6d., going badly at 5s. 6d. to 6s. 9d. One pen of cross-breds from the same place made 8s. Back Plains cross-bred wethers were marketable at 7s. 3d. to

8s., and Bowenville merinos fetched from 3s. to 4s. 3d., while the whole of the Clifton draft was withdrawn from sale."

Another report from Rockhampton puts the value of young sheep in that neighbourhood during the summer at 3s. to 4s., according to age, sex, and quality.

PIGS.

Thanks to the establishment in our midst of several bacon-curing factories with first-class plants, and to the success attending the efforts of the travelling dairy to widen the scope of our dairy operations (with which pig-raising is generally associated), a very large and increasing interest is being taken in this class of live stock.

Both in point of numbers and breed great changes are taking place. In 1847 there were but 200 in "Moreton Bay settlement"; we now have 110,855 (1897)—an increase on 1894 of about one-twelfth—but this is still under one-third of the number which the smaller colonies of New Zealand and New South Wales each possess. The increase from 1893 to 1894 was even more marked, being at the rate of 31·71 per cent. for the year.

According to the returns for 1896, the districts where the chief progress was made in the twelve months, and the respective increases upon 1895, were as follows:—Marburg, an increase of 529 head; Beaudesert, 794; Laidley, 346; Gatton, 483; Crow's Nest, 247. Of the total Petty Sessions districts, none were without "grunters"; and the practice of pig-keeping on a large scale is growing in many districts, of which the following may be mentioned:—Toowoomba, 5,294; Rockhampton, 3,918; Gatton, 5,201; Beaudesert, 5,309; Warwick, 3,453; Laidley, 4,214; Dugandan, 3,602; Brisbane, 3,507; South Brisbane, 2,755; Rosewood, 3,182; Marburg, 3,063; Crow's Nest, 1,667.

The breed which has been found most suitable to the climate, and which is preferred by buyers, is the Berkshire. But a few years ago this was a comparatively unknown sort; several imported specimens were, however, distributed throughout the colony by the efforts of the Government, bacon factory owners, and others, with the result that strains of this pig can be purchased in almost any town.

The Yorkshire, China, and other breeds common in Great Britain are to be met with, but they are not suited to factory requirements in this colony. Speaking broadly, their disability does not lie so much in size or colour as in their tendency to put on excessive fat. Contrary to public taste in the United Kingdom, and in most cold countries, the demand in Queensland is for *lean* meat, and reasonably so.

The price of pigs fluctuates somewhat according to the law of supply and demand, and is controlled by the various factories. The system generally adopted is for a buyer to go round each district in the interests of the factory, offer his 20s. to 27s. for all well-shaped beasts of 100 lbs. to 160 lbs., and make arrangements for the farmer to deliver (free of cost at the railway trucks, or other "rendezvous") any he may feel disposed to sell at the price. Sometimes the buyer is one of the factory staff, but oftener he is a resident in the district, and is paid a bonus of 1s. or so on each pig he purchases. So far there has never been a serious glut in this market, and in 1896 some twenty-one tons of pig products (principally hams and bacon) were imported for our own consumption, so that there is plenty of room for the extension of this industry with a view to home, but more especially foreign trade. The ratio of pigs to population is still very small—about as 1 to 4; but considering the utility of this animal as farm scavenger, his remarkable freedom in this country from disease, and the heavy protective duty—2d. per lb. for salt pork, 3d. per lb. for hams and bacon—which pig products from outside have to pay, the practice of pig-raising should, and is likely to, be much more general than it is at present. On some of the stations in the Moreton district, notably Buaraba, there used to be in former years, and I believe still are, large numbers of wild swine, the descendants of some which apparently got away into the dense scrub, beyond the control of their owners, and thus laid the foundation of subsequent droves. Similarly, on the Pioneer and Herbert rivers, &c., in the North, numbers are to be found roaming at large in the scrubs, the property of any one who takes the trouble to shoot them.

I may remark that these are the only class of live stock not required by law to be registered; even goats needing a registration fee of 5s. and a distinguishing mark within the precincts of the Brisbane and most other municipalities. The number of pigs per square mile averages about ·15.

EXPORT OF LIVE STOCK.

In view of the probable early renewal of efforts to establish this trade under more favourable conditions than hitherto, the following figures, from a report of some shipments from Sydney in January of 1895, may be of interest to our readers: the conditions being about equal in this and the neighbouring colony. The freight averaged £6 6s. a head, the fodder £2 12s., and other expenses brought the expenditure in Sydney up to £9 15s. 1d. a head. Estimating their selling value in Sydney at £5, this would make their cost to the consignors £14 15s. 1d. per head. The twenty-five bullocks were sold in London towards the close of February for an average of £21 12s. 1d., less £2 9s. 2d. per head for London charges.

Some nine head of Devons were very highly spoken of, as being good travellers, and "dressing out" well at the Deptford yards. These were of medium weight, and it was conceded that small, young cattle of the same quality would always command a ready sale at prices equal to the best American.

PART II.

Agriculture, Horticulture, Forestry, Pisciculture, &c.

SUGAR.

OF agricultural products this is our most important article of export— a position which it has held for many years. In point of area, sugar-growing is accountable for 98,641 out of a total of 371,857 acres under crop in 1897, and takes second place in this respect—maize being the favourite crop. During the ten years ending 1896, both area under cane and area crushed for sugar have increased steadily, the latter from 36,806 acres in 1887 to 66,640 acres in 1896—equal to 80 per cent. advance. The extent of land under sugar cultivation is an increase of 15,548 acres over the preceding year. The increased areas planted are situated in the Bowen, Ingham, Mackay, Childers, Maroochy, Cairns, and Port Douglas districts. An estimate prior to the opening of the 1896-7 crushing season gave the area available for crushing to be 71,975 acres, which is an increase on 1895 of 16,000 acres odd, and up to December 31, 1896, the yield from this assumed area was 100,774 tons of sugar—the largest yield which has so far been recorded in Queensland in any one year. The average return per acre of cane which was crushed was 1·51 tons of sugar per acre; this would give a return of about £18 per acre (export price). The year 1897 ranks next, with 97,916 tons, at the rate of 1·50 tons per acre. The above ratio is just under that for the ten years 1888-1897, and shows an advance of nearly a quarter of a ton (say £2 10s.) per acre upon the mean average return for 1876-1885. Estimating the value upon the 1897 basis (although much higher values than £12 per ton prevailed during most of the time), and reckoning the average number of acres crushed between 1887 and 1897 to be 46,000, this represents a gain of £1,243,930, which can only be attributed to better methods of growing and manufacturing; and, indeed, these have undergone most important and, it is generally considered, beneficial changes.

The first pound of Queensland sugar was produced in 1862, and although the quantity of cane grown was at first small, only 608 acres being utilized in this manner in 1866, its cultivation was, until quite recently, confined to planters with considerable capital, who more often than not owned the mill to which the cane was delivered. The indifferent quality of many of the makes of sugar, low prices, threatened competition, and unwieldy nature of many of the sugar estates, led to a consideration of the means to be adopted for the revival of the industry. Large plantations have been subdivided; and sold on the most liberal terms to farmers, with the understanding that the vendor binds himself to take from the purchaser at a fixed price per ton all the cane the latter can raise. In addition to this step, the Sugar Works Guarantee Acts, 1893 to 1895, which came into operation early in 1894, have enabled groups of cane farmers to combine for the purpose of erecting mills of the latest type, so that greater economy may result. Up to June 30, 1897, thirteen central mills had received an aggregate advance of £359,990, which sum is secured upon the joint and private freehold property of the shareholders, and in some cases by debentures, insurance policies, bonds, &c.

The following account, from the *Brisbane Courier*, of the Proserpine Mill, near Bowen, said to be the largest—as it is one of the latest erected —will be of interest :—

" The mill occupies a fairly central site on the south bank of the river, and is connected by tramway with a landing wharf five miles distant. The tram line, constructed by Mr. A. Mackenzie, of Bowen, was completed a few days before last Christmas. Unlike the Central Mill at Plane Creek, in the Mackay district, which has suffered much delay from a short supply of water in this its first season (1896), the location of this mill seems to have been judiciously chosen, and a practically inexhaustible supply of water assured. The capacity of the new mill is 5,000 tons, and with more cultivation, Mr. Fiddes, the Government engineer under the Sugar Works Guarantee Act, who has frequently visited this district since building operations commenced, has expressed the opinion that its capacity may be raised to 8,000 tons each season. The machinery has been supplied and erected by Messrs. Walker, Limited, Maryborough, whose work in connection with central mills is well known throughout the colony.

"The composition of the settlement is decidedly heterogeneous, embodying English, Scotch, Irish, Germans, Danes, Swedes, &c. They number slightly in excess of 400, and some idea of the progress made in cane-growing may be elicited from the fact that already 900 acres are under cane, all of which—should no undesirable flood or other visitant make its presence felt—is expected to yield at least 1,500 tons of sugar next season. Mera, Rose Bamboo, and Striped Bamboo are the canes most in favour here."

In reviewing the year 1896 the above "daily" said : — "*The mills erected under the Sugar Works Guarantee Act have been steadily establishing themselves; and a commercial start was made in those ready to take advantage of the crushing season.* One feature of the year has been the increase in number of small sugar farms, to supply which a large quantity of plant cane has been required; and in order to meet the demand it has been found necessary to add to the area under plant cane at the State Nurseries. The Department of Agriculture obtained from New Guinea a quantity of different varieties of cane. These, after propagation, will be distributed, and should they prove to be of equal worth to those formerly imported from the Possession and placed in the hands of cane growers, the additions to the varieties of Queensland cane will be of great importance. *The central sugar mills at Mackay—the pioneers of the central mill system—continue to progress, and are now more than able to hold their own. All liabilities to date have been paid to the Government, and a dividend has been declared.*"

Speaking of the latter, Mr. R. W. McCulloch, inspector under the Act, said, at the commencement of 1897 :—

" *A worse time could not have been selected for establishing central mills than when the first two—the Pleystowe and the Marian—started in the Mackay district.* The two successive seasons have been exceedingly adverse, but, notwithstanding this, both the companies have been able to make good their interest. The southern central mills have had a severe winter to contend against, yet they have been able to pay interest, and have credit balances of from £1,200 to £1,500 each. My impression of central mills is that they must come out all right. The mere fact of their being co-operative concerns will ensure their being worked to the best advantage for both sides. They are all of the most modern design, and can make a ton of sugar from as low a number of tons of cane as any other mills in any part of the world. Given fair seasons, I have not the slightest doubt of these meeting their engagements. One great thing they have achieved is to bring about a very considerable settlement on the lands around each."

In 1896-7, seven of these mills had crushings—two of them for their second season. The amount of sugar made by them may be put down as follows :—Nerang, 755 tons; Mount Bauple, 982 ; Gin Gin, 963 ; Plane Creek, 372 ; Pleystowe, 1,088; Marian, 1,860; Mulgrave, 1,433. Progress has been the order of the day, and mills have been erected at Nambour, North Isis, Mossman, Bellenden-Ker, Aloomba, Geraldton, &c.; several of which had already started operations in 1897. At the close of the preceding year there were fifty-three mills at work, without counting crushing plants which did not manufacture their own sugar. Of these, thirteen produced less than 500 tons each, seven over 500 and less than 1,000 tons each, fourteen over 1,000 and less than 2,000, and nineteen 2,000 and over. Several of the factories making under 2,000 tons have a very much larger capacity, and their low output was due chiefly to their having only just started, or to a short supply of cane owing to temporary unfavourable conditions. The following were the returns from the various districts during the above season :—

DISTRICT.	1894–5.	1895–6.	1896–7.	
			Estimate.	Output.
	Tons.	Tons.	Tons.	Tons.
Brisbane	2,650	2,140	3,000	3,700
Maryborough and Isis .	7,226	10,858	20,000	19,250
Bundaberg and Gin Gin .	23,618	23,361	30,000	28,700
Rockhampton . . .	665	1,580	1,500	1,600
Mackay	27,927	23,150	20,000	16,300
Burdekin	8,776	6,477	8,000	6,200
Herbert	13,695	9,900	11,000	10,500
Johnstone	5,215	5,357	7,000	8,500
Cairns	1,940	3,000	3,500	3,250
Total . . .	91,712	85,823	104,000	98,000

From the foregoing it will be seen that the crop realized 6,000 tons less than was anticipated in June, 1896, and this deficit is accounted for by the poor results from the Burdekin and Mackay districts. On the other hand, the Johnstone and Herbert districts have fully maintained their positions, and this is the more satisfactory as damage from the grub pest has been an unknown factor in altering results.

The above output for 1896–7 would represent about 75,000 tons for export, the average excess of production over export for the three preceding years being 23,000 as compared with 20,700 tons (the average for the three years previous to 1893–4). There seems little doubt that the consumption of the Colony is now well over 22,000 tons per annum, and this we understand is partly attributable to the establishment of additional jam factories in Queensland, and partly to the fact that the local production of beer has increased from three and a quarter million

The Growth of the Sugar Industry. Refrigerators and Machine Sheds in the Isis District.

D

gallons in 1892 to over five and a half million gallons in 1896. The cane crop was taken off 66,640 acres, giving an average sugar yield per acre of 1·51 tons, being but ·03 below that of 1895, and ·04 below the annual mean for the ten years ending 1895, a result which is not very high, but which is reasonably good under the circumstances. Crushings have occasionally given a yield of six tons of sugar per acre, and two tons per acre are frequently met with.

The price of sugar in the wholesale market is, under the new system, of very great interest to cane farmers. The Colonial Sugar Refining Company, who practically control the market, in 1896 notified to the retail trade a rise of 20s. per ton on all lines except "tablets," golden syrup, and treacle. This means that grocers, &c., are now paying for "tablets," £24 10s.; 1B (brewers' crystals), £17 10s.; 1X sugar, £17; 1A sugar, £17; No. 2 sugar, £15 10s.; No. 3 sugar, £14 10s. Contrasted with the average prices of eight or nine years ago, these are very low. As showing the difference in values even four years back, I may state that in 1894 an export of 1,298,200 cwt. was valued at £886,834, and in the following year—although the quantity had increased by nearly 46,000 cwt.—the total value was only £796,117.

On this subject a writer to the press has said:—"The price of cane has not been generally reduced. North of the Wide Bay District the farmers remain for the most part untouched. The exceptions are so few as not to bulk significantly. Millowners have voluntarily assumed the burden of the changed market, they have not had it forced upon them by concerted pressure on the part of the growers. This is a very uncommon departure from usual practice. The explanation is not single or simple, or all on the surface. Several reasons are in operation. One undoubtedly is the disclosure of the large profits made by the best mills. All the sophistry the millowners' intellect is capable of (though the millowners have mostly maintained a prudent silence) could not efface the deep impression that documents such as the balance-sheets of the Mackay central mills have made on the farmers and the public mind. On an output of 3,481 tons of sugar North Eton made a profit, allowing for depreciation of plant, of £11,418. Although the cane cost 15s. 2½d. per ton, the average cost of a ton of sugar, including Government and Bank interest, was only £8 19s. 10d. At £8 10s. for 88 per cent. sugar, the present price of North Eton sugar would be about £9 5s. The Racecourse mill presented still more impressive figures. The Homebush (C.S. Co.) mill is believed to have excelled both results. The output was more than double that of either of the central mills (a most important factor in

D 2

economy of manufacture), the quality of the cane was very high, and the management had the alleged advantage of chemical control and of the experience gained by the largest sugar enterprise in Australia."

It is a gratifying fact, however, that if the private millowners can make a profit at the low market rates which have been ruling during recent years, co-operative enterprise and a large turnover will be able to withstand a further fall, should such an undesirable event happen. Of a rise in value there seems little hope, in view of the persistent efforts being made to establish the sugar-beet in the southern colonies— up to the present our sole customers for surplus sugar, we may say. However, as a set off, there is the prospect of entering the port of Sydney duty free at an early date. The only solution of the difficulty appears to lie in greater economy in production, and ultimately in reduced prices for cane. Growers could in most cases accept a lower figure, and still make a fair living. Many of our scrub lands yield 30 to 40 tons of cane per acre. The poorer sugar lands yield about 10 tons. Incredible as it may seem to those unacquainted with the extraordinary fertility of our soils, as high as 108 tons of cane per acre have been obtained on Windsor plantation (Bundaberg) from virgin scrub soil, whilst crops of 15 to 20 tons of cane per acre have in other instances been successively taken from the same land for seven or eight years. The *Cairns Post* quotes figures regarding the sugar estate of the Hon. E. and R. De Moleyn (Hambledon plantation) which further illustrate the profitableness of sugar growing in the Colony : "These gentlemen put in 200 acres of cane some three years ago. From the first crop they cleared the whole cost of putting in the cane from the time of clearing up to cutting the cane, and this year the crop is averaging about 18 tons per acre. A contract was let by them, after cutting last season, to keep the cane clean up to cutting time this season, for £2 10s. per acre, and as the price paid by the C.S.R. Company for the cane is 9s. per ton, this gives them a profit of over £1,000 on the year's transactions, or as near as possible 50 per cent. on the original outlay." Owing to the absence of a return as to number of tons of cane cut in Queensland, I can only form an estimate of our average yield of cane per acre from the average tons of cane required to produce one ton of sugar. This may, I think, be fairly stated at 11½ tons, which on the 1896 basis would mean 17 35 tons per acre—figures comparing favourably with those of New South Wales for same year, viz., 17·60 tons per acre on a much smaller area. Cane prices vary. "Homebush" gives 14s. per ton delivered on the truck at the nearest point of the company's tramway, the company providing portable line for field use.

The central mills give about the same price. Other mills in the same district give lower prices, but, as the conditions of delivery vary, the comparison is not always easily made. At the Burdekin the price is 11s. at the rollers. At Cairns it is 8s. standing in the field. I think that disinterested investigators must come to the conclusion that the average price of cane in the North is a high one, and that the growers could accept a substantial reduction without being compelled to abandon their occupation. And it is more true of the growers than the millowners that they have not yet exhausted the resources of economy. A reduction of price might throw poor land, as it does small and wasteful mills, out of use, but there is plenty of good sugar land to sustain the industry. Given good land and good cultivation, cane-growing would be profitable though the farmer were called upon to share the burden of a worse than the existing market. The value of cane to the millowner varies according to the density of the juice, and in this respect it is interesting to compare the average tons of cane required on Louisiana sugar plantations to produce a ton of sugar (as exhibited by 202 samples quoted in 1889 by Dr. Peter Collier, of New York), viz., 13 tons, with our own results at North Eton: 1 ton of sugar from about 9 tons of cane; and at Mackay: 1 ton of sugar from about 8 tons of cane. The field labour on the larger plantations is mostly supplied by "kanaka boys," men who have been imported from the adjacent South Sea Islands. They are indented for a period of three years at a stated wage, being fed and housed by the plantation owner, who is responsible for their safety and comfort to the Inspector of Pacific Islanders in his district. During their time of service under indenture they are prohibited from working in the factory or otherwise usurping the white man's position. At the end of three years they may claim their wages and a free passage back to their island, or may sign on for a further period. A small proportion of time-expired boys bring their wives and families with them, with a view to making their home here. Although tribal fights have occurred sometimes, they are by no means a common occurrence; indeed, the behaviour of many of these "boys" is exemplary.

Amongst what are called "cane farmers" (i. e., small holders) kanaka labour is not much utilized; "where there's a will there's a way" being well exemplified in this matter. In the North there may be more ground for these importations, but it has now been admitted by sugar authorities in this colony that the colour line may be drawn at Townsville. Of course this is largely a matter of opinion. I do not think that disinterested onlookers can doubt that even in tropical Queensland a great deal

of the work in the cane-field can be done by white men. They are not
really so physically "soft" in high temperatures as is often imagined and
asserted. But some of the work, especially that which must be done
amongst the cane, where the air is still and the moist heat tremendous
through the summer months, is exceedingly distasteful to the unaccus-
tomed white constitution. Planters, great and small, would get on badly
if they were *confined* to the white supply. It is conceivable that a substantial proportion of the white labour offering itself in the sugar districts
is of indifferent quality. That is apt to be generally the case in regard
to the floating and shifting labouring population of new countries. In
the course of time employers may be able to command the services of a
much better class of whites, and if such occur it is likely that white
labour will gradually oust the black. What we want are the mutually
helpful elements—more labouring men of the reliable, intelligent class,
and new industries. The inevitable result will be, by increasing local
consumption and infusing greater intelligence, to assist existing industries,
and in new directions to make us more independent of imported goods
which are capable of local manufacture. The proportion of Polynesians
to Europeans and other white races has for the past two years been
nearly stationary, and at the end of December, 1896, stood at 1·82 per
cent. At that date they were estimated to number 8,003 males and
600 females, of which the greater number were employed in sugar cultivation. Besides these there were 3,796 white workmen employed in the
162 crushing and sugar-making mills and refineries of the colony (about
81 of which are used for crushing only), and over 4,000 white labourers
were engaged in growing cane. The 1896 returns show that £1,265,300
worth of machinery, of 9,760 horse-power, was employed in this industry,
and the total value of plant, machinery, &c., was £2,484,972. The value
of goods manufactured with this outlay of capital was £1,358,236.

The latter was £117,000 odd ahead of meat at the close of 1896, and in
1898 both meat and sugar production had materially increased in value—
the latter to some £1,500,000. Besides the mills there were, in 1896, five
rum distilleries, which produced from the molasses 105,826 gallons of
proof spirit. Apparently only 25,680 gallons were exported, and of this
461 gallons were sent to the United Kingdom. About 661 tons of molasses,
value £11,570, were exported to our near neighbours, and the balance of
the 2,195,470 gallons of molasses (after a portion had been used for rum
manufacture) was converted into "golden syrup," or consumed locally in
the raw state. The possibility of finding outlets for our surplus sugar
beyond Australasia has repeatedly engaged the attention of growers and

manufacturers, but so far has not been satisfactorily proved. Between January 1 and December 31, 1896, only £800 worth (mostly whites) went to the United Kingdom, out of a total export value of £863,080. The following extract from the Annual Report of the Chief Inspector of Distilleries—although only made up to June 30, 1896, in accordance with the usual practice of his Department—shows the various countries to which we exported between July 1, 1895, and June 30, 1897 :—

Where Exported to—		1895–6 Tons.	1896–7 Tons.
New South Wales	. .	26,597	32,689
Victoria	. . . .	23,505	31,211
South Australia	. .	4,175	1,983
Western Australia	. .	25	55
Tasmania	. . .	244	440
New Zealand	. . .	7,497	7,431
South Sea Islands	. .	4	4
British New Guinea	.	16	2
United Kingdom	. .	1	51
Total	. . .	62,064	73,866

As the quantity of sugar manufactured during the year ended June 30, 1897, was about 100,000 tons, of which 73,866 tons were exported, it will be noted that the sugar available for home consumption was 25,000 to 26,000 tons.

It is pleasing, however, to note that the Customs statistics for the year ending December 31, 1898, give the value of the 1898 exports to be £1,329,876, or £466,796 advance upon the figures for 1897.

Of probable buyers the United Kingdom is by far the largest consumer of cane sugar, of which she imported in 1895 no less value than £31,058,923. In 1887 the United States imported 84 per cent. of their sugar, equal to about 1,258,000 tons. Their consumption of this commodity per cap. was at that time 55·84 lbs., and this increased to 60 lbs. in 1890. I have not the figures for recent years, but, according to a statement in 1888 of the United States Consul in Sydney, the import into the States about that time would appear to be nearly 1,000,000 tons more than the above figures for 1887, and it is significant that whilst the population of the United States and the rate of sugar consumption per cap. are on the increase, this particular industry—

although artificially protected by a high tariff—is not in nearly so flourishing a condition there now as it was thirty to forty-five years ago. In fact, it has been stated that the United States consume fully one-fourth of the sugar product of the world. At the present time the solution of the sugar bounty difficulty is being awaited with much interest by this Colony, especially as the Royal Commission which was appointed to investigate the causes of the West Indian depression was presided over by our much-beloved ex-Governor—Sir Henry Wylie Norman. Besides the two large consumers above mentioned, the Dominion of Canada, portions of South America, and even of Continental Europe, China and Japan, would offer an extensive market for this product if greater economies in production could be practised, and tariffs did not prevent, or should the bounty on beet sugar be removed—as has long been desired. I have shown that our own consumption of sugar is only about one-fourth of the production, and is already much greater per person than that of most peoples, being 129 lbs. per cap. A large accession of population would be necessary to materially affect this industry, from which it is clear that oversea markets are of as great importance in this matter as in the case of, say, meat and dairy products. Even if the threatened competition from Australian beet sugar should be delayed a few years, it is only a matter of time when the production of cane sugar on this continent will more than cover the consumption, which is at present stated to be some 200,000 tons per annum.

The cultivation of sugar cane is carried on over a very wide area of coast lands—from Port Douglas, in latitude 16° 30′, to the southernmost boundary, in latitude 28° 8′. The number of Petty Sessions districts which have an interest in the sugar industry are 20, of which Mackay stood at the head in 1896 with 21,076 acres under crop; Bundaberg being second (17,987 acres). With regard to area crushed and sugar product, the position is reversed; Bundaberg sent the cane from 17,660 acres to the mill, for a return of 25,974 tons, whilst Mackay crushed the cane off 16,428 acres, and made 16.515 tons of sugar. The return of sugar to the acre is thus 1·47 and 1·01 tons respectively. The highest yield was in the Childers district—2·2 tons per acre. The port from which the heaviest shipments were made in the year 1896 was Bundaberg; £301,834 worth left that place—nearly double the value of the shipments from Mackay, of which the sugar export for 1896 was valued at £155,869. The port of Dungeness contributed sugar worth £106,481; Geraldton, £78,554; and Townsville, £75,890.

In the districts of Ayr, Townsville, Mackay, and Bowen irrigation has been practised with some excellent results, and it is to be hoped that cane-growers as a whole will recognize the advisability of following this practice in all but exceptionally favoured localities. According to the Registrar-General's Report for 1895, 7,464 acres (mostly cane) were irrigated in these four districts.

MAIZE.

As in the United States, a greater area of land is devoted to this crop than to any other. This has been so for many years, and may, in both cases, be accounted for by its adaptability to a wide range of climate and soil, freedom from disease, easy cultivation, and the small expense incidental to harvesting the crop. However that may be, it is generally the settler's first, and often his staple, crop.

About one-third of the land under cultivation in Queensland in 1896 was "in corn," and the proportion in the United States is even greater. The area of maize sown for grain in 1896 was greater than in any previous year of the history of the Colony, being 115,715 acres. The ratio of maize land to total cultivation in 1888 was rather better than two-fifths, but as the area under wheat has almost quadrupled since that year, it is conceivable that a portion of the last-mentioned crop is being raised by former maize-growers. The extension of sugar has also checked this crop. Besides the area planted in 1896 for grain 1,423 acres were planted for green food for cattle, and it is satisfactory to note a fairly uniform extension of the practice of hand feeding, as exhibited by the increased area of this and other green feeds. The average yield of grain per acre for the whole Colony was 26·49 bushels in 1896, having been only once exceeded in thirteen years, viz., in 1891 (30·3 bushels per acre). The mean average yield in New York State (U.S.A.) during a quarter of a century has been stated at 30·73 bushels. The relatively low prices which of late years have been realized for maize have, doubtless, been in a measure caused by over-production, in which belief a section of growers have turned their attention elsewhere. That this is by no means the sole cause of the fall is shown by the fact that in 1896—notwithstanding an import duty of 8d. per bushel—13,490 bushels (worth £2,167) were landed here from New South Wales and Victoria. As the fluctuations in the maize market have been considerable, much interest attaches to any method of storing the grain, and many systems have been tried, with more or less success. Judging from the comparative absence during 1896 of glutted markets, such as in former years paralyzed the trade, the holding of corn has been made possible by artificial means, so that a still steadier—if low—market may be looked for in the future.

This cereal is cultivated in 78 districts, extending over 13 degrees of latitude and 10 degrees of longitude. The heaviest returns for 1896 were obtained at Cairns, in the north, and Nerang in the south, which obtained an average of 42·09 and 35·36 bushels per acre over each district respectively. In twenty-four Petty Sessions districts the area planted with maize exceeded 1,000 acres, and of these the lowest average yield was 21·88 bushels per acre. Of districts producing over 100,000 bushels in 1896, there were the following, in order of precedence:— Warwick, Toowoomba, Allora, Gatton, Dugandan, Highfields, Killarney, Harrisville, and Marburg.

The total yield for the Colony in 1896 was 3,065,333 bushels. Not only has the area under cultivation increased considerably during the decennium, but a marked improvement is apparent in nineteen of the principal districts, as to the average number of bushels per acre in 1892–1896 compared with 1887–1891. The largest increase in 1896 as regards area planted was in the Allora district—2,713 acres. This district also takes the lead as regards increased yield of grain, viz., 107,024 bushels.

With regard to the prospects at the beginning of 1897 in the last-mentioned district, a correspondent stated that the crops ranged from 10 feet downwards, and that there was every indication of a record yield. From one of the cultivations a cob was cut which measured 8 inches in circumference and 14 inches in length; the grain was large and even. The increasing popularity of "home-grown" maize is shown by the fact that although in the last twenty years the population has risen about 160 per cent., the imports of this grain have fallen nearly 50 per cent., and still the grain holds first place as food for stock and even for man.

The following are some highly interesting remarks from the pen of Prof. Shelton, which appeared in the *Brisbane Courier*, respecting a trip made by him through what is known as the Fassifern district (about covering the Petty Sessions district of Dugandan). The visit took place on the 22nd and 23rd of December, 1896, when the forward state of the crop promised a bountiful and early harvest, so that his statements on the subject of this crop and methods of disposal have, in addition to the advantage of a long experience in one of the chief maize-growing countries of the world—the United States of America—especial weight as being the outcome of an intimate knowledge of local conditions,

Farm Life in Queensland.—The Home.

acquired in his official capacity of Instructor in Agriculture to this Colony :—

" The first thing which strikes one in this district is the extent and extraordinary promise of the maize crop. It seems now perfectly certain that the early and late, and what may be called the intermediate crop, will alike give a full yield of the highest quality of grain. What may be seen in the way of corn-growning upon the prairies of Illinois and Kansas can in a small way be viewed, at this time, from any commanding position in the Fassifern. Everywhere the rank, purple growth of maize covers hilltop and valley alike. Every field that has received anything approaching attention in cultivation is up to the high-water mark of cropping and promise of productiveness. . . . . .

"Upon the possibilities of utilizing the Queensland maize crop, I wish to advert briefly. In the first place, a glut in any one crop, be it maize, wheat, or potatoes, is a possibility in every agricultural community the world over. We have only to turn in memory back two years to see the Queensland wheat crop sacrificed at. prices, to the farmer, often considerably under 2s.' per bushel. In America, quite as much as in Queensland, the farmer has learnt the painful lesson furnished by over-stocked markets in some particular crop. I have myself, more than once, seen great crops of maize rushed upon the market at prices very much below 1s. per bushel in English money, and it always will be thus until farmers learn, by experience, that to grow altogether, or even largely, of some one crop is always hazardous and frequently disastrous.

" Cultivators will need to learn that to sell a crop or product directly upon the market is not always the most profitable of the means available to them by which that crop may be converted into cash. The American farmer, for instance, has learned that the corn crop may be converted into pork or beef (impossible here), or in a dairy district the whole crop of maize may be made into ensilage, which again is converted into high-priced milk and butter during the winter months following. Let us look briefly at certain of the methods open to Queensland farmers for marketing profitably the present maize crop.

THE EXPORTATION OF MAIZE.

" It is often urged that we may reasonably look to foreign markets for an outlet for our superfluous crop of corn. This is a matter which the Agricultural Department has frequently had occasion to study in recent years with a view to alleviating to some extent the pressure of this particular crop. As a general thing, and with rare exceptions, I am satisfied the Queensland-grown maize cannot be exported to London with the hope of profit. Our farmers, even in such favoured regions as the Fassifern Scrub, cannot produce maize so cheaply as their brethren and rivals upon the Western States of America. I need not go into details here. It is quite sufficient to state the fact. Some day, when our lands are cleared and stumped and the fields are larger, and we learn to make greater use of machinery, we may expect to alter the condition of things; but the facts at present are as above stated. It is alike doubtful if, during most years, we can compete with the States of the Balkan Peninsula, which supply, more than any other country, the maize which finds its way to the London market. For these reasons it seems clear to me that the hope of relief from the exportation of maize may not generally be entertained. Occasionally, with the scarcity of the crop in America or in Roumania, it might be done; but with the crops reported in America the present year, I conceive it to be hopeless.

TANKING.

" It is possible, as shown by a wide and very varied experience in all parts of the Colony, to put up well-dried maize in air-tight tanks with the assurance of its safe keeping. Many farmers follow the practice now, and merchants and speculators have been doing it for years past, often reaping considerable profits for their enterprise. It may always be questioned whether the farmer is justified in speculating even in his own crops and products, but when prices touch the very low levels to which this crop often attains, I believe that the cultivator is justified in preserving his crop for a rise which, judging by past experience, is inevitable. The cost, however, of tanking is considerable, but there is little doubt that when the price gets below 1s. per bushel, the returns fully justify the outlay. To preserve the crop in this way is sure to be a practice limited in its operation. It is only here and there, in the case of the fore-handed farmer, that resort will be had to a practice which commends itself rather to the merchant and grain dealer than to the man of the farm.

FEEDING THE CROP TO PIGS.

" This is the great resort of the Yankee corn-grower, and the practice of pig-feeding deserves in Queensland a much wider application than hitherto it has received. My own experiments in America, made upon a large scale, and covering several years of operations, with those of Dr. Miles and others, show conclusively that a bushel of shelled maize may be expected to produce somewhere between 10 lbs. and 12 lbs. of increase in the pigs to which it is fed. Taking the Queensland value for live weight of pigs, which at the present time is approximately 2d. per lb., we have a return of about 2s. per bushel for the crop thus fed; with the best quality of pigs, something better might be done. Perhaps inferior ones would do rather less for the farmer in feeding. This certainly will be counted a very handsome return for the maize, and the trouble involved in feeding the pigs. The cost of marketing the pork is certainly very much less than the cost of carrying the crop to the nearest railway station.

THE USE OF ENSILAGE IN DAIRYING.

" Very few Queensland farmers realize the enormous possibilities of the maize crop in the production of cheap and abundant supplies of this most nutritious fodder. Corn, whether put up in the shape of dried fodder, as is done so commonly in America, and to a certain extent in Queensland, or ensilaged according to the more modern practice, has feeding possibilities beyond the dreams of our stockowners. . . . . . Why should not this great, and for the present almost worthless maize crop be set aside for the needs of next winter? Why should not our farmers put themselves in such a position that, when milk brings 4d. to 5d. per gallon, as it almost certainly will during the coming winter season, they may be prepared to reap the golden harvest that falls in the lap of the fore-handed dairyman ? "

From the above remarks we gather that Queensland farmers have by no means exhausted the means now available for turning to profitable account this important product of the land, and I feel convinced that besides the methods mentioned by the Professor, a study of the problem connected with local distribution will do much towards bettering the position of growers, a remark which may be applied to most of our farm products, as shown by the following comparison by the Rockhampton *Bulletin* of ruling prices in that city and in Toowoomba—distant but 450 miles apart (mostly by boat). The prices given are the highest ruling in Toowoomba on Saturday, January 30, 1897, and the lowest rates quoted in Rockhampton on the same date :—Lucerne chaff, Toowoomba, £2, and Rockhampton, £5 10s.; oaten-chaff, Toowoomba, £2, and Rockhampton, £6; potatoes, Toowoomba, £1 15s., and Rockhampton, £4; maize, Toowoomba, 1s., and Rockhampton, 1s. 11d.; oats, Toowoomba, 3s. 11d., and Rockhampton, 3s. 9d.; eggs, Toowoomba, 4d., and Rockhampton, 1s. 3d.; butter, Toowoomba, 5d., and Rockhampton, 8½d.; cheese, Toowoomba, 6d., and Rockhampton, 7½d.; fowls, Toowoomba, 2s., and Rockhampton, 3s.; ducks, Toowoomba, 3s., and Rockhampton, 4s.;

turkeys, Toowoomba, 10s., and Rockhampton, 10s. The figures speak for themselves; but were we to give the *lowest* rates at each place compared the difference would be considerably greater than is shown in this table. Take, for example, potatoes. They could be bought in Toowoomba at £1 5s., or £2 15s. less than in Rockhampton. Then again butter could be bought at 3d. in Toowoomba. The lowest wholesale price here was 8½d. Cheese was selling in the southern towns at as low as 4d. ; in Rockhampton the cheapest price it could be purchased at was 7d. Coming next to poultry, we find fowls selling in Toowoomba at 1s. 4d., in Rockhampton at 3s.; ducks at 2s. 6d. in Toowoomba, 4s. here ; and turkeys at 5s. in Toowoomba, and 10s. in Rockhampton.

WHEAT.

Although in point of area sown for grain in 1896.(31,556 acres) and crop raised (601,254 bushels) this cereal does not come up to maize at the present time, the proved suitability of enormous tracts of land to the growth of the former, and the frequently recurring shortages as regards milling requirements, are certain before long to place it in the front rank.

Hitherto we have relied upon the adjacent colonies of South Australia, New Zealand, and New South Wales for requirements in excess of local production, but in the year 1896 a shortage in the first-named colony of about 500,000 bushels below their local requirements, and in New South Wales of more than twice that quantity (in common with our own still heavier deficiency), necessitated a large import from across the Atlantic, and notwithstanding an import duty of 4d. per bushel on wheat, and 20s. per ton on flour, this Colony imported 257,380 bushels of the former (value £57,650), and 30,867 tons of the latter (value £350,447) from the neighbouring colonies, besides some 2,028 tons of American and other foreign flour.

The slightly smaller area sown in 1895, and the disastrous effects of unfavourable weather upon the return per acre—which was less than one-fourth of that in 1894—led us not only to import flour, but grain ; and that to a large extent. Over £111,000 worth of American wheat found its way into the hands of local millers during the year 1896, from which it will be seen that, if immunity from that dreaded pest—rust—and from drought could be secured (and we believe that this is attainable), no grain crop holds out greater inducements than this one. The following will give a rough idea of the progress made with regard to the first-named trouble ; the second line shows approximate ratio of area affected with rust to the entire area sown with wheat :—

Year . .	1887	'88	'89	'90	'91	'92	'93	'94	'95	'96
Ratio per cent.	14	3	82	11	9	6	14	29	9	1½

A comparison of the average ratio of the last five of these years with that of the first five will disclose the fact that the proportion of rust-smitten wheat has fallen from about 24 per cent. to something like 12 per cent. This is in itself matter for much congratulation, but it is almost needless to state that a very much lower percentage of loss is looked forward to in the five years ending December 30, 1901. The most exhaustive experiments have been and still are being conducted by the Department of Agriculture with a view to eradicating this disease in our Colony, by introducing varieties of seed and methods of cultivation which do not favour it. A series of Wheat Conferences have been held throughout Australia to consider this and other questions affecting the industry — at which we were officially represented by Prof. Shelton—and nothing that science can suggest or money procure is being left undone, in order to place wheat-growers in a position to supply local requirements.

With regard to the second difficulty with which the wheat farmer has had to contend : want of early rain.

This will undoubtedly be fully met by the extension of irrigation systems. In the United States and in some of the Australian Colonies the most astounding results have been achieved by this practice, and whilst our own experiences are too recent to furnish thoroughly reliable data, enough has been done to show that in the scientific application of surface water lies one of the secrets connected with successful wheat culture. I have endeavoured to show that we are making progress as regards *methods* of cultivation; this is no less true as regards the area planted, and extent of crop.

Speaking broadly, the average area during the five years ending 1891 was 11,000 acres; from '92 to '96 it was 30,000 acres. 1895 excepted, a very satisfactory advance has been made in the output of grain, this having risen from 21,221 bushels in 1886 to a return for 1896 of some 601,000 bushels. The average for the first quinquennium was 185,041 bushels, for the second period it was 429,149 bushels per annum; as, however, the rate of local consumption (calculated over an extended period of years) is some five or more bushels of wheat per cap., this is yet a long way short of the quantity required for food alone.

In the Colony of New South Wales the yield of wheat rose from 10·45 bushels per acre in 1886 to 17·37 bushels in 1887; in our own Colony the rise was even greater, viz., from 3·13 bushels to 22·10 bushels (same dates). Our mean average, however, for the ten years ending December, 1894, was 14·9 bushels, which at recent prices—4s. to 4s. 6d. per bushel —means a return of 60s. to 67s. per acre.

In the year 1896 some high yields per acre were recorded from fairly large areas, such as :—An average of over 32 bushels on 28 acres at Dugandan ; over 24 bushels at Gatton; and 23 bushels at Laidley; even higher averages being sometimes recorded.

The ten years' average for New South Wales and Victoria was 12·0 and 9·9 bushels per acre, respectively, and, in view of these exceedingly low averages from two Colonies which are usually large exporters, there is no reason why Queensland should not become eventually a wheat-exporting country. Prof. Shelton has again and again emphasized the fact that the conditions which obtain here are as suited to wheat-growing as are those in California, Manitoba, and other great centres of this industry—perhaps more so. By averaging the yield for a period of ten years—1887 to 1896—Mr. Weedon's year-book shows conclusively the high average return of our wheat-lands. The following are that gentleman's figures :—Queensland, 15 bushels ; New South Wales, 11 ; Victoria, 9 ; South Australia, 6 ; Western Australia, 11 ; Tasmania, 17 ; New Zealand, 24. Amongst these colonies our own has, during the last 17 or 18 years, attained the distinction of being ten times at the head of the list, and only about three times at the foot of the same. The average for the United Kingdom is stated at about 28 bushels per acre, and I may add an average of yields in one of the American States—that of New York—extending over a quarter of a century, is stated upon good authority to be 14·86 bushels, whilst Mulhall gives the mean average for the United States as being 12 bushels.

The comparatively small area devoted to this crop here may, of course, have somewhat to do with such apparently high results; still, should an extension of the area affect the average to the extent of a reduction by one-third, we may still look for the development of this industry into a large and profitable one.

In view of the fact that we have *two or three million* acres of wheat-land open to selection or purchase on 20 years' terms by annual payments of £7 12s. 10d. on each £100 purchase money, the following statement of about December 16, 1896, is full of significance :—

" The *S. M. Herald* estimates the total acreage under crop in Australia this year, and excluding New Zealand altogether, at 4,234,409 acres, and

"Crossing the Line": Neptune and his Train, after the Ceremony.

the yield of wheat at 18,643,400 bushels, and sets down the probable needs of the colonies at 25,706,775 bushels, of which 4,602,895 bushels are required for seed. The foreign grain ordered or afloat is 2,323,610 bushels, which will have to be máde up by New Zealand or America. The reason why New Zealand is excluded from the computation is that at the present time it is impossible to obtain any reliable data from'that Colony as to the probable harvest, though there is every indication that it will be a good one."

But our wheat-growing area is by no means confined to the districts adjacent to the Southern border of the Colony. Very little, indeed, has been done in the Northern districts, even in an experimental way, but as far up as Hughenden a yield of 15 bushels per acre has been obtained from small plots. In the Central districts 22 bushels per acre were obtained at Springsure, 10 bushels at Rockhampton, 2 at Clermont, 3 at Barcaldine. This portion of Queensland, in the opinion of Prof. Shelton and others whose experience of the crop entitles them to judge, possesses some of the most productive wheat-lands of Australia.

Settlers are wanted. New South Wales obtained them from the adjacent colonies, and Queensland is even now receiving accessions from the Southern colonies, although mainly looking to Europe, and particularly to the British Isles, for agricultural settlers. We doubt if any other development could be mentioned which is so full of promise for Central Queensland as the building up of a great wheat-growing industry. And the pioneers are already putting in an appearance in the persons of several Victorian gentlemen and their families, who bring with them the experience of years, and all the mechanical appliances needful to the cultivation of this cereal on a considerable scale. One of these farmers— Mr. Griffiths—has formed an excellent opinion of the Central district of Queensland for wheat-growing, which he declares must ultimately become the granary of Queensland. The Messrs. Griffiths and Warwick have secured their seed wheat, which is of the Allora variety, at a cost of 6s. 6d. and 7s. 6d. per bushel, and to this has to be added the railway freight.

It may interest farmers who contemplate entering this field of industry to read the following report to the New South Wales Department of Agriculture, by Mr. H. L. White, of Belltrees, respecting the above-mentioned variety of wheat:—

"I have just finished threshing the Allora Spring wheat, the return from thirty-six acres of *poor land* being 310 bags, equal to 36 bushels per acre. This grain is a good sample, and I am offered 4s. 9d. per bushel by the local millers. The quantity of Allora Spring wheat sent to me in 1893 was a quarter of a pound ; yield in 1896, 310 bags." The report is corroborative of the experience of others with this early variety. When sowing must be done late this is one of the varieties most likely to succeed.

Intending wheat-farmers could not, however, do better than consult the Department of Agriculture on a subject to which much time and attention has been devoted. At the present time the seat of the industry may be said to be in the Southern division of the Colony, west of the main range. Toowoomba was shown in 1896 to have sown 10,736 acres for grain, 359 acres for hay, and 223 acres for green food ; Allora sowed 8,403 acres for grain and 450 acres for other purposes ; Warwick sowed 7,036 acres, besides a small area for hay and green food ; Killarney sowed 2,482 acres—all for grain.

To the east of the Range, 1,481 acres were sown with wheat, of which 937 acres were reaped. The average return of grain per acre was high, being 22·48 bushels per acre, as against an average of 17·37 to the west of the Range. A few Petty Sessions districts showed splendid results ; Dugandan, 32·25 ; Ipswich (small plot), 30 ; Gatton, 24·56 ; Laidley, 23·09 ; Nanango, 18·63.

As regards the cost of production, the following figures from the 1892 Report of the State Board of Agriculture in Massachusetts, U.S.A., as to the cost of cropping various cereals, &c., in Canada will be of interest. The total yield of wheat per acre is set down at twenty-eight bushels, of which the cost is about £3 6s. 6d. The principal items are very similar to those incidental to the better style of farming in Queensland—such as : Rent (or interest on capital), about 20s. 10d. per acre—a liberal allowance ; seed, 6s. 3d. ; ploughing, 12s. 6d. ; harvesting, 8s. 4d. ; threshing and cleaning, 11s. 5d. ; planting, harrowing, rolling, thinning, hoeing, and cultivating, are provided for at an outlay of another 6s. 11d., bringing the total cost *per bushel* up to a shade under 2s. 6d. From 'Queensland Past and Present,' 1897, I find that out of a number of growers who were recently questioned officially as to the cost of production in Queensland, some ten of the smaller farmers gave figures ranging from £1 0s. 6d. to £3 18s. 6d. per acre, whilst another batch of six large cultivators estimated the cost variously at from £1 to £3 8s. *Cæteris paribus*, that crop will be the heaviest on which the most money is spent, so that even at the higher cost, I think it will readily be admitted that there are "dollars" in this crop ; at all events, if our Canadian and American cousins find this so, what is to prevent our farmers doing the same ? The right class of soil and temperature are here, and nature's reservoirs need only to be tapped in order to yield an abundant supply of water. Aided by natural conditions such as these, labour-saving machinery and brains will secure a big share of the world's trade in breadstuffs.

It is apparent that the production of wheat has not kept pace with increase of population; this is strikingly shown by figures in the *Telegraph*, of Brisbane, anent the decided rise in wheat values, by which it appears that the world's visible supply on October 1, 1895, was but *two-thirds* of that on October 1, 1894; clearly demonstrating the enormous scope there is for extension in this industry.

On Oct. 1st.	European. Qrs.	American. Qrs.	Total. Qrs.
1896	6,130,000	8,500,000	14,630,000
1895	9,921,000	8,100,000	18,121,000
1894	9,062,000	12,650,000	21,712,000
1893 , . . .	10,900,000	9,784,000	20,684,000
1892	9,100,000	8,500,000	15,600,000*
1891	9,500,000	5,760,000	12,260,000

Later reports give the American visible supply in October of 1897 as 28,500,000 bushels, in October of 1896 it ranged between 60,000,000 and 70,000,000 bushels, and a marked fall has at the same time been taking place in the European supply, owing to unfavourable climatic conditions.

The milling industry in this Colony is yet in its infancy. There are now about fourteen mills for grinding and dressing grain, and a few spice mills worked by steam power, employing a capital of over £125,000 between them. The output of the first named in 1896 was 17,879 tons of flour, valued at £214,971, and 318 tons of other meal and rice, value £2,654, besides some £34,000 worth of bran and pollard. For further information the reader is referred to the Report on Agriculture and Live Stock, and other official publications.

OATS.

On the 1896 area sown for grain—1,881 acres—an average return of over seventeen bushels per acre was obtained, and 11,565 acres in hay-crop returned 17,836 tons of that article. In point of area sown and reaped for grain, the year was a record one.

Whilst considerably below the average of the United States, Great Britain, New Zealand, and Tasmania, our average yield per acre over a series of years closely approximates a like average for New South Wales and 'Victoria. The following will show the position; the figures are from Coghlan's 'Seven Colonies of Australasia,' 1895–6 :—

Bushels.

United States	.	.	.	.	.	.	.	24·3
New Zealand, mean (10 years ended 1894)	.	.	.	30·5
New South Wales	,,	,,	,,	,,	.	.	.	20·9
Victoria	,,	,,	,,	,,	.	.	.	22·0
Queensland	,,	,,	,,	,,	.	.	.	18 9
South Australia	,,	,,	,,	,,	.	.	.	11·1
Western Australia	,,	,,	,,	,,	.	.	.	17·4

On one occasion during the decade (1887) the year's average was 24·26, the least favourable results occurring in years of drought (1888 and 1895). The fairly uniform yield obtained during good years seems to point conclusively to the necessity for a reliable water supply if one would be successful with this crop. It is doubtful whether farmers in this Colony can raise oats as cheaply as is done in the United States: Iowa, 1s. per bushel; New Hampshire, 11d. per bushel; Maine, 1s. per bushel; and Canada, 1s. 1½d. per bushel; but as the grain maintains as a rule a steady value of 3s. 9d. to 4s. per bushel, there is a wide margin for extra cost—and profit too. It is worth bearing in mind also that the cost per bushel in New Hampshire and Maine as quoted above is more than half due to the fertilizer applied, although this again is counterbalanced by a heavy yield—40 to 42 bushels per acre.

Possibly the strongest plea for an extension of the area under oats for grain is the fact that every year we send away thousands of pounds sterling for oats and oatmeal. Though still a large sum, I note, however, that the import of these two commodities was some £13,000 less in value for 1896 than for 1894. At any rate, local requirements are yet sufficient to offer considerable inducement to the cultivation of the crop, the import duties of 8d. per bushel of seed and 4s. per cwt. of oatmeal—equivalent in each case to about 20 per cent. of their average values—contributing in themselves a good deal towards high market values.

As a fodder crop, oats are maintaining favour, an increase in area of over 18 per cent. having taken place in 1896, as compared with 1895.

BARLEY.

The area under cultivation for grain in 1896 was only 1,122 acres, and the average yield was 17·24 bushels per acre, or 9·43 below that for

1894; whilst the ten years' average is found to be over twenty-one bushels. The 1894 yield was remarkable, insomuch that it was second only to that of New Zealand (27·40), the difference being ·73 of a bushel per acre, and was considerably over the average 1894 yields in New South Wales, Victoria, South Australia, and Western Australia; respectively 17·25, 16·40, 15·73, and 7·53 bushels per acre. The 1878–1887 average yield in New South Wales was 20·25, and that of New York State (U.S.A.) for 1862 to 1888 was 22·38, so that this crop would seem to be worthy of a more prominent place on our farms; the future of this grain—and that a brilliant one—lies in the large and increasing local consumption of malt.

During the year ended June 30, 1897, the Inspector of Distilleries reports that out of 190,116 bushels of malt which were used, only 14,400 bushels were of local production. This is an advance upon the previous year's output of Queensland malt, which was then 12,988 bushels. The following figures show the opening which exists for the crop under consideration, and the present position of the brewing interests—with which this crop is so closely connected.

From returns received it appears that twenty-two breweries were in operation during the year ended June 30, 1897. Fifteen breweries were situated in the Southern, four in the Central, and three in the Northern districts. The quantity of beer brewed in the Colony during the year now reviewed was 5,378,115 gallons, being 554,558 gallons more than was brewed in 1896. The quantities of materials returned by brewers as having been used in brewing during the year are as follows :—

Malt, 190,116 bushels ; grain, *nil;* sugar, 46,117 cwt. ; hops, 302,285 lbs.

The value of the malt imported during 1895–6 would be worth some £40,000; the value of that consumed in 1896–7 would be about the same. Queensland is, however, by no means the only importer of malt and malting barley.

The chief exporting colonies are New Zealand, South Australia, and Victoria.

Three-fifths of the total area under barley in 1895 (or 1,397 acres) was destined for green food for cattle, and it is pleasing to note an increase of fully 90 per cent. over the area so utilized in 1894. The provision of artificial food for stock is a most important element in such climates as ours, and it is a subject for congratulation that farmers are beginning to recognize its necessity. The latest estimate of the total area under fodder crop (all kinds) in Queensland is 20,372 acres. The bulk of the barley in.

this Colony is grown on the Darling Downs, in the districts of Allora, Warwick, and Toowoomba. Small quantities have been tried in the Maranoa district, but with poor success. As a hay crop this has, however, been successfully grown as far north as Herberton (S. Lat. 17° 23′). I may add that the cost of growing a bushel of barley, as given by the Canadian authority already quoted—Simpson Reume, gold medallist farmer—is put down at 1s. 3d., a triumph of economy which our farmers would do well to endeavour to emulate. Recently, in the town of Warwick, a malting house has been erected by a gentleman who has had a long experience in the trade, and the establishment of this industry will mean the finding of a steady market for a considerable quantity of the grain. This maltster announced his intention of purchasing 5,000 bushels during 1897; 3s. to 4s. was being paid by him. The annual home requirements of barley are estimated to be of a value of £75,000.

RYE.

Although the returns from past crops have been high, these have experienced a decided falling off since 1891. In the latter year 12,434 bushels of grain were obtained from 538 acres (23·11 per acre). The mean average yield for the five years—20·73—is very high compared with that of other rye-consuming countries, say New York State, which showed between 1862 and 1870 a yield of only 15·17 bushels; between the years 1880 and 1888 the average in that State was only 11·94 bushels.

As regards rye sown for hay and greenstuff, I have to chronicle a considerable increase in output for 1897, equivalent to nearly 50 per cent. on the output for 1896. This satisfactory advance was mainly in the Southern district, and is an evidence of the attention which is being paid to the hand-feeding of dairy cattle and other stock.

RICE.

Prolific as the growth of this most important food product has proved here, it is a matter for surprise that its cultivation has made so little progress. The success of this crop in some portions of the Colony has been phenomenal. Yields of 60, 33, and 32 bushels per acre have been obtained during 1897; whilst in 1887 and 1886, 50 and 60 bushels per acre were recorded.

Going back to the year 1890, I find that we imported some 7,500,000 lbs., and exported about 215,000 lbs., leaving for home consumption over seven and a quarter million pounds, representing a money value of about £45,000. Deducting the odd thousands on account of

Banking in "the West."—A small Country Branch of the Queensland National Bank.

local production, we had in that year to bring in about 7,000,000 lbs. of rice at a cost of £43,000 odd. A glance at the 1895 figures will show how we stand by comparison :—

	lbs.		£
Imports	6,314,738	. . .	35,643
Exports	231,899	. . .	1,339
	lbs. 6,082,839		£34,304

To which must be added local production, in order to ascertain the quantity used for home consumption.

It may therefore be reasonably inferred that a very large portion of this Colony, especially where the agriculturist is favoured by a regular rainfall, is eminently suited to the cultivation of this grain.

The mean average yield per acre between 1886 and 1895 was little short of 37 bushels, while the average obtained in India does not exceed 12. Within the last few years the Indian Government have spent a large amount of money, time, and patience in trying to educate the natives out of their prehistoric methods of cultivating rice, with the result that where improved ploughs were used, and deeper cultivation given, a yield of 40 bushels per acre has been obtained. This only serves to show that with our rich soils and modern farming methods and appliances, an average yield of from 60 to 70 bushels per acre can, and should, be obtained. Mr. McPherson, in his experiments in Brisbane, obtained at the rate of 68 bushels per acre.

The few facts given above will show the *enormous scope* there is for rice-growing, which would find profitable employment for at least 30,000 acres. It might be added that all imported rice has to pay a duty of 1d. per lb., say 3s. 6d. per bushel. Already ten or eleven steam mills for the grinding of rice, coffee, &c., have been erected in the Colony, and for a high-class product not only Queensland, but all the Southern markets are open.

"The difficulty I have experienced for the past five or six years," says a prominent manufacturer, Mr. Walsh, of Cairns, "has been an insufficient supply of rice paddy to keep the mill going anything like full time ; in fact, up to the present I have not been able to secure enough to keep the mill going three months out of the twelve. I have, however, at last procured a rice which I am satisfied will meet the requirements of the Colony, and overcome the difficulties experienced by growers with the seed hitherto procurable."

The variety referred to is the " bearded " or " spiked " Java rice. Its productiveness may be imagined from the fact that one grower obtained 28 cwt. to 30 cwt. as the product of 80 lb. to 100 lb. of seed. The planter also supplied this important information : He found it would grow in wet or dry land equally well, it bore well to the acre, and would stand for months in the field when ripe, without laying down in windy or wet weather, or shedding its grain—a matter of the utmost importance to the planter, as the crop thereby will wait his convenience to harvest. Naturally the grain was difficult to thrash or strip, but Mr. Walsh concluded that this was the most economic and profitable variety of rice that could be introduced. For milling purposes he found this variety a white, plump-grained rice, free from the appearance of Japan rice, and the families who used it spoke in most satisfactory terms of its flavour, which they thought much superior to that of any of the imported rices.

Mr. Walsh is convinced that rice-growing in North Queensland will assume very great proportions, sugar plantations and others being large consumers, and will be found by growers to be a remunerative as well as a reliable crop. Rice paddy has the peculiarity of improving with age ; it will keep for years, and is not liable to attacks from weevils or other insects. Planting may be conducted from November to January, and it takes from thirteen to fourteen weeks for the crop to mature. It is of very great importance that it should not ripen for harvest until after the wet season, which generally ends between May 1 and 15.

Asked as to the commercial prospects of rice cultivation, Mr. Walsh said he had guaranteed growers to take the whole of their paddy at £7 10s. per ton. He could not compute the average yield per acre, because the immense possibility of the crop had never been tested beyond scratching the ground with a hoe. There were a few European growers in the Port Douglas district—notably Mr. Andrew Jack, a member of the Port Douglas Divisional Board—who had expressed themselves highly satisfied with the results of their rice-growing for the past few years in that district.

POTATO.

This is a very common crop with our farmers, and although sometimes a sufferer from fluctuations in the market, it is one of the " standbys " of the farm. Amongst a large section of those engaged in manual labour, potatoes, corned beef, and " damper " take a premier position in the larder, so that domestic requirements absorb a considerable portion of the crop ; and as to pig-feeding with this tuber, the extent to which it may be profitably practised is illimitable.

Official records state the 1897 yield to have been 2·26 tons per acre, whilst in 1896 it was 2·40 per acre (the five years' average being 2·29 per acre). Comparing these results with the known averages obtained in other parts of the world, we find that Queensland ranks after the United Kingdom, Canada, Germany, or France, approximates very closely to Austria, and completely outdistances the United States, in regard to yield of potatoes per acre.

Foreign-grown potatoes are subject to an import duty of 15s. per ton, and yet in 1895 there was an excess of imports over exports of 12,400 odd tons, of the value of £33,600 odd! Here, surely, is scope for enterprise.

It is undoubtedly true that many of the other colonies from which these supplies were obtained are better suited to the growth of this crop, but still, fairly remunerative prices might be always counted upon if in times of plenty a portion of the crops were turned into pig flesh, or carefully stored, instead of rushed on the market in the senseless way which is so often adopted. The chief seats of this branch of agriculture are at Highfields and Warwick, both west of the main Range, and Gatton, Redcliffe, Laidley, and Crow's Nest, all east of the Range—in the south of Queensland. At Winton (in the Central district) a small patch gave over four tons to the acre; and even six tons per acre is not uncommon.

At Townsville (in the North) just over two tons per acre was recorded, and on the Herberton table-land about 2¼ tons were obtained to the acre.

The potato is about as free from disease in Queensland as in any part of the world—"black heart" being about the only one which gives trouble, and this is no doubt to a great extent avoidable.

The area and production for 1897 were 8,197 acres for 18,520 tons—a significant contrast to the 283,000 tons of potatoes which the relatively small colonies of Victoria and New South Wales unitedly produced in 1895!

SWEET POTATO (*Ipomæa batatas*).

This is an edible tuber, of the convolvulus tribe, which is much in favour in this Colony, especially among the farming population, and also among the Polynesians, of whom it is often the main food.

Properly cooked, this root should be of a beautiful colour, varying from white to creamy, and of a flavour slightly resembling the chestnut. When broken with knife and fork it should present somewhat the appearance of a "floury" potato. The slightest degree of toughness is evidence of carelessness in having either more than sufficient, or insufficient water in the process of cooking. Almost needless to add, the sweet potato should

E

be cleaned and boiled *in its skin* in order to obtain the best results; it should not be cut with a steel knife, but broken, by preference.

The area under cultivation in 1897 was 3,581 acres, from which 17,466 tons of sweet potatoes were obtained. The average yield was 4·88 tons per acre, and although the market is somewhat limited, there are so many uses to which this root may be put on the farm—notably, for cattle and pig feeding—that the crop is an extremely profitable one.

COTTON.

Large areas were under cotton-plant in early years, but owing to a fall in the world's market, it was found that we could not compete at the price we had to pay for labour, and the plant almost passed out of cultivation.

Those who find a profit in the crop are mostly farmers with large families, who can do the light—although tedious—work of picking the balls of cotton.

The cultivation is stated to be no more troublesome than that necessary for most other field crops, and can all be done by plough, scuffler, and hoe. The returns of clean cotton per acre may be stated at 100 lbs. to 150 lbs., and the price lately ruling in the Queensland market was 1¼d. per lb.

The capabilities of Queensland for cotton production are stated to be fully equal to those of the United States, excepting possibly that labour and carriage to port of shipment are heavier on this side. Not only was Queensland an importer in 1895 to the net amount of about £292,000 worth of cotton in its manufactured and raw state, but most of the adjoining colonies are importers to a far greater extent, so that there is an enormous market for our cotton goods—and consequently a splendid opening for cotton culture.

ARROWROOT (*Canna edulis*).

Determined efforts are being made to find an oversea market for this root product, and when once the prejudice existing in Europe against any other preparations than those known as "arrowroot" is removed, we may expect a rapid development of the industry.

Practically none but Queensland arrowroot is used in the colony, and there are several mills which turn out a quality of flour fully equal to anything which could be imported. The imports in 1895 consisted of about 9,000 lbs. weight, of a value of £44, whilst the exports (mainly to neighbouring colonies) were valued at £3,173. The local consumption would appear to have been between 9,000 and 10,000 lbs. weight. The average production during the last three years has been something over 2,200 tons of tubers, and the wholesale value of the prepared arrowroot ranges from 13s. to 18s. per cwt. The plant itself forms a useful article of food for pigs.

The various Agents-General for this Colony have been at considerable trouble in bringing this article of commerce before the British public, and have personally, and by exhibits at shows, &c., advocated its claims. In a recent *Brisbane Courier* appeared the following very useful information on the subject from the pen of Mr. Thomas Lowry, Assistant Secretary to the Board of Inland Revenue, London. This gentleman writes to the Agent-General:—

" The term arrowroot, without prefix or qualification, should, strictly speaking, be restricted to the starch derived from plants of the genus Maranta. A purchaser asking simply for arrowroot would, presumably, by use and wont, expect to be supplied with Maranta starch. *Tous les mois*, or Queensland arrowroot, the product of *Canna edulis*, is quite a different starch, and its physical properties and appearance are distinct from those of Maranta starch. Inasmuch as the term 'arrowroot,' without a prefix or qualification, is now well established, the vendors of the Queensland article would, in the Board's opinion, best protect themselves by labelling it as 'Queensland arrowroot (prepared from Canna edulis).' "

TOBACCO.

The industry connected with this plant has undergone a great many changes of late years. Locally grown and made tobacco is being received with greatly increased favour, although the present production is small —the 1897 crop totalling but 5,703 cwt. from 755 acres, or a return of 7·55 cwt. per acre; this weight of leaf has several times been exceeded. Although largely grown by Chinese gardeners, the cultivation is not confined to them. The crop is one requiring almost incessant watchfulness, in order to prevent insect attacks, &c., but the patience involved in its culture is one which is well rewarded as a general rule.

Considerable fluctuations have to be noted in the price of the raw material, as high as 1s. and as low as 3d. per lb. having been given by manufacturers' buyers, but at 6d. per lb. (a very usual price) the mean average yield for 1888–97, which is 9·6 cwt. per acre, would give a cash return of about £27 to the acre. Indeed, it is a notorious fact that a Chinaman in the South of Queensland, working with the aid of fourteen of·his fellow-countrymen, realized £2,000 in one season from 60 acres of land. Of course, prices were then at a high point, but there is plenty of money even now in the crop, and once the right kind of leaf is grown largely and processes perfected, an enormous demand will set in from Great Britain alone. In 1894 the Government imposed a licence fee, and duty amounting to 1s. per lb. of tobacco, or 2s. per lb. of cigars or cigarettes, on manufacturers. Dealers in tobacco have to take out a licence, for which the fee is 5s. per annum.

COFFEE.

As an article of local consumption and export, this has a very promising future before it. The berry has been proved to be capable of production here in the highest state of perfection, and the range of climate in which the tree thrives is very wide. The value of our own net imports in 1895 was about £3,310, and the consumption may be set down at about 30 tons.

According to Mr. Weedon, the world's consumption of the coffee bean is over 500,000 tons annually, and is of a value of more than £40,000,000! Given the right class of soil and climate (which we have in abundance), it would appear that *thousands* might engage in this industry with profit in our Colony.

Only 60 acres were recorded in 1895 as being planted with the shrub; in 1896 this increased to 138 acres, whilst in 1897 as many as 311 acres were under cultivation.

The following is culled from the report of an interview with the before-mentioned Mr. Walsh. This gentleman said "that three selectors sent in a little over half a ton of berries. These came from the Russell and Barron rivers, and from over the Range. He roasted and ground them, and they were found to be of good quality and excellent flavour. Considerable attention is now being paid to its cultivation around Cairns, on the Russell River, and at Kuranda. From what he could learn from growers, based on the price he was prepared to give, coffee ought to be worth from £60 to £80 per acre per year. To use Mr. Walsh's own words, ' Coffee grows there like a weed, and only requires some care in pruning and nipping the young shoots.' " The North is at present, and probably will always be, the principal seat of this industry. Besides the 57,065 lbs. weight from the district of Cook, and 16,962 lbs. from Cairns, there were over 5,000 lbs. of "parchment" gathered in the Maroochy and Mackay Petty Sessions districts, whilst six other districts contributed 2,447 lbs. The average return per acre in Cook was over half a ton per

A portion of Queen Street, Brisbane, during a "lull."

acre, and in Mourilyan and St. Lawrence the yield was 672 and 336 lbs. respectively.

Coffee from Kamerunga, Mackay, has attracted much attention in England, notably at the London "Dairy Show," and a fine sample of the berry is now on view at the "Greater Britain" Exhibition.

A few healthy-looking coffee shrubs may be seen in and around Brisbane and Rockhampton.

HAY, ENSILAGE, AND GREEN FODDER.

Although differing essentially as regards process of manufacture, the material from which the first two forms of stock food are obtained, and their ultimate use, are often so similar that it may be as well to consider them together.

It is probably not more than fifteen years since ensilage-making attracted any attention in the Colony, and from figures it would seem that, to some extent, it is taking the place of the first-named system of feed preserving. In 1893 the production of hay was 42,353 tons, and in 1894, 1895, 1896, and 1897 it is put down at 55,696 tons, 50,966 tons, 43,054 tons, and 94,339 tons respectively. The mean average return of hay per acre between 1891 and 1897 was just short of 2 tons, which may be considered fairly satisfactory. In 1894 (not our best year) our return of 1·99 tons was heavier than that of any of the other six Australian colonies. Our average for the above period compares favourably with that of New York State for 1861–1888, viz., 1·19 tons.

Of course the above figures do not give any idea of the big yields which are obtained in isolated districts, both in Queensland and in New York State.

At Stanwell, near Rockhampton, 2½ tons of lucerne hay per acre are frequently gathered; at Scrubby Creek, in the Rockhampton Land Agent's district, 3 tons of oaten hay have been obtained in good seasons; and similar results have been recorded at Herberton in the far North.

It is a very common practice to cut lucerne four times in one year, each cutting yielding about 2 tons of green stuff per acre.

In the same way, the Agricultural Experiment Station of the State of New York reports a yield of 15 tons of green-cut lucerne (equal to about 5 tons of hay) per acre—probably aided by artificial manure. Lucerne and oats appear to be pretty general favourites for hay crops, both here and in the States, where the former is known also as "alfalfa." The proportion of these two to total area of hay crops in 1897 was about 80 per cent.

The imports of oaten chaff, which were formerly very considerable, are now being reduced. There was, however, £18,000 worth imported in 1895 from neighbouring colonies.

As regards ensilage, the quantity cured in 1897 was 1,197 tons, being a considerable increase upon that for 1896. In 1893 the amount was only some 419 tons.

Readers who wish to gain information regarding the best methods of saving fodder and making ensilage, &c., should consult Bulletins 12 and 24, from the pen of Prof. Shelton. These invaluable publications may be obtained free from the Department of Agriculture, Brisbane.

The last few years have experienced a considerable advance as regards area sown for green fodder. In 1894 the area was but 12,029 acres; in 1897 it was upwards of 19,000 acres.

Lucerne, sorghum, maize, and oats take the lead, but the varieties of crops sown for "green stuff" are naturally very numerous, including barley, sugar cane, panicum, rye, and wheat.

FRUIT AND VEGETABLES.

The varieties of fruit, &c., which may be, and are, grown in Queensland are infinite, and the quality of many of these is unsurpassed. Owing, however, to the vastness of our territory, "squatting" was for very many years considered the only industry to which the country was adapted, with the result that horticulture was greatly neglected, and it is only of late years that it has shown signs of becoming a most important factor in our national prosperity.

With the advent of Mr. Benson as fruit expert, who brings to bear on his duties a wide colonial and American experience, there may be said to open up unlimited possibilities to the fruit-grower, and the action of the Government in appointing so highly qualified a gentleman is evidence of the recognition of the above fact.

Mr. Benson has already done good service in visiting the various fruit districts of the Colony, making himself acquainted with the prospects and difficulties of the growers; and since the destruction of insect pests is of even prior importance to the judicious marketing of fruit, the pamphlet on 'Fruit Pests and the Methods of dealing with Them' which has emanated from his pen will be welcomed by those who cultivate fruit for profit, as it will enable them to produce a better quality of fruit, so that they may take their rightful place in the world's market.

It is not the purpose of these pages to give an exhaustive account of all the fruits and vegetables which might be grown here successfully (for

they are almost endless), but rather to give au account of what is now
being done in that way, and the tremendous scope which exists for
extension on those lines. Referring to the well-known fruit district of
Cleveland Bay, comprising some 600 acres under fruit, the *Courier* says:

"In the Macleay orchard are sugar bananas that have been growing
seven years, now in good bearing, and perfectly free from disease. The
mango thrives to perfection. Amongst the many kinds of oranges
imported by Mr. Corrie from Florida, it will be of much interest to
orchardists to learn that a number have proved quite suitable to and at
home in this climate, and are now bearing heavy crops. They are the
Majorca, Garey's Mediterranean sweet, Valentia late, Maltese blood,
Beech's No. 2, Bell, Foster, Omasassa, Saul's blood, and Magnum Bonum."

Speaking at Wellington Point, Mr. Benson said that after careful
observations made in going through the district that week, he would like
to tell them what fruits to grow. The soil had distinct capabilities of
growing citrus fruits, more especially the orange, to perfection, mango,
banana, pine, custard apple, and tomato. The lemon would not do, but
the Tahiti lime did well, and they could not grow too many of that fruit.
The orange ripened early in Queensland, and commanded the Southern
markets during the months of May, June, and July, before the crop was
available in New South Wales for competition.

As regards the position and prospects on the "Downs," Mr. Benson
recently stated at a public meeting held in Toowoomba: "He believed
they could grow suitable oranges upon certain soils, and in suitable
positions, sheltered from the westerly winds; he also believed they could
grow Lisbon lemons. The soil was likewise capable of growing to advantage certain varieties of American grapes, and figs. In addition to the
fruit he had mentioned, plums of various sorts would grow well, and he
believed they could produce a first-class dried prune. In California this
was the finest industry, and, from what he had seen, there was no reason
why in Queensland we should not be able to grow for both local market
and export. He was also surprised to see the way in which pears grew;
they grew here easier, were more prolific, and stronger than in New
South Wales."

A most interesting review of the fruit industry was given at the
beginning of the year 1897 in the *Courier*, from which the following is
an extract:—

"Already, we find the oranges of the Wide Bay district in steady
demand in the Southern colonies; the pineapple of Nundah, Zillmere,
and other districts around Brisbane still supplies a large portion of their

consumption; oranges and bananas from Buderim Mountain, and the districts on the southern shores of Moreton Bay, have also a profitable market outside our own borders; while the Darling Downs—extending from the Main Range, south to Warwick and Stanthorpe, and westward to Roma—are becoming famous for many of the fruits of a temperate climate, and some portions are proving specially suited to the vine. The green fruit exported from Queensland during the year 1896 represented £66,965, as against £58,555 worth in the previous year, and in addition to this we have every year a larger quantity used locally, either for domestic consumption or in the manufacture of jams and jellies.

"If the vendors of 'soft' drinks could be persuaded that North Queensland limes are as good as Sicilian lemons, and might be got far cheaper, we believe a large supply of that wholesome fruit could even now be obtained from the Herbert River, Cairns, and Cooktown. The annual output of these districts in citrus fruits represents, according to latest returns, 6,195 cases of oranges and 300 cases of lemons, and a considerable proportion of this was exported. In tomatoes a very profitable trade has been carried on, as the season is so much earlier in the sheltered coast lands than in the Southern colonies, and in the early spring there is a good demand in Sydney and Melbourne. Mangoes also are already largely grown in these districts, but with them—more even than with other species of fruit—quality is everything."

Nor is fruit-growing restricted to the places hitherto mentioned. Around and about Nanango—approached by coach from Esk (Brisbane Valley Railway), Jondaryan (Western Railway), or Kilkivan (North Coast branch railway)—the most splendid fruit-growing soil and climatic conditions abound, and upon a recent visit Prof. Shelton stated that he was very greatly impressed by the excellent condition of the orchards, which abounded in orange, apricot, peach, and plum trees of the finest description.

Again on the Gregory River, in the Gulf of Carpentaria (between the 18th and 19th parallels of S. Lat. and on the 139th meridian of E. Long.), there is splendid land awaiting the orchardist. It has already been proved by Mr. Barrett, of Gregory Downs, that orange, lemon, and banana trees grow rapidly in what is called the Gulf Country, in the northern part of the Colony, and in due season yield a prolific crop of fruit. Grape vines, too, take kindly to the soil and climate. I have had the pleasure of eating as fine a sample of grapes locally grown as may be found in the vineyards about Brisbane. Need it be added that all kinds of vegetables grow luxuriantly, except, of course, during the very warm months? A market for potatoes, maize, fruit, cabbage, butter, cheese, fowls, &c., could be found at Burketown, Normanton, and Croydon.

Brief reference has been made to bananas and grapes, and although the former constitute at present a very large, and probably the most important section of our fruit industry, vine culture will in all probability soon take the lead. A shipment of the dried fruit of the banana has just reached London in safety; but until the taste for dried bananas (of which excellent samples are turned out at Buderim Mountain) has grown considerably, the market for this fruit will be limited. Not so with the fruit of the vine. Besides the historic use in the form of wine, there is a good opening for the dried fruit. As stated by Mr. Benson, some localities are not so suited to the growth of the very finest sorts; but in our broad extent of country suitable soils and climatic conditions can be found for the production of the best qualities of raisins and currants. The quantities and values of all kinds of imported fruits in 1895 (green excepted) were as follows:—Bottled (equal to 15,855 dozen qts.), value £5,128; dried, 410,313 lbs., value £10,077; currants, 1,535,087 lbs., value £12,001; raisins, 941,783 lbs., value £9,851; pulp, 108¾ tons, value £2,111; total, £39,186. Of these it will be noticed that grape products constitute more than half the value, so that the importance of the trade is very apparent. The growing of suitable sorts and the erection of drying apparati are going on apace, and the finished product is in great favour. I should mention that successful experiments in this direction have been made by Mr. Lester, of Roma, and Mr. Searle, of Mitchell.

The position of VITICULTURE in Queensland has been very ably dealt with in a series of papers—written at the request of the Agricultural Department—which appeared in the *Brisbane Courier*, from which I have taken the liberty of making the following extracts (the writer is Mr. Henry A. Tardent, of the Wine-growers' Association, of Roma):—

"In the northern part of the Colony the vine grows luxuriantly, giving an abundance of shoots and leaves. On the eastern coast of South Queensland the vine is grown profitably in many places, especially the American varieties. The principal drawbacks here are the absence of sufficient frosts to give a rest to the sap, and superabundance of rain—not seldom at vintage time; still, the results obtained by men like Childs and Capner, Cox, Lambert, and others, in the neighbourhood of Brisbane, show that pluck and energy can, to a certain extent, overcome those difficulties. On the Dividing Range, at a height of some 2,000 ft., the vine is more at home. About Warwick there are already a few vineyards (Kircher's and others), situated on granitic soils, which have made a name for their products, some of which are being already exported to Scotland. North-west of those places extends the plateau of which I have spoken above. It slopes gently towards the centre of the continent, and comprises over 100,000 square miles, nearly all included in the basin of the tributaries of the Upper Darling River. Numerous and of vast extent are the patches of soil here suitable for the vine. The town of Roma, on the Western railway line, 320 miles from Brisbane, occupies nearly the centre of it, and, strange to say, it is here that the wine industry has made a start, and come to stay. I intend to dwell more particularly on vine-growing in this particular district, not only because I know it better than other places in the Colony, but also because it is unquestionably at the present time the principal vine-growing centre in Queensland. The average rainfall is about 26 in. annually, and the aggregate heat necessary to bring the grape to maturity is here obtained in about five months' time —from September to February inclusive."

After describing the introduction of the vine to the district, about the year 1872, and the varieties planted—mostly table grapes, such as Black Hamburg, Black Prince, Doradillo, White Syrian, and Sweet William —Mr. Tardent states that about sixteen years ago new kinds of winemaking grapes were largely planted. These are the Black Cluster, Black Hermitage, Carbenets, Pino, White and Green Solferino, Verdeilho, White Portugal, Reisling, &c. "Our Black Cluster, known elsewhere under the names of Mataro and Espar, originated, I think, in the south of France and in Spain. In cold districts it gives a somewhat harsh wine; but here in our sunny climate it has proved to be an excellent acquisition. It shoots late, is hardy, and fairly prolific. When well treated it gives an excellent red wine of a claret type, especially when judiciously blended with Black Hermitage. This latter, called also La Petite Sirrah, from its original habitat in Persia, has formed for centuries the main "cepage" of the celebrated Hermitage vineyards in France. Here it thrives well, and gives large crops of superior fruit, provided it is pruned long and given plenty of room."

With greater railway facilities, such as would exist if direct communication were effected with Melbourne or Adelaide in the South, or Port Darwin in the North of the Continent, we should be able to supply the Southern capitals for some weeks prior to their own season, and even faraway "Londoners" might with the aid of Australian shipments enjoy this princely fruit for at least eight months of the year.

The production of grapes in 1897 was equal to some 2,286 tons. Many of our grapes are extremely luscious, and bear carriage remarkably well, and are, therefore, admirably suited for eating in a raw state. The output of wine in the above year was 207,945 gallons. On looking at our statistics for 1895, I find that there was an import to the value of £27,188 ; 4,304 gallons of sparkling wine having paid a duty of 10s. a gallon on entry, and 39,269 gallons of still wines a duty of 6d. per gallon! Surely a much larger home production may be expected in the next few years, and this large sum of money be retained in the Colony!

ORANGE.

As has been already stated, this fruit has made its way to the Southern markets, and there established a reputation which doubtless will grow with years. At the present time a large proportion of our output is absorbed by shipments to the adjacent colonies when the fruit is scarce in their markets, but with additional openings for the disposal of this crop, a very great extension of the industry would be at once made possible.

Many parts of Queensland are as eminently suited to the perfect development of the orange as are the shores of the Mediterranean, and better methods of gathering, packing, and shipping will place us in a position to command a market in these latitudes during their winter season. With the object of testing the Canadian market during the out-season, a few shipments were made by Messrs. Huddart - Parker's steamers, but owing to an alteration in the service, these were not carried out to a successful issue. Upon the first opportunity, however, our indefatigable Department of Agriculture will doubtless take up the matter again, and now that commodious cold-storage is provided on the British India Co.'s steamers running between Queensland and London, the successful landing of this fruit is only a question of time.

The principal district devoted to orange culture in the Colony in 1897 was Maroochy, in which the yield averaged something over 250 dozen per acre on an area of 234 acres. Next in point of area was the far-famed Maryborough district, with 209 acres ; then followed Nerang, 145 ; Gatton, 129 ; Cairns, 127 ; Bowen, 121 ; Rockhampton, 104 ; Cleveland, 100 ; and Douglas, 89 acres (Northern district). It will therefore be seen that the cultivation of this fruit is carried on over an enormous extent of country, covering each of the three great divisions of the Colony. The area in 1897 (2,196 acres) was a very marked advance upon that of former years, over 1,200 acres of orangeries having been added during the short space of ten years. A fair crop on small areas would vary from 1,000 to 2,000 dozen per acre.

In some districts, notably Charters Towers and Cardwell, quite phenomenal yields have been obtained, the former averaging 4,026 dozen, and the latter 3,000 dozen per acre.

A special feature of this crop is the great success attendant on small areas to the west of the Main Range.

The following extract from a paper read by a Mr. Biddles at the Maryborough Agricultural Conference of 1891 gives, in a few concise words, the practical aspects of orange culture: "We will say a man takes one acre and plants it with seventy-five trees; it can be well done for £20. Another £15 or £20 a year, at the outside, for five years will bring it up to £100, or thereabouts. You can then count upon a tree bearing 100 dozen; that at 3d. a dozen is 25s. a tree, or £90 15s. for one acre a year. I have taken from one tree 500 dozen a year for the last three years, and that is not a third of what you hear of sometimes. I put this estimate low, so as to allow plenty of margin for a few years. As the population of Queensland increases the demand for this most popular fruit will become greater, and will far exceed the supply. In my opinion, any one going in for orange-growing could not call it a venture, for if they make it a legitimate business it is a certain success."

PINEAPPLE.

Generally a great favourite, and source of some splendid incomes, this crop has seen many "ups and downs." The gross production in 1897 was 351,524 dozen. The area occupied with this delicious fruit was 909 acres, of which 465 acres were situated in the Brisbane district; the average yield for the latter was 422 dozen per acre, whilst in the Cleveland district as many as 986 dozen per acre were gathered. From a report of the proceedings of the Rockhampton Agricultural Conference, previously referred to, I clip the following joint testimony as to the profitable nature of the industry in Queensland:—

Mr. Jones said he had it on very good authority that one gentleman in the South, who had eleven acres of land planted, had been exporting pineapples for some years past to the annual value of £1,100, while another grower, who had only three acres, realized £300 a year.

Prof. Shelton said that, having had occasion to inquire a good deal into the operations of pineapple growers in the Southern part of the Colony, he could throw some light on the matter. Some weeks ago he visited an establishment near Nundah. The owner had only five acres of ground under cultivation, and his income from that patch was never less than £700, and often went over £1,000. He had asked about a

Open-air Culture of the Pineapple.

dozen growers what an acre of pineapples was worth per annum, and the lowest figure was £60. Land that grew pineapples about Brisbane cost from £60 to £120 an acre. The other day he visited a pineapple garden of three or four acres, a few miles up the north coast from Brisbane, and found that the owner, on this small patch, was keeping a family and paying interest on the purchase of his land, which cost him £125 an acre.

Several attempts—more or less successful—have been made to ship the pineapple to distant countries, where their advent in a time of scarcity would ensure a splendid price. All attempts, under ordinary conditions of temperature, have come somewhat short of expectations, some few lots arriving in condition, whilst others were totally spoiled. Recent developments in oversea carriage have made possible a big trade with Great Britain, as was shown by the safe arrival of a trial shipment in the refrigerating chambers of the British India Co.'s steamer the "Jumna." The shipment consisted of 18 cases of pines and 19 cases of mangoes.

The industry of canning pineapples is now being carried on by several Queensland firms. A really excellent article is turned out, and a small but growing export trade is being established.

In 1895 some 214 packages of locally preserved pineapples (value £105) were exported. Speaking at Rockhampton in 1891, Mr. J. S. Edgar, a gentleman of practical experience in fruit culture, stated that Messrs. John Moir & Sons, of London, had expressed their willingness to take all the preserved fruit which could be sent from a certain factory, and yet, owing to lack of fruit at the time, this factory had not received the support to which it was entitled. To keep up a supply for one factory several hundred acres would require to be put under cultivation. There is abundance of land close to the railway lines eminently suited for the purpose. The variety most favoured by preservers is the Queen, on account of its superior flavour and evenness in the size of the fruit. For local consumption, or shipping to the Southern colonies, the Providence, Smooth-leaved Cayenne, Sugar Loaf, Black Jamaica, and Trinidad are good sorts. The fruits of some of them grow to a large size. At certain seasons of the year, when plentiful, the pineapple may be purchased wholesale for 3d. per dozen, good-sized fruit, or ½d. each retail. Besides being a pleasant table fruit, it is stated to possess valuable properties for the cure of diphtheria. Pineapples grow to a very large size in certain parts of Queensland, 10 lbs. to 18 lbs. being no uncommon weight for them to reach, and in Mackay they have been known to weigh 30 lbs.

MANGO (*Mangifera indica*).

As a dessert fruit, as a condiment, and even as a medicine, this is rapidly taking a prominent position.

As stated by Mr. L. A. Bernays in his 'Cultural Industries for Queensland,' there is no doubt that the mango is one of the greatest delicacies of the vegetable world, and it is a notorious fact that a liking for this fruit—once acquired—is undying. Its native habitat is India, but so readily does it adapt itself to varied conditions of climate that it thrives on the Southern and Central seaboard of Queensland; although, naturally, it attains its highest degree of perfection nearer the Equator. This will be apparent from the following averages, obtained in 1895 :— Northern district averaged 1,400 dozen per acre; Central, 1,108 dozen per acre ; Southern, 345 dozen per acre. So numerous are the varieties of this fruit, that even an acknowledged authority, such as the gentleman above named, has not attempted the task of classifying them. It may be sufficient to say that the best mangoes are of good size (20 to 30 oz. weight), free from fibre, and when the peel is removed (which may be very easily effected) the pulp should be of a soft, creamy consistency, so as to enable it to be readily taken off the seed with a spoon. The flavour and juiciness of a good mango are the delight of an epicure. The total crop of this Colony in 1897 was 358,315 dozen (off 235 acres), a considerable increase on former years, thus showing its growing popularity. In speaking of pineapple exportation, reference was made to a consignment of mangoes, which duly arrived in London, and of which a portion was presented to Her Majesty the Queen. This leads me to the subject of foreign markets, and the following extract from a scientific journal will serve to show the possibilities of engaging in the export of mangoes for medicinal purposes. The *Medical Press* said:—"We are told that a determined effort is to be made in the wholesale fruit trade next year to bring the Indian mango to London in sufficient quantities to be of commercial consideration. Its introduction would undoubtedly be the signal for its use as a medicinal agent. The rind of the fruit contains a volatile principle, allied in action to pure terebene, and a bitter crystallizable substance to which the name of 'Mangostin' has been applied. A decoction of the fruit is commonly employed in tropical climates as an astringent, and is found useful in sore throat, nasal catarrh, and other allied conditions. Mango chutney is used as a condiment, and is found efficacious in the treatment of many forms of dyspepsia. Dr. Murrell, who has obtained a small supply of the fresh fruit from India, finds that it may be given with advantage in the treatment of chronic bronchitis and winter cough."

In the form of "mango chutney," as shown above, there is a brilliant future before this fruit both in the Australasian colonies and in England.

At the Sydney International Exhibition of 1879, Messrs. Acheson and Allen (two Queensland growers) were rewarded by prizes for their preparations of chutney and preserved mangoes; and Prof. Shelton has demonstrated in a practical way the ease with which the fruit lends itself to every method of preservation. So impressed is the last-named gentleman with this fact that in the course of a lecture on "canning and fruit preserving," he said that if he were going to plant an orchard along the coast, he would have five or six mango trees to every one of any other sort.

Propagation by seed being somewhat unreliable, inarching is the commonly employed method. According to the previously quoted authority—Mr. Edgar—plants which were taken up from the seedbed in April, May, June, and July (the "winter" season in Queensland), and planted in the open ground, throve very well.

The mango flowers from September to December, and the fruit is generally ripened during January, February, and March—and occasionally even earlier. The tree does not mature sufficiently to produce a crop of fruit for from three to six years.

COCO-NUT (*Cocos nucifera*).

Over 5,000 dozen of these were gathered in 1897. Much attention has been bestowed upon this invaluable variety of the palm tribe. The Cingalese have a saying that this tree serves for ninety-nine known uses; the hundredth cannot be discovered by man. However this may be, its oil, fibre, and food producing qualities are such as to justify the extraordinary trouble to which our Government have put themselves in the acclimatization of this exotic. At the date of the first annual report of the officer in charge of these operations over 10,000 coco-nuts had been planted on the islands adjoining our coasts, and these have since been added to, so that when maturity is reached the production of nuts will be greatly augmented. As is well known, the value of the tree does not lie only in its fruit, and the consumption of the various by-products— such as coco-nut fibre, copra, oil cake, oil, &c.—is so large that in this industry alone Queensland may be said to have a magnificent future before her.

OLIVE.

Repeated attention has been drawn to this tree as a most valuable subject for the attention of Queensland pomologists. For several years the olive has fruited in the neighbourhood of Brisbane and on the Darling Downs; it is only lately, however, that any extensive groves have been planted, and as the tree does not fruit for from 10 to 17 years after planting (according to Major Chapman—Bulletin No. 10 of the Department of Agriculture), there are no results worth chronicling. Another authority—Mr. L. A. Bernays—states that in South America a fair crop of oil is obtained at the fourth year. The average yield of an acre of olives is variously stated at 60 to 64 gallons of oil; this, at the moderate estimate of 8s. per gallon, would, as shown by the latter gentleman, give a handsome and ever-growing return. Although the olive lives to a greater age than man, and gives an increasing yield of fruit if well cared for, it does not invariably bear every year, a good season being counterbalanced by a poorer one, and *vice versâ*.

The two writers above mentioned give the fullest information regarding methods of planting, harvesting, and preparing the products of the olive. At present, Queensland does not possess any mills for crushing the olive, linseed, sunflower seed, coco-nut, &c., but with the extended cultivation of these oil-giving products it is reasonable to expect that the machinery will be forthcoming.

The following extract from the *Age* shows that Victoria is already finding an oversea market for linseed and other oils of local manufacture: "On the English market Victorian linseed oil is worth £16 10s., and that obtained from sunflowers, £17 per ton. The residual product of the former oil-cake makes the industry a highly useful adjunct to dairy farming. The oil-cake contains 7 per cent. of oil, sometimes as much as 10 per cent., and forms a first-class fattening food for cattle. Some which was produced in this colony brought £6 per ton in the English markets about three months ago. The oil industry, though still in a purely initiatory stage, seems to have a very promising future before it."

FIG (*Ficus carica*).

This eminently Mediterranean tree is similarly placed (with regard to Queensland fruit-growers) to its compatriot the olive.

Although growing luxuriantly in this part of the world, its cultivation has not been systematically pursued, and imported figs in a dry state continue to have a small demand, whereas locally produced fruit—equal in quality and lower in price—might readily be had for the growing.

Indeed, that the flavour of some of the locally raised fruit is quite equal to that gathered fresh on the Mediterranean shores I can personally vouch for. It is a matter of difficulty to ascertain even the *approximate* area under this crop, but from a comparison of the returns for two or three years it would appear that 9 or 10 acres is about the extent of ground really devoted to the crop. The production varies from 500 to 1,400 dozen per acre, which at 3d. per dozen when fresh, or say 2d. per dozen in a dried state, might be considered a fairly remunerative crop for the extremely small attention which fig culture involves. In its native habitat this tree attains a great age, and the writer has seen on the shores of the Mediterranean Sea the most prolific crops taken off apparently barren soil—stony ridges of which a sunny aspect and excellent natural drainage seemed to be the chief features.

LIME, LEMON, CITRON, SHADDOCK, AND CUMQUAT (OR KUMQUAT).

These fruit-bearing trees—all of which are of the citrus family, and well known commercially—are so admirably suited to this climate as to form in portions of Queensland and the adjacent islands immense natural orchards. In the neighbourhood of Ipswich there were formerly large quantities of the wild lime to be had for the picking—unhappily now all but extinct, owing to the ruthless way in which the trees have been treated. The shaddock also finds in Queensland a congenial climate, and in the neighbouring islands of Fiji is reported to be so prolific that the seedling trees are covering the river banks.

Speaking of the year 1895, the Registrar-General reported that one grower made 300 gallons of lime juice from the product of three acres planted with limes—which, at a low estimate, should mean a return of £10 per acre.

The lemon crop in 1897 totalled 47,252 dozen, and averaged 1,000 dozen to the acre—say, equal to £12 10s. per acre. The cultivation of this fruit was carried on in the Northern, Central, and Southern districts, and the best average returns were obtained in the Northern and Central portions of the Colony, the handsome average of 1,300 dozen per acre (say £16 5s.) having been obtained. Of the citron it may suffice to say that requirements can be amply met by local production—the perfection of the Queensland-grown citron and the excellence of local peel manufacture being such as to warrant the hope of a more than local demand for candied citrus fruits.

Other methods of curing are sometimes adopted by Southern colonies, and might be so by us with advantage. Mildura growers of oranges and lemons have not many months ago realized high prices for stocks held by them, lemons netting up to 16s. per case, and oranges between 14s. and 15s.; of the latter, a Mr. Fitzpatrick preserved 200 cases in dry sand.

The demands of the London market are shown in the following, under date January, 1897: "All the manufacturers of orange, lemon, and citron peel buy their fruit in brine. Citron comes from Corsica and the coast of Morocco. The most esteemed comes from Corsica. It is shipped to this market in casks containing 8 cwt. to 10 cwt. of fruit. The fruit is simply cut in halves, put into the casks, and, when full, brine is poured in of a strength sufficient to float an egg. The price in a normal year would be about 25s. per cwt. Oranges and lemons come from Madeira and Messina, in pipes of 6 cwt. to 7 cwt. of fruit. They are prepared in exactly the same way as the citrons. In a normal season the prices would be 20s. to 21s. per cwt. of fruit."

The cumquat is a very heavy bearer, but as the demand is at present small there would not appear to be much scope for extension, except perhaps for the growers' own consumption in the form of a preserve, of which it furnishes a most delicious example. The yield in 1895 was 1,400 dozen from an acre.

The shaddock is not in great favour for eating purposes, although a palatable preserve can be prepared; but its use for stocks on which to graft allied fruits has been advocated, and it would seem that for this purpose a limited demand may arise.

MELON (*Citrullus vulgaris*).

The cultivation of this favourite is mainly carried on in the Southern and Central littoral districts. The best average return in 1897 was obtained in the South (East of the Range), where a yield of 116 dozen per acre was recorded. This is the chief seat of the industry.

A considerable trade is done with Brisbane and some of the larger towns, where (at a low estimate) a net average of 3s. a dozen, wholesale, is realized the season through. The returns at the above price would be close on £18 per acre, but many growers within driving distance of the metropolis are personally known to the writer to have made considerably more than this amount by supplying the fruit trade with early melons.

PASSION-FRUIT (*Passiflora edulis*). GRANADILLA (*P. quadrangularis*).

The first mentioned is in considerable demand, both locally and in the Southern colonies. The vine from which it is obtained is of rapid

A Young Cherry Orchard, Ballandean.

growth and fairly hardy, very leafy, and a prolific fruit-bearer. Screens of this warmth-loving plant may be seen on many a verandah in the South of Queensland, and quite a large quantity of fruit thus passes into consumption which cannot possibly be included in the annual returns. As far as records go, 21,000 dozen were produced in 1897 from eight acres —a fairly satisfactory yield considering that the wholesale price is rarely less than 1d. per dozen. Experiments conducted by Prof. Shelton in 1893 demonstrated the keeping qualities of this fruit under artificial cold for a period amply sufficient to land them on the European markets, so that if the taste for Passion-fruit and the closely allied Granadilla could be cultivated sufficiently, we might look to a large extension of the area under vines.

In size, the first named resembles a small egg; whilst the larger variety of this species (*Passiflora macrocarpa*, Masters) has, on the authority of Mr. F. M. Bailey, attained a weight of 8 lbs.

PEACH (*Prunus persica*) AND ITS ALLIES.

These include the nectarine, almond, cherry-plum, plum, cherry, and apricot, and, with the exception of the peach, may be said to be cultivated solely in the South of Queensland.

The 1897 agricultural returns give the area of peach orchards as 38 acres, from which the yield was 44,775 dozen peaches. Of these about 35,000 dozen were produced from 22 acres of land in the Southern portion of the Colony (West of Main Range), or at the rate of 1,590 dozen to the acre. Peaches being, however, one of the commonest of garden trees on the Darling Downs and other localities, there are immense quantities of the fruit which are passed into home consumption, and in that way do not find their way into the agricultural schedules.

Nectarines, plums, cherries, and apricots showed on an average 60 dozen, 22½ bushels, 16 bushels, and 321 dozen per acre respectively. Of cherry-plums and almonds no detailed statement is made, but all the above are heavy croppers between the Range and the Southern border—in fact on the Darling Downs generally.

Many are the varieties of peaches and plums grown here, some of them thriving on the coast lands; but few can excel the " Toowoomba peach " for size and lusciousness. " China Flat " peaches are well suited to our climate, and largely grown, and as this fruit ripens several weeks earlier in Queensland than in New South Wales, where as much as 17s. the half-case has been paid in the off season, a remunerative opening exists for those who will produce only *the best* of fruit, and go to the trouble of careful marketing.

From the accompanying newspaper clipping of quite recent date it will be seen that there is also a market in London, if our shippers will comply with the technical requirements of the trade in tinned fruits. It is pleasing to note that we have had a gentleman in our midst so well qualified to give instruction in present-day American canning as Prof. Shelton :—

"Apricots : There is also a good demand for this fruit, both whole and in halves. Prices for 3 lb. tins run from 6s. up to 9s., according to quality. A large trade is also done in this country in apricot pulp. This is packed in five-kilo tins (ten tins to the case). The preparation is very simple, namely—the fruit is cut in halves, the stones removed, and then the halves are put into the tin. No sugar or other matter is added. The tins are, of course, processed in exactly the same way as for the fruits.

" Peaches : There is also a good demand for this fruit, the finer kind being what is called the 'Lemon Cling,' where the stone clings to the peach. Prices of these range from 6s. to 10s., according to quality.

" Cherries : There is only a moderate demand for these. Prices are from 7s. to 9s."

Whilst on the subject of fruit preserving, I quote the following *re* samples of the best class of French pulp fruit, which were imported for the Victorian Department of Agriculture with a view to opening up a similar trade between that colony and Great Britain :—

" The samples sent were 10 lb. tins of apricots, raspberries, and plums, and it was reassuring to find that there was nothing in the quality of the pulp which Victorians may not with care easily hope to rival. The best tin of apricots was, no doubt, of good quality, rich in colour, and the fruit when cut in halves retained its attractive appearance. This, Mr. Knight (the fruit expert) pointed out, was a great consideration, buyers being able at a glance to note the character of the fruit, and see that it was free from blight. The pulp is worth from £12 to £15 a ton in London, and these rates, fruit-growers say, will pay well. The tins in use by the French are 6 in. by 10 in., and ten of them in a case hold just 100 lbs. of pulp. It is likely that a quantity of pulp will be shipped from Mildura this year."

PERSIMMON (*Diospyros kaki*).

This is a fruit of recent importation—sometimes called Japanese date-plum, from its country of origin—which has, however, proved itself to be so thoroughly at home in our climate as to induce cultivation to a large extent. Naturally, in the space of a few short years, little more than the supply of local requirements has been possible, but the fairly remunerative market which still exists will probably lead to heavier plantings.

The yield during 1897 in the Southern division was 8,288 dozen, off 27 acres (average 369 dozen per acre). None were reported in that year as growing in the North, or to the West of the Range, in either of the other divisions. According to our Colonial Botanist the tree requires a free, rich soil, and not much pruning. The rank-growing sorts will be much assisted in fruit-bearing by judiciously pruning the roots.

APPLE (*Pyrus malus*) AND ITS ALLIES.

This fruit, together with the pear, quince, and medlar, are practically confined to the Western side of the Main Range—adjoining the New South Wales border.

Of apples, the Southern district (West of the Range) produced 41,036 dozen from 75 acres, say 547 dozen per acre, and, strange to say, the average production (412 dozen per acre) and the *total* production were greater in the North of the Colony than to the East of the Southern district.

This Colony is not, perhaps, so well suited to the production of fine-flavoured apples as are the neighbouring colonies of New South Wales and Tasmania; but, as far as yield is concerned, we have no reason to complain, and there may yet be found localities where this fruit will grow to perfection. Occasionally some excellent apples are met with of local production, but it must be confessed that many are wanting in the delicacy of flavour so apparent in those from colder climes.

As an encouragement to present growers to aim at producing the best at their command, it may be stated that one large local fruit-preserving firm, at least, is making a special feature of evaporating apples, apricots, and peaches, and eventually hopes to produce cooking and dessert raisins, to the exclusion of the £32,000 worth returned as imported in one year (1895). From the end of March till early in May there is practically no fresh fruit in London which can come into competition with Australian fruit, and colonial growers have, therefore, an excellent opportunity of doing business in this direction. During one season Tasmania shipped about 140,000 cases, and Victoria nearly 14,000 cases of apples, and the prices realized averaged, for the best shipments, about 11s. 6d. per case. The various items of expense to Victorian growers were as follows: Freight, ocean, 4s. 1d.; cost of special export case, 7d.; tissue paper for wrapping apples, also lining paper and paper shavings, including rail freight on material, 3d.; freight to Port Melbourne, say, 3½d.; charge for allotting space, supervising shipment, exchange, &c., 3d.; dock dues, &c., London, 6½d.; commission and insurance, say, 9d.; total, 6s. 9d. At 11s. 6d. per case, this left 4s. 9d. net for the apples at the garden; but some individual growers averaged 12s. to 15s. 6d. per case in London, which netted them 5s. 3d. to 8s. 9d. per case at the garden. Mr. Nepean Smith estimated that the expenses per case in connection with the small shipments from South Australia last season amounted to 7s. 1d. A shipment per "China" realized 12s. to 20s. per case in London.

The pear (*Pyrus communis*) has not, so far, been grown to nearly the same extent as the apple, possibly because it does not carry so heavy a crop. The remark made with regard to flavour in the apple applies equally to the pear; but should a trade be impracticable in the green fruit large quantities might be marketed in the tinned form. This is the most popular amongst this class of goods in the London sale-rooms, and the best Californian pears were fetching 14s. a dozen at the close of January of 1897. Although the price is only 10s. to 12s. per dozen 3 lb. tins, when in fair supply, the trade might be worth trying for; but for inferior sorts, it must be remembered, the demand is almost nil. This class of fruit is packed twenty-four tins to the case. The method of canning could be better described by our Instructor in Agriculture.

Quinces (*Pyrus cydonia*) are slow of sale in the colonies, as well as in Great Britain (tinned). The production, of which details have not apparently been given since 1895, was 1,888 dozen from five acres; no increase may be looked for at present.

The medlar (*Pyrus germanica*) grows fairly well in the colder localities, but is not a favourite. No record of this crop is taken.

RASPBERRY (*Rubus idæus*)

Is grown in many Queensland gardens. There is also a native species (*Rubus rosæfolius*, Sm.) which is found over a large extent of country. Sometimes it alternates with the Cape gooseberry as a spontaneous crop from newly cleared land. The indigenous variety being wanting in flavour, and the European variety being successful only in a few localities (such as the Downs), a cross has been suggested by our Colonial Botanist, which would doubtless lead to an extended cultivation for market. A few American blackberries, of which "Lawton's" may be mentioned as an example, fruit freely around and about Brisbane. It would appear that a judicious choice of sorts of the latter, which belong to the same family as our raspberry, as well as some of the American "Black-cap" raspberries (*Rubus occidentalis*) might result in valuable additions to our fruit list.

STRAWBERRY (*Fragaria vesca*)

Has been grown with great success on some of the volcanic loams of the coast; also on the Darling Downs. A fairly good market exists for good samples, a favourite dish in the largest towns being "strawberries and cream."

GOOSEBERRY (*Ribes grossularia*) AND ITS ALLIES.

The cultivation of this fruit is confined to the South of the Colony, and to a small extent at present. The yield recorded in 1897 was 450 quarts per acre. In common with the red currant (*R. rubrum*), black currant (*R. nigrum*), and white currant (*R. rubrum, var. album*), it succeeds well on the Darling Downs near the Southern Border, and in a few favoured localities East of the Range—but not on the coast.

RHUBARB (*Rheum rhaponticum*).

Although it is not the fruit, but the leaf-stalk which is used for culinary purposes, the above is of interest to Queensland fruit-growers inasmuch as the plant thrives in the Southern districts, and is in no very great supply so far.

ROCK MELON (*Cucumis melo*) AND ITS ALLIES.

This is not so great a favourite here as in Europe; but by those who have a liking for the fruit it is readily obtainable, and it will produce abundant crops of fine-flavoured fruit in the South of the Colony, if European-raised seed be sown. The cucumber (*C. sativus*) grows almost like a weed, and is very much in favour here. The average 1897 yield was 503 dozen per acre. Of the same natural order (*Cucurbitaceæ*) are the pumpkin (*Cucurbita pepo*), the vegetable marrow, and the gourd; also the Chocho, Chouchou, or Chayota (*Sechium edule*)—all of which give good yields in this Colony.

The return of pumpkins for 1895 was 4,501 tons—at the rate of nearly 4 tons to the acre. West of the Range, in the Southern district, over 4 tons per acre were harvested. Little demand exists for the Chocho as a vegetable.

ENDIVE (*Cichorium endivia*) AND CHICORY (*C. intybus*).

The former is not much in demand, although growing successfully. The latter is also grown very successfully in the Southern part of the Colony; one gentleman—Mr. Samuel Grimes, M.L.A.—having as many as 14 acres under crop. An exhibit of chicory root and the chicory of commerce by this manufacturer was highly spoken of at the recent Brisbane International Exhibition, and was awarded the Gold Medal. The yield for the Colony in 1897 was about 1 ton per acre.

ONION (*Allium cepa*) AND ITS ALLIES

Give abundant crops in this Colony, and, when closely cultivated, produce splendid bulbs. Notwithstanding the inducements towards growing the above, imports worth several thousands of pounds sterling take place annually, so that there is evidently an excellent opening in this direction. The 1897 average yield was 2½ tons per acre. The leek (*A. porrum*), garlic (*A. sativum*), and shallot (*A. ascalonicum*), also thrive in Southern Queensland, and are worthy of more extended cultivation.

CELERY (*Apium graveoleus*)

Grows to perfection, and has a moderate sale, but no particulars of the production are published.

CABBAGE (Genus *Brassica*).

Under this popular term may be considered the many varieties of vegetables known as cabbage, broccoli, cauliflower, Brussels sprouts, kale, kohl-rabi (*Brassica oleracea*). By far the most important position, from a commercial standpoint, is that of the first named, of which 81,420 dozen were produced in 1897, according to the Registrar-General's report on that year. The bulk of this crop was obtained in the Southern district, in which the average yield was 499 dozen per acre.

The return of cauliflowers was about 4,000 dozen, and the others were not grown in sufficient quantities to warrant detailed notice.

Closely allied to the above are the turnip (*B. rapa*) and the swede (*B. campestris*), which are neither of them so extensively grown as their suitability to our natural conditions and their high nutritive value would seem to warrant.

The yield per acre, as shown in the 1897 returns, was about 56 cwt. of turnips, and about 7½ tons of swedes. The cultivation of these is practically confined to the south-eastern corner of Queensland.

Ferns and Foliage in the Acclimatisation Gardens, Brisbane.

PARSNIP (*Peucedanum sativum*).

This vegetable yields a heavy crop, and is met with in the markets as an article of household consumption, but is not grown for cow feed, as in Jersey and other countries. Its value for milk production is such that farmers would do well to devote their attention to it as a crop. No figures are available regarding the quantity at present grown, as it may be said to be practically nil.

CARROT (*Daucus carota*).

Another valuable cattle food. Can be grown over a large area, and offers great inducements to extensive culture.

The cultivation of this is at present on a very small scale, yielding (in 1897) about 600 dozen to the acre.

TOMATO (*Lycopersicum esculentum*).

Fairly large quantities of this fruit are raised annually, the returns for 1897 being 3,720 cwt. from 96 acres. A large portion of this, as well as unrecorded crops, pass direct into the hands of householders, and a good deal of tomato sauce of very superior quality is made in the home, and by preserving works in bulk.

The average yield in the Southern district, where this is principally grown, was about 39 cwt. to the acre.

BEAN.

The scarlet runner (*Phaseolus coccineus*) and the French—or haricot— bean (*P. vulgaris*) are mostly cultivated in South-Eastern Queensland. The return in this district for 1897 was about 82 bushels to the acre (all kinds). The results obtained in the Central Coastal districts were not quite so favourable.

PEA (*Pisum sativum*).

This is a favourite South Queensland garden crop, and gives a good monetary return to the grower. The average yield per acre in 1897 was 46 bushels in this district, and, as with most of the fruits and vegetables under review, in more favourable seasons a much higher yield would be obtained.

SUNDRY TROPICAL AND ECONOMIC PLANTS.

Amongst the former may be mentioned as growing to perfection in the North of the Colony:—The Jack Fruit tree (*Artocarpus integrifolia*); Bread Fruit tree (*A. incisa*); Alligator or Avocado Pear tree (*Persea gratissima*);

F

Litchi (*Nephelium litchi*); and Longan (*Euphoria longana*, Lam.), sometimes classed as a Nephelium with the Litchi, to which it is, however, said
to be much inferior in flavour. Both the Date Palm (*Phœnix dactylifera*)
and Papaw (*Carica papaya*) have been planted in most latitudes within
the boundaries of the Colony, and, as far as the writer is aware, have
fruited in the Southern as well as the Northern districts. The last-
mentioned tree yields from 350 dozen to 100 dozen per acre.

The Indian Tamarind (*Tamarindus indica*) is a large tree, from the pods
of which a pulpy substance is obtained which has a medicinal value as a
laxative. There is also a fruit called by colonists Queensland Tamarind
(*Diploglottis cunninghamii*).

The Whampee (*Clausena wampi*), for its fruit; the Divi Divi (*Cæsalpinia
coriaria*), for its pods (worth £10 to £13 per ton); the Cassava plant
(*Manihot utilissima* and *M. aipi*), for its tapioca product; and the Arnotto
shrub (*Bixa orellana*), for the colouring matter which it yields, might be
extensively cultivated here, as they have been successfully grown in most
of the Coastal districts, and only require trial on a commercial scale. The
Cassava has yielded 2 tons to the acre.

Many kinds of Pepper thrive remarkably well here — both of the
climbing order (*Piper nigrum;* order Piperaceæ) and the Capsicums, viz.,
the "Chili shrub" (*C. frutescens;* order Solanaceæ), the Bird's-Eye
Pepper (*C. baccatum*), and the Bell Pepper (*C. grossum*).

Of Ginger (*Zingiber officinale*), a few acres planted in the North
yielded an average of 2,240 lbs. to the acre.

Yams (*Dioscorea alata*) and Taro (*Colocasia antiquorum*) are used by the
South Sea islanders in their native land as food, and for this purpose are
sometimes cultivated in the North of this Colony, where they grow to
perfection.

The Pea Nut (*Arachis hypogæa*) is cultivated in the North and South
of the Colony, and its great value as the source of the "nut oil" of
commerce should gain for it a wide popularity. Between a sixth and a
third of its weight consists of oil, and besides the latter a large quantity
of nitrogenous matter is contained in the nut—facts which are so highly
appreciated in the United States that several millions of bushels are
annually raised! Reckoning 22 lbs. to the bushel, our 1897 crop averaged
over 74 bushels per acre.

Cowpea (used by many as a vegetable) and Kaffir corn yielded
respectively about 19 and 20 bushels per acre. As regards the latter, as
much as two crops can be obtained from one sowing. Broom millet has
lately been introduced to the Colony; the yield in 1897 was 400 lbs. per

acre. There is a steady demand for the stems for broom making; and as the standard of manufacture becomes higher, so is the demand likely to increase materially.

Of seed and fibre producing plants which are successfully grown, and give much promise, the following may be mentioned :—Rhea fibre (*Boehmeria nivea*); Jute (*Corchorus olitorius*); Hemp (*Cannabis sativa*); Queensland hemp, or "Sida retusa" (*Sida rhombifolia*); Flax or Linseed (*Linum usitatissimum*), &c. Other economic plants include the Quinine tree (*Cinchona calisaya*, &c.); the Camphor tree (*Cinnamomum camphora*); the European Walnut (*Juglans regia*); the Hazel or Filbert Nut (*Corylea* tribe); and the Sweet or Spanish Chestnut (*Castanea sativa*). The three last mentioned thrive well on the Downs.

HORTICULTURE.

This affords a means of livelihood in many of the large towns of the Colony, and the establishments of several of our metropolitan nurserymen, in particular, are veritable fairylands. These are as remarkable for the luxuriant outdoor growth of tropical and sub-tropical plants of exquisite colours or stately magnificence as for the variety of "old country" favourites which we here meet with. Most of the *useful* products of our gardens have been dealt with in detail; it therefore remains for me to touch briefly upon the *ornamental* department—embraced under the term "Floriculture"; and to this end I cannot do better than quote from the admirable digest of this subject by Mr. Theodore Wright as follows :—

"In the Darling Downs district many of the most popular florists' flowers of Great Britain attain to great perfection, and amongst the successes may be specified pansies, violets, carnations, pinks, picotees, balsams, cockscombs, amaranths, phloxes, Canterbury bells, petunias, geraniums, heliotropes, dahlias, sunflowers, Indian and Chinese pinks, mignonette, sweet peas, hollyhocks, portulacas, penstemons, chrysanthemums; in short, an almost endless variety of annuals, biennials, and perennials from every clime grace the ornamental borders; edgings of box and other British favourites help to maintain the charm of early associations. Amongst the flowering shrubs in all temperate localities of the colony, the rose in its many varieties is deservedly popular and quite at home. The rose of old England is loved as much for the country it represents as for itself, and some of its species and varieties thrive over the greater portion of Queensland. But on the Darling Downs may be seen the lilac, laburnum, laurustinus, camellia, honeysuckle, weigelia, veronica, abutilon, berberis, deutzia, duranta, euonymus, gardenia,

F 2

rhododendron, hibiscus, hydrangea, holly, ivy, jasmine, laurel, magnolia, spirea, viburnum, and hosts of other ornamental trees and shrubs in great variety, besides an endless assortment of conifers and taxads from almost all the countries under the sun.

"Sub-tropical Queensland is very favourably circumstanced for the cultivation of flowers. During winter many of the old favourites, such as pansies, asters, ranunculi, primulas, cinerarias, violets, and other soft-wooded annuals and herbaceous plants, thrive admirably; and in the summer, plants which are only to be seen in hothouses in the British Isles are regular occupants of the border. The same remarks apply to shrubs and ornamental trees. Roses in very great variety succeed admirably. Many of the handsome flowering and ornamental trees and shrubs from the Brazils, East and West Indies, Mauritius, and Cape of Good Hope are thoroughly at home in the sub-tropics; and gardens well stocked and tended can be made to show to as good if not to better advantage than in more temperate climes, for these shrubs keep up a display the year through. Where in Great Britain and on the Continent there are conservatories, there are less costly, but quite as attractive structures in Queensland called 'bush' or shade houses. These are made in various styles, and generally of very inexpensive materials. They are very frequently used as ferneries, and with taste and skill in arrangement it is quite surprising what an attraction they can become.

"Balsams, cockscombs, zinnias, portulacas, petunias, verbenas, geraniums, antirrhinums, phlox drummondi, and a few others do very well in the tropics, and so also do many hothouse bulbs and herbaceous plants. Begonias, colei, and a host of other ornamental foliage plants are well adapted to grace the borders and parterres; and for shrubberies, an immense variety of ornamental shrubs and trees are suitable. The gaudy crotons from New Guinea occupy much the same place in Northern gardens and shrubberies that the laurel and holly do at home. In the tropics, in the spring time, instead of the laburnum and the horse-chestnut, there is the gorgeous poinciana regia with its brilliant display of scarlet bloom, and the jacaranda mimosæfolia with its garment of cerulean hue, also the lagerstrœmiæ, in their many varieties of growth and colour; and the shrubs and large trees bloom profusely most of the summer through. Among smaller shrubs there are poincianas, poinsettias, hibiscus, alla-mandas, hoyas, gardenias, francisceas, many varieties of palms, conifers, and taxads; also a great variety of grotesque and huge cacti. British stove plants are more at home in the open borders in North Queensland than in the best-kept stove-heated winter garden in Europe. One of the

Refreshment Kiosk in the Queen's Park, Brisbane.

Refreshment Kiosk in the Queen's Park Brisbane

great attractions of the North at the present time is the variety of indigenous orchids there; and in that climate their cultivation is of the simplest and easiest character imaginable. Orchid-houses, such as the bush-house already described, will ere long be a marked feature in all good collections in the North; and pretty nearly all the famous varieties grown could easily be accommodated there with all that is needful to make them vigorous and floriferous. The same remarks apply equally to ferns; and many choice varieties of this beautiful family of interesting and attractive plants may be easily grown there by the veriest 'tyro' in horticulture. Roses are now being cultivated for perfume in the south-eastern portion of the Colony, and there seems likelihood of an important industry becoming established."

FORESTRY AND TIMBER EXPORT.

In concluding a review of the resources of Queensland which belong to the vegetable kingdom, reference must not be omitted to the wealth of timber she possesses. There are upwards of 800 varieties at present known to our naturalists, and the number is continually being added to. Exhibits have been made at various times, and have attracted a considerable amount of attention, notably at the Colonial and Indian Exhibition of London, and the Centennial International Exhibition in Melbourne. The enormous extent of forest country yet available for commercial purposes is beyond the grasp of the mind of man, and it is satisfactory to note that—young as our Colony is—the Government have shown in many practical ways their intention of adding to these resources. State nurseries for the cultivation of forest trees are situated in various parts of the Colony, and a day is annually set apart (Arbour Day) which all State schools observe as a holiday, the occasion being celebrated by the public planting of ornamental trees in the school grounds.

Many beautiful shade and timber trees have been imported from the Old World and acclimatized, but the variety of native timbers is such that they only require to be better known in order to create a large export trade. Already our timber merchants and others have received inquiries from Natal and the Cape re railway sleepers, &c., and from Philadelphia as to wood-blocking. Our nearest neighbour—New South Wales —has made a definite start in the trade, a gentleman engaged in this industry having brought with him to England specimens of grey iron-bark, spotted and grey gum, tallowwood, blackbutt, mahogany, and cedar. The value of these for various purposes was brought under the notice of leading engineers here, with the result that orders were given for supplying certain of these timbers. The principal demand comes from the railway companies for sleepers. Timber for wood-paving the streets is also required, and since his return very large orders have been received to supply timber. The price obtained in England is satisfactory, and far in advance of what is paid locally. The opening up of this trade is regarded as of much importance to the district and colony, and already there is increased activity in the timber business on the Clarence River (an important centre of this industry).

All the timbers mentioned above are obtainable in Queensland *in large quantities*, so that we may fairly expect to get a share of "the good things going."

A trial of New South Wales hardwood has been made in the erection of a large goods shed at Manchester for the Great Northern Railway Company. To those unacquainted with the mechanical value of our timbers, the following particulars respecting a few of those which are common to the latter Colony and ourselves may be of interest. The figures are derived from a work by the U.S. Consul in Sydney, published under the authority of the Government of New South Wales, and may, therefore, be taken as fairly accurate.

The " proof transverse strength " was the weight (pounds avoirdupois) which a 1 in. × 1 in. bar of perfectly dry timber could sustain between two supporting points, one foot apart, without having its fibre or elasticity impaired. The "modulus of rupture" was *eighteen times* the load required to *break* the bar.

	Proof strength.	Modulus of Rupture.	Weight in lbs. of a cubic foot.
Large leaved iron-bark (*Eucalyptus siderophloia, variety rostrata*)	313	6,858	72
Narrow leaved iron-bark (N.S.W. "Grey iron-bark ") (*Eucalyptus orebra*) . . .	364	8,568	69
Blue gum (N.S.W. "Grey gum " or " bastard box ") (*Eucalyptus tereticornis*) . .	285	6,300	71
Blackbutt (*Eucalyptus pilularis*) . . .	245	5,544	56
" Mahogany " (*Eucalyptus resinifera*) . .	238	6,300	70
Cedar (known in the English trade as "Moulmein cedar ") (*Cedrela toona*) . . .	140	3,296	28
Common yellow wood (*Flindersia Oxleyana*) .	217	5,346	50
Moreton Bay or Hoop pine (*Araucaria Cunninghamii*)	196	4,212	48

Besides the above, there are many more deserving special notice, amongst which may be mentioned the Spotted Gum (*Eucalyptus maculata*), of which the timber is utilized in a large number of ways—for ship, carriage, and bridge building; wheelwrights' requirements, and street paving cubes. "Bloodwood" (*Eucalyptus corymbosa*) is believed to be suitable for the latter purpose.

Another of the Eucalypti, of which we have so great a variety, is the Turpentine tree, sometimes known as Peppermint (*Eucalyptus microcorys*); by the natives it is known as "Tee." The timber is largely used by ship and house builders, and by wheelwrights; it is strong, handsome, and durable.

Stave wood (*Tarrieta argyrodendron*) is plentiful in the Queensland scrubs, and in New South Wales. The name by which our neighbours know the tree is "Black Stave" or "Ironwood," and the timber is used by them for posts, sleepers, tiles, and bridges. It is said to be tough in texture, and capable of great resistance to the action of water; may be used for the same purposes as the English beech.

Several thousand pounds' worth of machinery, &c., is now engaged in wood-working. Out of a total of over 300 establishments (employing some 2,400 hands), rather less than half were in 1897 engaged solely in saw-milling, of which the total capital value was set down, roughly speaking, at £400,000. A fair average price for sawn timber at the mill per 100 ft. super., hardwood is 12s. 5d.; cedar, 18s. 4d.; pine, 10s. 2d.

The *Townsville Bulletin* mentions one log containing 2,984 ft. of cedar, from which a "flitch" measuring 1,000 ft. had been sawn. Our contemporary speaks of a tree from which eight or nine logs, each from 12 ft. to 14 ft. long, had been cut. The butt measured 7 ft. 6 in., and the diameter of the smallest end was about 4 ft.

THE HARVEST OF THE SEA.

Specially written by

D. O'CONNOR, Esq.,

"Duporth," Oxley, Queensland.

IN marine fish Queensland is very rich as regards variety, abundance, and excellence. At Southport, Caloundra, and many other places on the coast, the disciples of good old Walton may indulge in their favourite sport to their hearts' content. Most of our fresh water is, however, not so well supplied. The celebrated Palmer (*Lates calcarifer*) may be caught in the Burnett, and in rivers north thereof. This is a fish of rare excellence, and may be regarded as unrivalled, whether we view it from a sportsman's or an epicure's point of view. It attains a considerable size, sometimes exceeding fifty pounds in weight. The Ceratodus is an extremely ancient fish, being one of the oldest forms of life in existence; it is regarded as a connecting link between the fish and the reptile. Unlike other fish, it breathes by means of a lung as well as by gills. The Ceratodus is found only in Queensland, where it was until recently confined to two rivers—the Burnett and the Mary; it has, however, now been placed in half a dozen other waters. This was done in the hope of preserving it from extinction. Its native name is "Teebine"; it is known on the Burnett as Salmon, on account of its pink flesh. In 1886 and 1887 attempts were made to acclimatize Trout, English Perch, Carp, and Tench in the Gold Creek and Enoggera reservoirs. A number of young fish brought from Ballarat and some Perch from Hobart were liberated, but unfortunately destroyed by the numerous shags which were allowed to infest these waters. The Acclimatization Society of Southern Queensland, whose headquarters are at Warwick, have successfully introduced the English Brown Trout and the American Rainbow Trout into the streams on the Downs. It is expected that Trout fishing will in the near future be one of the sports of Queensland. The above excellent Society is also engaged in the acclimatization of feathered game, having already imported Pheasants, Partridges, and Californian Quail. Another attempt to acclimatize the Gourami in Queensland is contemplated on a sufficiently large scale to ensure success. This justly celebrated fish is kept in a domesticated state, and is consequently always available. It is held in high estimation wherever it is known.

The fishing industry in Brisbane has recently received considerable impetus through the establishment of a fish market by Messrs. Geddes & Co., in connexion with their freezing works. We still, however, continue to import fresh fish from England and Canada, most of the tinned, salted, and dried fish also being imported. This should not be the case, as we occasionally meet with locally preserved fish of the highest excellence; the writer having once eaten mullet which had been caught and preserved by a South Sea islander, equal to any Yarmouth bloater, Findon haddock, or Tasmanian trumpeter he ever tasted. This proves what can be done with care and intelligence. With the abundant " harvest of the sea " that always awaits garnering it is marvellous that the people of Queensland should have to rely to so great an extent upon the antipodes and other colonies for their fish supply. Smoked Blue Cod is sold in Brisbane at a shilling a pound; this fish is sent in a fresh state from the Bluff in New Zealand to Melbourne, where it is slightly salted and smoked, and thence re-exported to Sydney and elsewhere; it always commands a high price. During the cold season, when fish may most easily be preserved, our coasts, bays, and rivers teem with Mullet in countless thousands; they are in excellent condition, of large size, and are easily caught. The mullet is captured by means of a seine, and occasionally the take is so great that the larger part has to be abandoned, the boats being overfilled. Our coasts are periodically visited by vast shoals of Anchovies and other fish, which might be turned to very profitable account by large numbers of fishermen and fish curers.

Edible fishes form only a portion of the great " harvest of the sea." Several species of oysters abound from one end of Queensland to the other. *O. glomerata* are of especial value, and have for years past formed an extensive and profitable industry, a very large quantity being exported to the Southern markets, especially to Sydney and Melbourne. The pearl oyster fishery has also attained large dimensions. The Trepang fishery has been carried on with considerable vigour. Turtles abound, but are seldom sought. Sponges are plentiful, but none are gathered. It may well be said, "The harvest truly is plentiful, but the reapers are few."

The following list comprises some of the food fishes of Queensland. There are several species of many of the following, but few are ever offered for sale :—

Anchovy.

Barramundi (several different fishes are called Barramundi), Bony Bream (a herring), Bonito, Butterfly Gurnard, Bream, Black Trevally, Bat Fish, Black Fish.

Ceratodus, Conger, Cat Fish, Cardinal, Cooktown Salmon.

Deep Pouter, Diamond Fish, Dory.

Eel, Epaulette or Pearl Fish, Eel-Cat Fish, Emperor.

Flounder, Flying Fish, Flat-head.

Gar Fish, Giant Herring or Milk Fish, Giant Mackerel, Grey Mullet, Groper, Gurnard.

Herring (*Clupea sundaica*), Huzzah, Hair-tail, Horse Mackerel.

Javelin Fish, Jew Fish.

King Fish.

Loter, Lysan, Ling (*Congrogadus subducens*), Long Tom, Leather Jacket.

Mackerel (*Scomber antarcticus*), Murena, Moon Fish, Mullet (Grey and Red), Murray Cod.

Ox-eye, Old Wife.

Parrot Fish and Perch in great variety, Paradise Fish, Palmer or Giant Perch.

Queen Fish.

Rock Cod, Red Mullet, Rifle Fish.

Sole, Stranger, Sea Cat Fish, Sand Smelt, Surveyor, Stone Fish, Sting Ray, Sweep, Snapper, Sea Pike, Samson Fish.

Tassel Fish, Trevally, Tongue Sole, Tailor or Blue Fish, Tarwhine.

Whiting (*Sillago ciliata*), Wirrah.

Yellow-tail.

PART III.

Mineral Wealth.

THIS has been written about so often and so ably that it would seem almost a superfluous, and certainly a difficult task, to revert to the subject. If, however (as was reported in the columns of the press), a distinguished visitor from Great Britain to Queensland, well informed in most commercial matters, was so little acquainted with our magnificent and inexhaustible mineral resources as to inquire whether we "had any coal or gold mines in Queensland," it would appear that we have all the justification and needed encouragement to again present the claims to universal recognition of a few of our most prominent mining fields.

Mineral production accounts for a considerable share of the annual wealth of Australasia — rather more than one-eighth, according to Coghlan—and Queensland takes no mean place amongst her neighbours in this respect. Of the £15,000,000 odd attributed in 1897 to minerals, our Colony produced £3,059,104—more than a fifth; and between the dawn of gold mining in Queensland—but a few years ago—and the present time over £45,000,000 has been wrested from the soil of this Colony in the form of gold! Another £9,700,000 may be said to represent the value of minerals, other than gold, raised in Queensland since 1860.

The output of gold in 1898 showed an advance of 110,180 ounces (£385,630) upon that of 1897, and is the largest which the Colony has ever seen, whilst the yield of gold per head of population is all but the highest in Australasia. The gold winnings, per miner employed, are considerably over double those of Victoria, and more than three times as great as those of either New South Wales or New Zealand, while Queensland is third among the colonies in the aggregate mineral production. With these facts so plainly before us, we are led to speculate where Queensland would be if we had a mining population equal to that of either Victoria or New South Wales.

Men and capital are what we need. On all hands it is admitted that few of our mining "shows" (to use a popular term) have been developed to their full extent, and that many are little more than "surface scratchings." In the large majority of instances the choice of fields has been so great and the reasonable expectations of successful prospecting so tempting that our present mining population and invested capital, whilst producing magnificent results, are inadequate to gathering the harvest of former sowings. As has been suggested, had we a population like our next-door neighbours, New South Wales and Victoria—either of which is two and a half times as populous as we are—we should probably hold the mineral record of Australasia, *and of the World.* In confirmation of this remark, it may be noted that the population and age of the colonies which surpass us in point of aggregate mineral productiveness are, in each case, greater than our own, and—strange to say—whilst the gold production of the two most important is shown by the following table to have been fluctuating heavily and on the decrease, that of Queensland has increased uniformly with the increase of population, a fact which speaks volumes for the exceptional inducements offered by our goldfields to the mining world :

Colony.	1861 Oz.	1871 Oz.	1881 Oz.	1891 Oz.	1897 Oz.
Queensland . .	1,077	171,937	270,945	573,439	807,928
N.S. Wales . .	465,685	323,609	149,627	153,336	292,217
Victoria . .	1,967,453	1,355,477	858,850	576,400	812,765
N. Zealand . .	194,031	730,029	270,561	251,996	251,645

The 1898 official figures for some of these colonies are not yet to hand.

GOLD.

Gold mining is at present our most promising—and has always been our most important—single industry, as it finds employment and support for some 68,000 persons. 8,623 miners' rights were issued in 1897, and steam power of 10,115 horse power, with machinery for mining, crushing, reducing, and dressing ore, &c., of a total value of £1,067,106, was employed in the industry. The annual fee for a mining licence is 5s. The number of companies engaged in mining increased from 179 in 1884 to 229 in 1896; subscribed capital £5,852,847.

It is difficult to obtain the aggregate amount of dividends which the mines of Queensland have paid to investors, but according to the sworn returns made under the Dividend Duty Act, £4,826,213 15s. 6d. were distributed between September, 1890 (commencement of Dividend Duty Act), and 31st January, 1897, or about £752,000 per annum.

QUEENSLAND 1897
Charters Towers, (Brilliant)

Buildings at the Surface of one of the leading Gold Mines.

The value of gold raised per miner (excluding assistants, such as carters) was £250 per head in 1898, and this has previously been even higher. Upwards of 2,000 distinct quartz reefs have been proved to be auriferous; 1,943 of these are detailed in the Official Statistics for 1895, and incomplete as the figures are acknowledged to be, fully 13,000 square miles of auriferous country have been worked in the reef and in the alluvial. In the early days the latter predominated, but at present quartz or "reef" gold constitutes about 95 per cent. of the whole output. The average return of gold per ton of quartz was 1 oz. 4 dwt. 5 grs. in 1894 and 19 dwt. 19 grs. in 1897 ; the value, all round, may be put at £3 10s. per oz. The average return per miner engaged in reefing was some £300 per annum in 1894, 1895, and 1896. The March quarter of 1897 showed the gratifying increase of nearly 20,000 oz. over the corresponding period in 1896, since eclipsed by the average increase during 1898.

CHARTERS TOWERS and CAPE RIVER goldfields. During 1897 alone these fields contributed a total of 360,369 ozs., of a value of £1,030,191. In 1898 the yield increased to 455,028 ozs., valued at £1,150,000. Before 1872 Charters Towers was a bleak, nearly barren, desolate run for a few head of cattle, with grass too poor and "seedy" for sheep. The Hon. Hugh Mosman and some friends found reefs and secured some gold from the outcrops. It is little more than a quarter of a century since these gentlemen reported the find, and yet at the end of 1898 it was officially recorded that 4,399,725 ozs. of gold had been won, of which the value was about £15,179,051. With figures of such magnitude, little wonder that the "Towers" field holds the premier position among all Australasian goldfields, and, what is more to the purpose, is in a position to retain that proud place by the aid of her deep ground below the 2,000 ft. levels. This phenomenal field occupies the edge of an area of granite and syenite rocks, which simultaneously with their upheaval displaced many lines of auriferous quartz reefs, the whole disturbance causing convulsions and faults in the previous over-lying strata upon a gigantic scale. Under such circumstances, therefore, it was first maintained in theory, and later by practical work, that to as great a depth as the quartz miner can ever hope to penetrate he will find a continuance of these reefs. Indeed, within the past few months a shaft "bottomed" on the reef, having been sunk but a few feet from the original estimated depth of 2,200 ft. vertical. Charters Towers miners, with a veritable network of reefs to work upon, and the knowledge where to find them at deep levels, may be said to have brought mining within the category of commercial or industrial enterprise. £13,000 is said to be paid weekly in miners' wages on the above field.

Next in order of importance is the MOUNT MORGAN goldfield, of which the bulk of the yield must, of course, be credited to the great Mount Morgan mine itself. During 1897 this property yielded over 165,000 oz. of gold, making a grand total of some £7,882,980 worth, and it is remarkable that for many years past the annual returns have been on the increase, the 1897 yield alone being an advance of 17,486 oz. upon that of the previous year. In 1896 the ordinary ore averaged 19 dwt., the mundic 4 oz. 4 dwt., the slimes 1 oz. 19 dwt., and the low grade 11 dwt., giving an average per ton of stone treated of 1 oz. 8 dwt. The unparalleled richness of this Company's property has dazzled the world. Princely dividends have been paid out to the lucky original shareholders, some of whom at least are now living in affluence in various parts of the world. It has paid between September, 1886, and the present time some

£5,000,000 IN DIVIDENDS, OR £5 PER SHARE.

Work at other places outside Mount Morgan has demonstrated, as it has outside Gympie, Croydon, and the " Towers," that the gold does not end with the area within which the principal operations are being carried on in the respective localities. Right in the midst of agricultural and pastoral centres are to be found mines which to a greater or lesser degree are adding either to the gold, the silver, the coal, or the copper output of the Colony. Mount Morgan has not inaptly been called the "Mountain of Gold." In its early days the mine yielded £100,000 to £125,000 per month in dividends on 1,000,000 shares at £1 each. Immense sums of money have been lost as well as made by speculators in these shares, who often purchased at a high price with a view to a further rise. The Company has for some time past been paying £25,000 per month (6d. per share), and has been able at the same time to do some heavy prospecting, to lay down the most expensive machinery, erect an inexhaustible reservoir of water, &c. The number of employees during 1897 was 1,611, all receiving fair wages, and the town itself of about 5,000 people may be said to be supported by it. The works are lighted throughout by electricity, so that—to those at least who prior to 1882 knew this little group of hills in all their pristine peacefulness—the " fairy land " simile, so often applied to this far-famed mine, would seem to be justified by its present busy aspect. It may be mentioned, incidentally, that the 640 acre selection, of which the ground now being mined formed a portion, was sold (subsequent to the finding of gold " colours ") for £1 per acre !

The ROCKHAMPTON goldfields, in the neighbourhood, comprise: Ridgelands, Rosewood, Morinish, Canoona, Coonyan, Blackfellow's Gully, New Zealand Gully, Stanwell, Ulam, Cawarral, Mount Wheeler, and a few less important places. From the latter a nugget of 250 or 260 oz. weight was secured, and a writer thus describes the finding of it :—" In a claim which had been pegged off near the top of one of the spurs of Mount Wheeler, early one Sunday morning, a miner's little boy took up his father's pick to try if he could use it, and, standing just within the boundaries of the claim, drove the pick into the black volcanic soil among the grass roots, and felt it stick, so that he could not lift it. The point of the pick was found to be embedded in a weighty nugget of the value of about £1,000. It was an oblong piece of pure gold. On the upper side it was dark, where the black volcanic soil had covered it, but on the other side it was of a bright yellow ; it appeared like a splash of molten metal suddenly cooled when brought into contact with a cold surface."

From 1883 to 1898, inclusive, the total output of these fields, including Mount Morgan, is stated at 2,222,045 oz. of gold, and their permanence is strikingly shown by a comparison of the first eight years with the subsequent eight years of the period, which yielded respectively 844,862 oz. and 1,377,183 oz.—a very noticeable increase for the last few years.

GYMPIE and the neighbouring small goldfields next claim our attention. The year just closed (1898) shows a return of some 105,540 oz. of gold, of which the value was £369,000. At present Gympie is almost entirely worked by companies and syndicates of Queensland residents—a large proportion being engaged in actual mining on the property they are financially interested in, or an adjoining claim. In all this district there are very few mines supported by English capital. These companies distributed over £168,000 in dividends during 1897, whereas the calls on shares amounted to but £84,186, an exceedingly moderate sum when it is considered that a tremendous amount of deep ground prospecting was done. The 1898 calls amounted to £124,570.

In common with all Australian fields, the gold was first found in alluvial drift, and the ease with which it was obtained gave many a poor man a " lift." Mr. J. Nash, the discoverer of Gympie (in 1867), put together, it is said, £8,000 in a couple of years, and many similar instances occurred. Nuggets of all sizes were found, one weighing as much as 804 ounces and worth £3,000.

For several years gold continued to be found in the alluvial in sufficient quantities to support a large number of miners, but when at last the supply ceased, the bulk of the men moved on to other fields, or spread out on all sides in the hopes of making new discoveries.

Attempts were, of course, made to find the reefs from which the alluvial gold was judged to have originally come, with such success that the present population is nearly as great as that in Gympie's palmiest alluvial days, and the prospects are far better than ever they were under that class of gold-getting. The estimated population at the close of 1897 was over 13,000.

The history, present position, and prospects of some of the most notable of the claims, as briefly sketched in the *Brisbane Courier* of 17th February, 1897, fully confirm the above view:—

"The 'Lady Mary' was the first quartz reef found, being discovered in November, 1867, by Messrs. Pollock and Lawrence. A few days afterwards this find was followed by the exposing of the 'Caledonia.' Exceedingly fine specimens were taken from these near the surface. The result was further prospecting, with the consequent unearthing of others. How rich these were may be imagined from the fact that 10 tons from 'Dodd's Caledonia' yielded 998 oz.; 3 cwt. from 'No. 1 California' gave the magnificent return of 367 oz. Dodd himself extracted 1,100 oz. from 10 tons, and three crushings from the 'Caledonia' p.c., aggregating 3,164 tons, yielded 75,936 oz. or 24 oz. to the ton.

"Gympie has, of course, had its periods of depression; but there are always some of the mines turning out good payable stuff. At present the prospect is unusually promising. For instance, the 'Wilmot Extended' have recently had a breaking-down which for richness would be difficult to beat. It is the same break which about ten years ago turned out £70,000 in dividends, although only 70 ft. of stuff was taken out. At this particular place there is a great stretch of country — about 800 ft. to the southern boundary. It is right on the Russell reef, too, which gave such sensational returns years ago, and which has since given from 10 oz. to 12 oz. to the ton. It is, in fact, in the centre of the golden belt, with the 'Ellen Harkins' on one side, the 'Smithfield United' on another, 'No. 1 North Phœnix' (which has paid princely dividends and never made a call) on the north, and the 'Monkland' line on the south." The "No. 1" has paid about £431,750 in dividends.

In 1897 the old 'Phœnix No. 1. North' made a clear profit of £10,000.

As showing some recent results it may be mentioned that in 1897 Brennan's "Caledonia" mine gave an average return of 16 oz. to the ton; the "Caledonia and Smithfield" distributed £44,000 in dividends; and the "South New Zealand Junction" crushed 393 tons of stone for a yield of

1,528 oz. of gold, of the value of over £5,300. The North Smithfield Co. obtained 13,837 oz. of gold, and paid £33,414 in dividends in 1896. "No. 1 North Glanmire" paid 3s. per 5s. share in the same year, and has altogether paid over £12 per share. The "Phœnix Golden Pile" paid away £20,000, and the "Columbia Smithfield" £19,800 in dividends during 1896. Adjoining the former of these two claims is the "Phœnix," which distributed £6,666 amongst its shareholders that year. To the crushing machinery on Gympie, a few cyanide plants have not long been added, and have proved a decided success, the cost of treatment being reported to be as low as 4s. per ton. This development was first suggested by noticeable losses from the ordinary treatment of the stuff raised by the Gympie Gold Mines (previously known as the Eastern Monkland). The character of the gold here is extremely fine and pure, and it is remarkable for the absence of the usual slate formation by which the Gympie gold is accompanied. The present depth of this claim is over 1,450 ft., a depth which has been exceeded by four other mines on the field. Elsewhere the gold is very free and extraordinarily coarse. In every case it can be found in conjunction with black shaly slate. Reefs several feet in width can be traced in the workings for hundreds of yards, yet their value is infinitesimal without the presence of the slate. Often the slate is no thicker than a sheet of brown paper, yet coincident with it are rich gold veins.

In about eight years the dividends paid by Gympie companies total nearly £1,000,000, whilst the aggregate yield of gold from 1867 to 1898 has been 2,311,900 oz., of the value of £8,091,650.

As has already been incidentally mentioned, many—if not most—of the miners on Gympie are also shareholders in some concern or other; frequently they are found sitting as directors of the board in control of their " boss "—the manager. It is significant, too, that notwithstanding this intermixing of interests, trouble rarely occurs, as the men have a very fine perception of where their duty as wage-earners begins and ends. As was remarked by a writer during the period of depression: " The spirit which animates so many on Gympie is the true bond of fraternity, and to this may be ascribed the freedom from labour disputes which the field has enjoyed for so many years. The greatest harmony has always prevailed between employer and employee, for the simple reason that it is hard to tell where one leaves off and the other begins. Even to those unacquainted with the field it will readily be observed how the interests of one are bound up with those of the other, and how promptly this fact is realized on both sides."

It may be remarked incidentally that the year 1898 was among the most successful which Gympie has seen, the yield being greater than that of 1897 by nearly 10,000 oz., or £35,000.

CROYDON is a relatively young, and by no means the least promising goldfield of the Colony. Thirteen years have passed since it was proclaimed (Jan. 1886), and at the close of 1898 official returns gave the total output to that date as being some 761,064 oz., whilst the value of gold won in the year reached the sum of £140,516.

The ratio of calls to dividends is also most satisfactory. In 1896 the former only amounted to £14,000, whilst the dividends paid reached the substantial total of £63,000. The average value of the gold is £2 3s. 6d. per oz., and it will be seen that, although it is impossible to foretell future returns, the very highest hopes may be entertained of the prospects of this field.

In common with many of our goldfields, this one covers an enormous area of gold-bearing country, which needs capital and men to develope it. So numerous are the reefs that good payable claims have often been abandoned directly the stone became poor, instead of which a little persistence would, in the majority of cases, have been handsomely rewarded. In other cases the want of capital to provide pumping machinery has stopped the work of prospecting before a return was obtained. Some 268 claims had crushings during the year 1897, whilst nearly 400 claims and other mining areas were on the register. So important is this field considered that it has been made the subject of an exhaustive report by Mr. William H. Rands, of the Geological Survey of Queensland, and to this interesting work readers are referred for further information. One thing is certain: except for its out-of-the-way position, Croydon would long since have received attention at the hands of capitalists, the underground wealth would have been unearthed in vast quantities, and the field would now, perhaps, rank as the " premier " in the Colony. The old transport difficulties are now largely done away with; deep sinking has proved to be an unqualified success on similar auriferous country; and capital and pluck will reap a rich harvest when brought to bear on the unquestionably extensive deposits of the precious metal occurring here. The conservation of water on a large scale is one of the most urgent needs of the field, and were capital turned in this direction alone, a very great increase in the year's returns would be immediately apparent. The estimated population at the close of 1897 was about 1,847 men and 2,296 women and children.

The ETHERIDGE, WOOLGAR, and GREEN HILLS may be said

Custom House, Brisbane.

to have splendid resources, which a combination of difficulties have greatly retarded in development. About 1,000 men and 700 women and children are at present on these fields, which, according to the estimate of the warden at the close of 1895, carried sufficient gold to support a similar number under the present state of things for the next fifty years. An average of over 20,000 oz. of gold has been turned out annually for the past twenty years, and (as in the last-mentioned field) capital only needs to be applied in guarding against droughts and otherwise putting operations on a more satisfactory footing. The Etheridge field is described as an area of enormous extent, saturated with gold from the surface downwards. The principal centres are situated on high ground, and being exceptionally healthy, should offer inducements to try this field. Prospecting has been very imperfectly done, and good finds are frequently reported as being made on new ground. Recent reports speak most encouragingly of the renewed vigour exhibited on this field; in fact, many " shows " which have been idle for twelve or more years—notably about Georgetown and Charleston—are again being worked most remuneratively. These two mining centres were supporting some 350 and 200 persons respectively at the date of last reports ; the latter township is about 26 miles from Georgetown. The difficulties referred to at the outset are, it is pleasing to state, being steadily overcome, and the outlook generally is very good. Alluvial workings at Green Hills have largely assisted in the renewed prominence of the field, over 300 miners getting a good living at this place. There are similar indications of a revival on the Woolgar goldfield. The output for these fields in 1898 was 21,679 oz., say £60,701 sterling ; making a grand total of 601,034 oz., or £1,682,895. The estimated value of machinery was £44,750 (1897).

The RAVENSWOOD goldfield possesses an enormous advantage over the Etheridge, inasmuch as it is connected by railway with the port of Townsville, from which it is only 78 miles distant. In common with many of our richest fields, it has had " ups and downs," but at the date of 1898 report of the Under-Secretary for Mines (1897) it was the means of supporting about 2,943 persons, of whom only 163 were Chinese. A small quantity of alluvial gold is still found here—mostly worked by the Chinese—but the mainstay of the field is, and will be, reef mining. The yield for 1898 was 27,673 oz., which was greater by £24,000 (say 37 per cent.) than that of any year since the proclamation of the field in 1870. The total output to 31st December, 1898, aggregated 497,725 oz., of a value of £1,742,037.

The report of the warden for 1897 states that the prospects of the field may be considered very promising. Most of the leases now held need but a little capital to develope them and to cause a stir on the field.

The key-note has been struck when it is said that capital is all that is needed to make most, if not all, of our goldfields the wonder of the world. Gympie had this need, and, being near the populous centres, secured it, with what splended results every one knows. And yet it cannot be said that either Gympie or Charters Towers offered any more certain return for the outlay than do the above and many more fields in our Colony. The difficulties of treating the somewhat refractory Ravenswood ores led some time since to the establishment of large chlorinating works, besides which a good deal of new machinery has been put up during the last two or three years.

CLERMONT is another good field and—contrary to the last-mentioned —is almost exclusively an alluvial one, and as such may justly be considered the leading " poor man's goldfield " of Queensland. At date of the 1898 report the warden stated the population to be 4,357 persons. One locality is reported to have given from 1 oz. to 7 oz. 12 dwt. per load, and at White Hill 2 oz. and 3 oz. a load have been obtained. A certain claim washed 18 oz. for two loads, obtained at a depth of 70 ft. The wash is fully a foot wide, and the average washing is from 1 oz to 3 oz.

Clermont enjoys similar facilities to those at Ravenswood, being but 62 miles from the main Central Railway, and 227 miles from the port of Rockhampton. There are some six or seven centres here—McDonald's Flat having in time past been the pick of these. It formerly supported a large population, and now that the water difficulty has been in a great measure overcome, will do so again. Deep sinking here is assuming large proportions, and claims that are but 100 to 160 ft. in depth are on splendid gold, and the permanence is fully established of this portion of the field. This camp has the advantage of an excellently managed provisional school, averaging about 40 children. Black Ridge and The Springs are some 15 miles out of Clermont, whilst Copperfield is only four miles. The gold here is alluvial. At Copperfield there is a cyanide company at work, doing fairly well on the old tailings. Several new finds of gold took place during 1897, amongst these being those at Mount Clifford, Logan Downs, and Leo Flat. Altogether, mining affairs on Peak Downs have a very encouraging appearance, and after the recent rains, fossickers and gully-rakers should be able to get a good bit of gold in the old workings. At the same time it is the opinion of the warden and of the "old hands" that the alluvial workings are as yet in their infancy, and that they will provide a fair living for many a long day to come. The 1898 yield of gold from this field was 31,876 oz. The total yield of gold to the end of 1898 was of the value of £716,873.

Considering that the EIDSVOLD has been a proclaimed field for less than a dozen years, the aggregate result of 104,709 ozs., valued at some £379,570 for about 94,000 tons of quartz crushed during that period, may be considered fairly satisfactory, although individual crushings have given as high as 10½ ozs. to the ton. Several companies whose scrip is regularly quoted on "Change" are engaged in further developing the splendid resources of the above field, as well as at St. John's Creek (13½ miles from Eidsvold township as the crow flies) and Dykehead (27 miles from the township). These various centres support a population of close upon 1,000 Europeans, besides a few Chinese, and when development of the reefs has taken place there will be room for many more. There is latterly a decidedly upward tendency in the output of this field, the returns of one mine alone, the Minerva, having totalled 1,126 ozs. during the month of October, 1898. New "shows" are also being opened up, so that the prospects may be considered to be fairly bright. Two of the most prominent of the claims were in 1896 consolidated under the title of the "Mount Rose and Stockman Junction." One company, now defunct, paid away the respectable sum of £12,750 in dividends during its 4½ years of gold-producing, and the original Mount Rose and S.J. Gold Mining Co. paid £34,000 in "divi's" during the seven years odd ending December, 1896, say 11s. 4d. per share, totalling £4,500 per annum. The crushing machinery comprises an aggregate of 84 head of stampers. The steam power on the field equals close on 200 horse-power. The machinery is of a total value of £19,910, including a very complete cyanide plant.

It may also be mentioned that there is some prospect of the construction of a railway to this field, viâ Mount Perry, from which it would be distant about 50 miles along the proposed route. Two or three alternative routes from various points on the Mount Perry to Bundaberg line (at present 67 miles in length) have been reported upon.

The 1897 yields of a few of the other goldfields (at present giving small returns) were:—Gladstone, 6,051 ozs.; Coen, 5,386 ozs.; Russell, 1,750 ozs.; Mackay, 262 ozs.; Russell Extended, 695 ozs.; Mareeba, 537 ozs.; Tate, 44 ozs.; Cloncurry, 570 ozs.; Balcooma, 725 ozs.; Palmer, 2,497 ozs.; Hodgkinson, 3,206 ozs.; Paradise, 1,434 ozs.; Normanby (Bowen), 326 ozs.; Pikedale, Talgai, Mount Shamrock, Tenningering, and other small fields, 1,554 ozs.; Horn Island, 1,301 ozs.; Cooktown, 274 ozs.; and Mulgrave, 127 ozs. During 1898 the yield from the Palmer gold-field was but 3,183 ozs., although at an early period of its history it pro-duced £3,000,000 worth in a couple of years. Rapid development may be expected when alluvial digging gives place to " reefing." The Hodg-kinson yield increased to 4,169 ozs. in 1898. Coen and Gladstone stood at 5,337 ozs. and 4,781 ozs. respectively. Details may be obtained from the annual report of the Under-Secretary for Mines, and the geological bulletins issued by the Government Geologist. Of the latter, No. 4 (on the Hodgkinson) and No. 5 (on the Palmer) may be specially cited as obtainable on application at the office of the Geological Survey, George Street, Brisbane; or in London.

I cannot conclude without special mention of the WARWICK gold-fields, which are remarkable on account of age (about 34 years), proximity to the metropolis, and particularly from their position. To take the last point first. It will be seen from the map that nearly all the goldfields of Queensland are situated to the East of the Dividing Range, whilst this one is situated on the other side, being on the Western watershed at the head of the Condamine river. Some six or seven centres have been established, and in past years big nuggets have been found in all of them. At the present time both alluvial and reef work are carried on, the former with fair success (if one may judge from appearances), the latter—owing to the primitive methods employed—probably being less remunerative. In 1897 some 226 men turned out about 680 ozs. of gold from all sources, the crushings of quartz yielding over 16 dwt. of gold to the ton. The district over which the gold is spread is an enormous one, and there can be no doubt that the most favourable openings exist here for the judicious expenditure of capital in opening up the reefs which have been already laid bare, or in underground prospecting.

Even under present conditions, nearly 4 ozs. to the ton were obtained from a crushing at Talgai; a claim on Thane's Creek area has yielded 220½ ozs. for 238 tons of stone, and another has given 36¼ ozs. of gold from 45 tons of stone. Canal Creek and Lucky Valley are mostly occupied by fossickers and alluvial miners, whilst reefing is also carried on at the Palgrave field. Little is being done at Leyburn. Another point very greatly in favour of these goldfields is their proximity to the metropolis, and as they are all within driving distance of the important town which gives them their name, the drawbacks, experienced by many fields, of high cost of living and expensive freights are unknown here. Recent developments give a very hopeful outlook to the field.

R. L. JACK, Esq., LL.D., F.G.S., F.R.G.S.,
Government Geologist of Queensland.

From a Photograph by Elliott & Fry.

(Reproduced by kind permission of the *British Australasian*.)

MINERALS OTHER THAN GOLD.

Although gold is the foremost, it is by no means the only mineral of which we have untold wealth. Besides traces—as yet not followed up—of nearly all the minerals known to commerce, sufficient quantities of some of these have been unearthed to justify the proclamation of a large number of mining districts, each under the jurisdiction of a Mineral Lands Commissioner, whose duties are to safeguard the interests both of the miners and of the Crown.

From the latest available statistics, I learn that the total value of TIN exported between 1872 and 1898 is approximately £4,412,000, thus taking rank next to gold in this respect. The principal tin-producing districts, in order of importance, are :—Herberton (mainly lode tin), Cooktown, Stanthorpe, Ravenswood and Star, Port Douglas, and Kangaroo Hills. The value of the tin raised in 1897 was £37,509 (1,203 tons)—a somewhat smaller output than that of the preceding year ; the value of tin exported in 1898 was £29,880. In the early days of this industry our production was as high as 9,000 tons, of a value of £606,000, in a single year, and the present small output is in no way due to the exhaustion of supplies (which are practically illimitable), but solely to the long and severe depression in the tin market, now happily at a close.

Next in point of total value is COAL, although as regards present output it holds pride of place. The deposits of this mineral, with the exception perhaps of ironstone, are the most extensive in the Colony, and may fairly be said to be inexhaustible. At present a very small portion of these are worked ; still, a sufficient and increasing quantity is being raised for our own requirements : this was 358,407 tons during 1897—value, £139,889, and the export of the mineral is likely to be an important feature in our commerce. The most important centre of the industry is Ipswich. Next in order is the Wide Bay district (the Burrum fields, near Maryborough), and then comes Clermont. There are a few workings at Warra and Clifton in the Darling Downs district, and others between Ipswich and Toowoomba, but the output is too small to deserve detailed notice. Coal has also been raised at Moggil and on Flagstone Creek (near Helidon), and is known to exist on the Bowen River (near Mackay), at Cooktown, and on Callide Creek. The heating qualities of the Queensland coal are very good, and much which is not suited for domestic purposes produces excellent gas and coke.

OPAL MINING has come to the front of late years ; indeed this item has only figured in the mineral returns since 1890, although isolated finds were noted previously. These highly prized gems have been met with in many localities, mostly in the Western districts, and the area of opaliferous country is estimated by an expert as being a belt of some 200 miles in width, where tens of thousands of pounds' worth only await systematic search. The principal fields at present are those in the Fermoy Commissioner's district (latterly known as Opalton), from which stones roughly worth £41,000 were obtained in the three years 1895-6-7. The population is between 200 and 300, and has been greater. The second district in point of importance is that of Thargomindah, which contributed opal to the value (on a rough estimate) of £24,000 in the same time. The two centres—Duck Creek and Gowal—support something over 200 miners. Another field is situated in the Jundah Commissioner's district, which at date of last report (1897) had only produced £500 worth during the past two years, and the population was very small. But recently a sensational find of opal has been made, the value of the single specimen being placed at £3,000 to £4,000, whilst the weight of the stone was so enormous as to require the strength of several men to carry it off the field. This piece of " pipe " was said to be several feet in length.

SILVER is found in abundance in the Stanthorpe district; indeed the bulk of the production comes from this locality, which bids fair to become as important a silver district as in former years it was a tin-producing centre. Queensland did not become a steady producer of silver till 1880, and in the short space of 19 years she has raised silver to the value of £686,548. The last of these years (1897) is credited with an output of £25,118 worth, towards which Stanthorpe contributed £12,839; the Hodgkinson, £4,995; the Herberton district, £3,736; Ravenswood district, £2,940; and various fields, £608. The first-mentioned field consists of two or three claims, one of which, the " Silver Spur," Texas, gives employment to over 50 men, and shows no signs of giving out; the leasehold covers an area of 30 acres. There have been some excellent smeltings of ore at the Pikedale mine, some £4 2s. 6d. worth of matte being turned out per ton of ore put through, and in the short time which has elapsed since the commencement of active operations a prosperous community has been formed. The output of silver at Herberton experienced an increase of over 12,000 ozs. during 1897 ; and as the construction of the railway between Mareeba and Chillagoe has made progress so has the feeling gained ground that this district has a splendid future before it. With regard to the Ravenswood district, silver mining still prospers at Ukalunda. The most noticeable claim is that of four men (all miners) who, between them, each year divide from

£3,000 to £4,000. At Ravenswood proper, silver has been abandoned for the superior attraction of gold, which is likely to be constantly happening as long as prices keep low.

Besides the above, silver is found on the Coen River, in the extreme North, on the Gilbert River (back of Ingham), at Gin Gin (near Bunda berg), and in combination with gold, copper, and bismuth ores in many localities. At Lawn Hill, in the Burke district, yields of 35 ozs. of silver and 72 per cent. of lead to the ton were obtained from a shipment of 33 tons of stone; the returns from later shipments have not yet been officially made public.

COPPER holds an important position as regards total production, although, owing to the low state of the metal market for a considerable period (not to any lack of ore), the output has been affected similarly to that of silver, tin, and lead. The subject of these few lines divides with coal the honour of being our earliest mineral export, the total value of the copper output from 1860 to 1897, inclusive, being £2,020,761. In 1897 the Herberton mines (Chillagoe district) furnished £7,890 worth; Port Douglas (Mount Molloy copper mine) furnished £351; Stanthorpe, £3,534, and sundry localities, £870, making a total of £12,645 for the year, whereas in 1872, when the price was nearly half as much again as it is now, the value of the output was £196,000. Deposits of copper exist on nearly every degree of latitude south of the 17th, and in very various longitudes. The greatly improved, stronger tone of the copper market is already producing an improvement, and we may soon hope to see the noted Cloncurry, Mount Perry, and Peak Downs copperfields supporting something like their former number of miners. The chief obstacle to the development of the Cloncurry mines, in the manner to which their richness entitles them, is the want of railway communication and consequent high cost of living and cartage of ore. The quality of the latter is, however, considered equal to any which has been raised in the famed mines of the United States, and—given a good price—these fields will prove a powerful factor in the progress of the Colony. Mount Perry, as has been already stated, has railway communication with Bundaberg, and the Peak Downs is connected by rail with the port of Rockhampton, so that the repeated rises in copper, which has lately ranged from £70 to £80 per ton, should prove a blessing to a large number of miners. At Emerald Creek, near Mareeba, a 3-ton sample from a 4-ft. wide copper lode showed 22 per cent. of pure copper, and an abundance of flux is to be had within 1½ miles of the claim.

Prospecting is also being carried on with fair success at Lucky

G

Valley, and if the find proves satisfactory it is expected that work on a large scale will be entered upon in the locality.

Other minerals, not as yet constituting any large portion of our production, are: LEAD, of which the total output in 1897 was valued at £4,117; BISMUTH, £3,258 (1895); MANGANESE, £1,506; and WOLFRAM, £195. The first mentioned having lately risen to £14 or £15 a ton, a larger output may be expected during the current year. Between 1873 and 1894 ANTIMONY was raised to a gross value of £35,258, although there does not seem to have been sufficient inducement to continue the industry since then. Similarly, in 1892 and 1893, gems worth £9,000 were unearthed; but either from a scarcity of gem hunters possessing the requisite knowledge, or from the want of a market, little has been done, although rubies, garnets, specimens of the Oriental emerald, topazes, sapphires, and even diamonds, have been found, it is said, as far back as the "seventies," and continue to be found at intervals. Agates are found so plentifully in some parts as in one locality on the Etheridge to have furnished the name of a creek, known as "Agate Creek." Besides Wolfram (Tungstate of Iron and Manganese), Chrome Iron, Hæmatite, Magnetic Iron, Carbonate of Iron, and Clay Iron ore are found abundantly scattered over the Colony; but owing partly to these not occurring in close proximity to the coal and limestone which are required in the reduction of the ore, and partly, I understand, to the low price of the imported iron, no attempt has yet been made to work the deposits. CINNABAR, occurring at Kilkivan, is another mineral of which we have a large quantity; at present only worked for local requirements. ZIRCON has been found at Eungella head station, near Mackay. COBALT has been found in small quantity, but its production has not yet become an established industry. MOLYBDENUM and PLUMBAGO are met with, but have not been commercially utilized. PLATINUM, ASBESTOS, and KEROSENE may also be mentioned as possible mineral assets in the future. Quarrying for BUILDING STONE is carried on in various parts of the Colony. Felstone porphyry is mined in two or three localities about Brisbane. Bluestone is obtained from the districts of Ipswich, Toowoomba, Dalby, and Rockhampton; Freestone or Sandstone from Gatton, the Diamantina, Maryborough, and Normanton; whilst Limestone is raised in the Petty Sessions district of Paradise. Several deposits of crystalline limestone of a white and of a black colour occur on some small islands off the Queensland coast, near the Tropic of Capricorn, and in various parts of the mainland. Excellent white marble is obtained near Warwick. Besides the above building stone, there are many others which are highly ornamental, such as granite (very abundant), porphyry, serpentine, diorite, syenite, elvan (granitic porphyry), and dolomite. Slate is also found, but, in common with the above, has not so far been utilized for building purposes.

The following return, obtained by favour of the Department of Mines, shows at a glance the localities from which minerals (other than gold) were obtained during 1897 :—

MINING DISTRICT.	Nature of Ore or Mineral raised.	Quantity.		Value of various Minerals.
		Tons.	Ozs.	£
Burketown	Silver	—	3,181	345
	Lead	58	—	696
Charters Towers	Silver	—	637	69
Clermont	Coal	3,934	—	3,787
Croydon	Nil	—	—	—
Cooktown	Tin ...	146	—	5,835
Eidsvold	Silver	—	351	38
	Copper ..	5	—	120
Etheridge	Lead	1	—	12
	Silver	—	63	7
Fermoy	Opal ..	—	—	6,000
Gladstone	Manganese ...	300	—	1,125
Gympie	Silver	—	36	4
Herberton	Lode tin } Alluvial tin } ...	935	—	27,967
	Silver	—	32,507	3,436
	Lead	252	—	2,521
	Copper ...	154	—	7,890
	Lead	18	—	216
	Silver	—	2,774	300
Hodgkinson	Silver	—	49,950	4,995
	Lead	56	—	672
	Wolfram ...	13	—	195
	Bismuth ...	⁴/₈	—	134
Ipswich and Darling Downs ...	Coal	277,172	—	97,411
Jundah	Opal	—	—	200
Kangaroo Hills	Tin	19	—	570
Paradise	Silver	—	970	105
Port Douglas	Tin	20	—	711
	Copper ...	42	—	351
Ravenswood and Star... ...	Silver	—	29,400	2,940
	Tin	30	—	1,260
	Silver	—	6	—
Rockhampton	Copper ...	4	—	200
	Manganese ..	97	—	381
	Silver	—	92	10
Stanthorpe	Tin	53	—	1,666
	Silver	—	113,822	12,839
	Copper ...	72	—	3,534
Thargomindah	Opal	—	—	4,050
Wide Bay	Coal	77,301	—	38,691
Other Sources	Copper .	11	—	550
	Silver	—	276	30

PART IV.

Cities and Towns of Queensland.

[In quoting Railway Fares, the single second-class rate is given. The cost of a first-class fare will be rather more than one and a half second-class fares; return fares, in each case, will be about one and a half times that for the single journey. Steamship Fares are somewhat variable, but the usual single saloon charges are given.]

BRISBANE.

THE Metropolis naturally calls for our first attention, for not only is this the seat of Government, but it is here that the visitor from the other Australian colonies (and from the furthest corners of the earth, for that matter) generally makes his first acquaintance with Queensland. That which most strikes the eye of strangers is, perhaps, the number of hills within the city area, and the more venturesome will be amply repaid by the many beautiful views to be secured from these eminences. A short ascent from the Central Railway Station (in Ann Street) brings one to the Albert Park—of many acres in extent—situated upon Spring Hill. In these grounds stands one of the most historic buildings of the city— the Observatory—which was erected (according to Mr. J. J. Knight, the author of 'In the Early Days') about 1829. This was originally a windmill, but for some years, owing to defective machinery, it was worked by tread-power, supplied by gangs of convicts. By many, the eminence on which the Observatory stands is known as "Windmill Hill." Another relic of early days exists in the Colonial Stores, in William Street, situated between the Museum and the Offices of the Department of Agriculture. They were built by convicts in 1824, on what is believed to be the site of the first halting-place of Lieut. Oxley's expedition from Redcliffe. Happily all traces of this element in the population have long since disappeared.

Considering that the total length of streets is only 52½ miles, and the population within a five-mile radius is under 100,000 persons, Brisbane is lavishly supplied with public gardens and recreation reserves. The largest of these is the Victoria Park, on the outskirts of which are many

Northern Entrance to the Houses of Parliament, Brisbane.

North-west Wing of the Houses of Parliament, Brisbane

places of interest, viz., the Brisbane General and Children's Hospital, Albert Sports Ground, Acclimatization Society's Gardens (otherwise known as Bowen Park), National Agricultural and Industrial Association's Exhibition Building, together with a large area of land possessing an excellent cycling track; also three large educational establishments— the Christian Brothers' College and Boys' and Girls' Grammar Schools, respectively. Next to Victoria Park in point of size is a large reserve situated in South Brisbane. As in the case of the former, the pressure of population around it has not been sufficient to rob it of its somewhat raw appearance, but there is no doubt that in a very short space of time this will be one of the most popular "breathing spots" of the metropolis. Within its limits are the Goal reserve, the Diamantina Orphanage, South Brisbane Cemetery, the Pound, and Dutton Park. Musgrave Park is likewise a place of growing beauty, many beautiful trees having been planted here which will make it one of the favourites among city gardens. The above faces Russell Street, about half a mile distant from the southern end of Victoria Bridge. Another reserve is situated just off Stanley Street East, and goes by the name of Woolloongabba Park, taking its name from the district. A pleasant hour or two may be spent here. By far the best known, however, are the Botanical Gardens and Queen's Park, situated in the heart of the city on the river bank. Here are tennis, cricket, and football grounds, conservatories for the cultivation of some of the more delicate productions of nature, a kiosk for the refreshment of weary pleasure-seekers, and beautifully laid-out lawns and flower beds. Adjoining are the Houses of Parliament, Government House, the Masonic Hall, and the Queensland Club—all fine buildings of their class, but the Houses of Parliament, which were erected at a cost of £100,000, are especially so. Round and about Brisbane are to be found many places of surpassing beauty and interest: Moggill Creek, with its wealth of verdure; White's Hill, affording panoramic views of far and near; One-Tree Hill, with its charming ruggedness and bracing air; and Enoggera Reservoir, famed for its unequalled inducements to picnic parties. Besides the Treasury buildings and Supreme Court, the mineralogical collection of the Geological Survey Office at the corner of Queen and George Streets will be found well worth a visit, as will the Natural History Museum hard by—in William Street, the Government Printing Office (admission by order), the Technical Museum of the Department of Agriculture, the Town Hall Picture Gallery, Parliament House Library (by "member's order"), and the School of Arts and Technical College (containing some 19,000 or more volumes). Besides the latter there are Public Libraries and Free Reading Rooms in Stanley Street, South

Brisbane; at the Mechanics' Institute (about 4,000 volumes); and in Brunswick Street, Valley, at the Oddfellows' Hall. To these should be added the National Public Library which is in course of formation, the trustees under Government having been granted the use of temporary premises pending the choice of a suitable site. Passes, giving admission to the Reading Room of the Y.M.C.A. (Treasury Chambers, George Street, opposite the Treasury), may be obtained, free of charge, upon application to the General Secretary. To those interested in land selection, &c., the Map Room of the Department of Public Lands is accessible from 9 A.M. to 4 P.M. from Monday to Friday, and from 9 A.M. to 12 noon on Saturdays. Enquirers may be sure of a courteous attention to any matter upon which they desire information. The head offices of the Queensland National (cost £40,000) and other banks in the heart of the city are also worthy of note, the architecture of many of these buildings rivalling that of the edifices in the older colonies. The Opera-House, Theatre Royal, Gaiety Theatre, Centennial Hall, and Norman (late Protestant) Hall are all substantial and commodious places of amusement. Of places for religious worship there are a large number, chief among which are the Anglican pro-Cathedral (St. John's), St. Stephen's (R. C. Cathedral), St. Paul's (Presbyterian), Albert Street Church (Wesleyan), the Synagogue, the Lutheran Church on Wickham Terrace, the Tabernacle (Baptist), Wharf Street Congregational Church, and the Headquarters of the Salvation Army, known as "The Temple."

The wants of gymnasts are liberally catered for by the Brisbane Gymnasium and German Gymnasium.

A score of newspapers are published in the capital, the leading dailies being the *Brisbane Courier* and the *Telegraph*.

At Nudgee, on the railway line to Sandgate, some nine miles out of town, are situated the Orphanage of St. Vincent (under the management of the Sisters of Mercy), and the Christian Brothers' College for boys; whilst at Nundah the "Home of the Good Shepherd" undertakes the training of girls; all of them well worth a visit, both on account of the work carried on and their surroundings. The terminus of this line of railway is at Sandgate, a delightful and favourite seaside resort.

Another place of interest is to be found in Lytton, down the Brisbane River, where are situated the reformatory for boys and military fortifications commanding the mouth of the river. Outside the entrance are the islands of Dunwich and St. Helena, devoted to the care of the aged poor and the custody of criminals respectively. These spots are noted for the picturesqueness of their surroundings, and tickets to visit may be obtained at the Treasury.

Roman Catholic Cathedral, Brisbane.

IPSWICH.

Fare from Brisbane, 2s. 7d.; distance, 24 miles. A short ride brings one to Ipswich, at one time a determined rival of Brisbane for the seat of Government. From the historian previously referred to we learn that the first sale of land here took place in 1843, at which 6s. to 23s. a perch was realized, and in 1846 the population consisted of 64 males and 39 females, as compared with some 7,000 or 8,000 to-day. The town is situated on both sides of the Bremer River, and is known as North Ipswich and Ipswich proper. There are many valuable coal mines in this neighbourhood, and the surrounding districts of Limestone, New-town, Blackstone, Bundamba, Sandy Gallop, and Churchill, afford opportunity for many delightful excursions. Commercial enterprise has obtained a very firm hold on this town. On the north side of the river are the mills of the Queensland Woollen Manufacturing Company, Ltd., the Phœnix Engineering Co., and Messrs. Hancock Bros.' sawmills; here also are situated extensive Government railway work-shops. On the main side are scores of large commercial concerns, amongst others the mills of the Queensland Cotton Co. and the vast business of Messrs. Cribb and Foote, general merchants and storekeepers.

The Waterstown Coal Company, one of the more prominent coal mines on the northern side of the Bremer River, near Tivoli, have recently been sinking for the purpose of opening up new seams of coal, and in 1897 they struck the old "Tivoli seam" at a depth of 570 feet; the seam was in former years successfully worked by Mr. James Gulland. This portion of it is fully 5 feet in thickness, and the coal which it carries is of excellent quality.

Many other large coal properties exist at Blackstone, Bundamba, &c., one at least of which is worked on purely co-operative principles, and these have been found to give very satisfactory results. Although mining absorbs a large proportion of the working population it by no means holds the monopoly in this district. Cotton growing offers good inducements owing to the presence of a mill ready to purchase at a fair price, and, as the soil is adapted to this crop, cotton is likely to reach an even more important position as the staple production of Ipswich farms. Dairy farming is annually gaining favour, and creameries are springing up on all sides. Those at Millbong, Flinders, Coochin, and Bellevue are actually proprietary concerns, but a system of bonus payments has been adopted by the owners, by which the suppliers on one occasion received an additional ½d. per gallon for the month's supply of milk. In the case of all these creameries the cream is dispatched to the metropolis, where it is converted into butter at a central establishment. Dairymen in the immediate vicinity of Ipswich have a ready market for milk or cream at the recently established butter factory in North Ipswich. As this has been incorporated with the old-established Ice Works on that side of the Bremer River, and the very best butter-making machinery erected, a first-class product is turned out, and a good price is realized—a very important matter to the milk supplier as well as to the factory owner. Shipments of this brand have found their way to the London market.

A great impetus has lately been given to farming by the prominence accorded to fruit and milk products, and a small portion of the excellent land which is to be found in the jurisdiction of the Ipswich Land Agent's Office was recently thrown open and briskly competed for. To show the esteem in which this land is held, it may be mentioned that cash amounting to £4,487 10s. 4d. and land-orders for over £12 were deposited for rent and survey fees of the above eighty-eight "blocks."

The social institutions of Ipswich are very numerous and important. Art, music, and literature are largely engaged in by the residents. The Press is ably represented by the *Queensland Times*, the *Advocate*, and the *Standard;* and societies for the encouragement of all manly sports are innumerable.

LAIDLEY.

Fare from Brisbane, 6s.; distance, 51 miles. On the route to this important farming centre a tract of fine dairying country is passed through, back of which again on both sides of the railway line are numerous fertile valleys and luxuriant scrubs, affording the means of subsistence to a large number of farmers, dairymen, and timber-getters. What is known as the "Rosewood Scrub" contains some of the finest agricultural land in the Colony, and has enriched thousands. Before the better-suited northern lands were put under cane a considerable amount of sugar was produced here. At the present time maize, cotton, and hay crops receive a good deal of attention, and to these may be added the cultivation of the grape vine, the credit of which may largely be given to the Germans, who have settled in this locality in large numbers.

An abundant supply of running water, the ease with which fodder can be raised, and a ready access to the metropolitan market, will combine to make this essentially a dairy-farming and fruit-growing district. At Hatton Vale, a neighbouring settlement, pig-raising is largely carried on, and supports a well-equipped factory. Rosewood Railway Station is 36 miles from Brisbane, and is the centre of a quiet, but prosperous little

Supreme Court, Brisbane (Northern Entrance).

township, consisting of a few general stores, a couple of hotels, two saw-mills and a moulding-mill, churches, &c. Creameries have been established here, at Lanefield, and Grandchester (near the line of railway); and many others at some little distance away. Amongst the latter may be mentioned the Co-operative Creamery at Rosevale Plains (on the south side of the line), which is worked by steam power, and at date of last report was putting 500 gallons of milk per diem through the separator.

The petty sessions district of Laidley accounts for a very large pro-duction of maize, and is probably the chief producer of hay and chaff (especially lucerne) in Queensland. The output of English potatoes is also considerable, being something like the fourth in the Colony in point of importance. To show the amount of trade which is done, it may be stated that during 1896 there were forwarded from the Laidley Railway Station 11,504 bales of hay, 17,596 bales of chaff, 4,457 bags of chaff, 45,153 bags of maize, 4,175 bags of potatoes, and 9,378 gallons of cream.

As might be expected, a thriving township forms the outlet for all this agricultural wealth. Several of the Brisbane produce merchants have a resident buyer here, and on recognized market days the place pre-sents quite a lively appearance owing to the number of farmers and farmers' families who come to sell and to buy. Some half-dozen stores, the inevitable hotels, a post office, a school of arts, two or three saddlers and other caterers for domestic and farm requirements, go to make up one of the busiest little townships in the Moreton district; and nowhere could these hard-working, honest folk find an abler champion than in their valued local paper, the *Lockyer Star*.

Passing through FOREST HILL, where dairying is largely in evidence, the traveller will next reach GATTON—distant about 61 miles from Bris-bane; fare, 7s. 1d. As regards maize and fodder growing, this petty sessions district holds a very important position, but it is the potato crop which may be said to be the staple. Of late years, however, fruit-growing has been entered upon, side by side with the older-established branches of agriculture, and with so much success that Gatton oranges and grapes are in great demand, although the industry is still in its infancy.

Of late, however, interest centres in Gatton principally on account of its being the postal and market town of the Queensland Agricultural College, which is distant about three and a half miles. The area of the reserve upon which the College Farm is situated is 1,692 acres, and both the buildings and land are eminently adapted to imparting a thorough knowledge of general horticulture and agriculture in their scientific as well as practical aspects. The district is healthy, and well supplied with churches of the Protestant and Roman Catholic faiths, several well-stocked stores, a School of Arts, a Bank, the usual educational facilities, creameries, &c.

The situation of this township of about 300 people is delightful. Hard by flows a tributary of the Brisbane River—Lockyer Creek—which ensures at all times an abundant supply of water. Many of the river bends are extremely picturesque, and in its waters some fine mullet, &c., may be caught at certain seasons of the year.

HELIDON.

72 miles; fare, 8s. 7d.; is reached in something under 2¾ hours from the metropolis, and the first stoppage is made here by the Sydney "Mail" after leaving Ipswich. Being on the high road from Brisbane to Toowoomba, it was at one time a busy place, but the advent of the railway has, of course, much reduced the traffic from teams and travellers, as well as the number of stock passing through. Special interest attaches to important quarries in the vicinity, locally known as "Pearson's," from which a very large quantity of stone has been and is being trucked to Brisbane, for use in the building of the large bridges and other public works constructed of late years. Near these quarries, and in the various glens and nooks with which this country at the foot of the Main Range abounds, the most charming scenery is found—majestic tree ferns, stately palms, roaring waterfalls, and lichen-covered rocks seem to open out to the delighted visitor a veritable fairyland, and many are the picnic parties which make a starting-place of this or the adjoining stations of Murphy's Creek or Spring Bluff. In the vicinity of Helidon several mineral springs have been found, and are commercially utilized. By the courtesy of the proprietors the best known of these is open to all comers, and is credited with so great vitalizing powers that a trip to the Downs could not be considered complete without a call at this place of interest. Some 20 miles from Helidon is the settlement of Ravensbourne, and although the road is somewhat rough the visitor will find himself well repaid by the rugged grandeur of the hill country over which he passes, whilst to the naturalist new wonders in the three worlds open out at every turn. The above is eight miles distant from Hampton Station on the Crow's Nest line; fare, 3s. 3d. to Toowoomba. Ascending the Main Range on the railway line a series of panoramic views which are excelled in few parts of Australia unfold themselves before the delighted eyes of the traveller, and these are scarcely lost to view when one reaches

TOOWOOMBA.

Fare from Brisbane, 11s. 8d.; distance, 101 miles; altitude 1,921 feet above sea level. The capital of the Darling Downs, and, as such, of considerable importance. The estimated population at the close of 1895 (including the shires of Middle Ridge and Drayton) was 12,300 persons, and the number of dwellings 1,975. The borough of Toowoomba enjoys the distinction of having been one of the first proclaimed, and for its relatively short existence of thirty-eight years has been a marvellously prosperous one—commercially, agriculturally, and socially. Although by no means the only town which can lay claim to the title, this is undoubtedly the favourite sanatorium of Southern Queensland. The vice-regal party usually spend the hottest months of the year in the neighbourhood, and much of the prosperity of the place must be attributed to the constant influx of visitors. Substantial flour and saw mills receive in a steady stream two of the most prominent products of the soil; some half-dozen tanneries convert into a finished article the hides and skins from surrounding districts; whilst the products of the orchards and market gardens find a ready outlet at one of the many stores, or at the preserving works in the centre of the town. To these must be added the various foundries, smithies, tin-plate working establishments, breweries, aërated-water factories, soap factories, fell-mongeries, boot and furniture factories; and if the visitor arrive on market day (Saturday), he will be confronted by a scene of such intense activity as will leave no doubt in his mind as to the prospects of a town which is said to have once aspired to the position of metropolis. Many public buildings—not without architectural merit—are found here. The Grammar School (cost £9,058), Town Hall (cost about £4,000), School of Arts (£3,800), Lunatic Asylum (accommodates about 400 patients, and cost something like £107,050), Post Office, Banks, Court House, Hospital (53 beds), Masonic Hall, and various churches of the Protestant, Roman Catholic, and Jewish persuasions are mostly substantial and attractive buildings. The town is lighted throughout with gas, for which the charge has lately been fixed at 9s. 2d. per 1,000 ft. (subject to the usual rebate of 10 per cent.). The water supply is abundant, and is supplied from waterworks which are situated on high ground adjoining the hospital.

Public baths, and extensive public gardens (Queen's Park, in the centre of the town, containing 70 acres, and a reserve of 32 acres on the Range), provide healthful recreation, whilst literary and scientific tastes are catered for by the School of Arts Library of 4,387 vols. (end of 1895), the meetings of the "Gordon" and other literary clubs, several newspapers —amongst which the most prominent are the *Chronicle*, the *Darling Downs Gazette*, the *Settler*, &c.—and the various meetings of a couple of agricultural and several church societies. Besides the Public Schools there are some thirteen private scholastic establishments.

The suburbs of Toowoomba, including the populous district of Highfields on the north, and the prosperous settlements of Emu and King's Creek to the south, are occupied chiefly by a farming population. In the suburbs there are several beautiful gardens that would do no discredit to any country in the world. Here will be found growing in abundance apples, pears, apricots, peaches, nectarines, mulberries, lemons, oranges, figs, plums of all varieties, loquats, quinces, the walnut, &c. The grape grows here luxuriantly, and is cultivated with great care and attention by several German colonists, who have also manufactured wine of excellent quality. Some of the gardens are places of public resort, and are a sort of Baden-Baden on a small scale.

Highfields, in addition to its agricultural resources, has vast quantities of timber, giving employment to a large number of hands. It has two sawmills, and supplies the district for miles around with the most valuable timber.

As may be seen from the map, this railway station is an important junction. It is the starting-point for the Western line, the Pittsworth branch line, and the Crow's Nest line (Highfields branch), besides being an important station on the main line to Sydney, Melbourne, and Adelaide. Continuing on the Southern line, some pretty country is passed through—timber-covered mountain spurs alternate with picturesque valleys through which limpid streams wend their way. Here may be seen the snug little farmhouse, and there the fields of lucerne or maize with their varied tints, whilst scattered over the landscape are the dairy cattle to which the district owes so much of its prosperity. Under the new order of things butter and cheese making promise to take a still more prominent position; for whilst there are still some excellent makes of "farmers'" butter and cheese, the bulk of the milk now finds its way to the numerous creameries and butter and cheese factories dotted along the line. Amongst these may be mentioned the Gowrie Junction Butter, Cheese, and Ice Factory, Daly Bros.' Factory (Jondaryan-Western Railway), the Westbrook Creamery, the Southbrook Creamery, and Pittsworth Dairy.

Further south—at GREENMOUNT, in the neighbourhood of KING'S CREEK—two of the largest dairying concerns in the Colony are situated.

The Greenmount Dairy Co., Ltd., distant about two miles from the railway station of that name, has become celebrated for the quality of its cheese, whilst the Pilton Dairy Co., Ltd., "The Glen," KING'S CREEK, is producing butter of equal merit. During a recent year suppliers to the latter received from 2½d. to 6½d. per gallon of milk (the average being 4⅙d.), and the company carried forward a substantial credit balance. The Greenmount cheese factory has a storage capacity of 18 tons. From CAMBOOYA (125 miles from Brisbane, fare 14s. 2d.) a coach runs three times a week to the Leyburn goldfields (population about 500 persons). The route covers a distance of about 29 miles, and the coach fare is 10s. This is the most accessible railway station from the above fields. Adjoining Leyburn are the Thane's Creek and Talgai goldfields, to which the nearest township of importance is Pratten—the centre of what is known as Darkey Flat, beautifully situated on the Condamine. It is reached from Hendon Railway Station by a coach running twice a week; the fare is 2s. 6d. The "repurchased" agricultural Toolburra lands are on this coach route, and contain 11,000 acres of land. Yearly payments equal to £7 12s. 10d. on every £100 of purchase money are being accepted by the Government from purchasers of these excellent agricultural selections, so that principal and interest will be defrayed in 20 years.

CLIFTON.

Distant 143 miles from Brisbane, fare 36s. 11d.; is a thriving agricultural township. The chief resources of the district are wheat and maize culture. Deposits of coal occur near here, but these do not appear to be very actively worked at present. Besides the usual stores and hotels, &c., there are in the township a School of Arts, a State School, a Divisional Board Hall, and Churches. ALLORA, lately connected by railway with Hendon (Southern railway), is within easy driving distance, and there the richest black soil abounds, so that a great variety of crops can be grown to perfection. In depth it varies from 5 to 10 ft., and in addition to the water of Dalrymple and other smaller creeks an abundant supply can generally be obtained 30 or 40 ft. below the surface. The estimated population of this municipal borough at the close of 1895 was 1,000 persons, and the number of dwellings was 230. The township comprises some well-appointed general stores, butchers' and saddlers' shops, several hotels and churches, Municipal Chambers, a Bank, State School, Post and Telegraph Office, and School of Arts (1,182 vols.). The manufacturing industries are well represented here by a flour-mill, a couple of dairy factories, a soap and candle works, and a soft drinks factory. Referring to the dairying industry, it may be said that no part of the world is better suited than is this for the production of abundant green feed. Lucerne, wheat, oats, barley, maize, and panicum grow luxuriantly; and a fairly good rainfall, combined with streams of the purest water, offer exceptional advantages to the dairy farmer. The presence of numerous factories and creameries, and proximity to the markets of Warwick and Toowoomba, ensure success to the careful man. The Press is represented by the *Allora Guardian* (weekly)—a name to which the latter is thoroughly entitled, for its spirited advocacy of the claims of the district, as well as its consistent support of every forward movement.

WARWICK.

Fare from Brisbane, 18s. 9d.; distance, 169 miles. This is an important centre for the farming, mining, and dairying districts by which it is surrounded. The town is prettily situated on the River Condamine, wherein is found an abundance of cod and other fish, and is, perhaps, more substantial in appearance than any other town in the Colony. The public buildings—among which may be noted the Town Hall, Masonic Hall, Police Court, the Banks, several handsome Churches, a Convent, a Hospital, &c.—are mostly built of a durable stone found here in abundance. The use of the latter is not confined to the larger buildings of the town, many of the private residences being apparently built for succeeding generations, and an air of quaintness is thus given which is peculiar to Warwick. A School of Arts, with a library of some 3,767 volumes, the *Argus* and the *Examiner* (both of great merit), and various societies minister to the educational needs of the town; two tastefully laid out central squares afford healthful recreation to residents, whilst the annual show of the local Agricultural Society, and the Caledonian Sports—also an annual event—are the occasion of large gatherings from far and near. As at Toowoomba—although in a lesser degree—the cultivation of the grape vine is pursued side by side with other branches of agriculture, several of the Warwick vintages being well known throughout the Colony for their excellent quality. Indeed, some of the surrounding hills would seem to be the "beau ideal" of the "vigneron." The remarks regarding crops at Clifton and Allora are generally applicable to the whole of this district. Warwick had at the close of 1895 an estimated population of 4,000 persons, and about 830 dwellings. An abundant supply of really excellent water is laid on to every house within a certain radius. The pumping works, having a reservoir capacity of 96,552 cubic ft., were completed in 1883, and the cost to end of 1895 was £19,598.

A couple of flour-mills turn into well-known brands of flour the wheat of the district, in which the wheat-growing industry is an important one. A large brewery is also doing a considerable local trade. Warwick is well supplied with stores, stationers, jewellers, &c. The medical and legal profession, tobacconists, and the Press are also represented; the latter, as stated, by two ably conducted papers. Much of the commercial activity of this thriving town arises from the traffic to and from Goondiwindi, as well as from that with Thane's Creek, Talgai, and other adjacent goldfields. The malting of grain is now taking a prominent position among the industries of the place.

KILLARNEY.

Fare from Warwick, 3s. 6d.; distance, 28 miles. Nestling among the timber-clad hills which give rise to the Condamine, this township seems to invite the tourist by its irresistible charms. Here are the "Dagmar" and "Brown's Falls"; imposing in their grandeur, or charmingly playful—as the time of year decrees. Not far away on the heads of the river are the trout "hatcheries," a visit to which will well repay the visitor. Here may be said to be the home of the apiarist, for here it was that bee-keeping received its first real impetus, and Killarney honey ranks in our metropolitan markets amongst the best. Two of the largest apiaries are well worth a visit, which may be made by the stranger in full assurance of a courteous welcome. Tobacco growing also occupies in this district a most important place. Nor would a brief sketch of this historically named locality be complete without reference to the "lakes" or lagoons, which would seem to have been responsible for the name "Killarney." A few miles from the township—on the Canning Downs Estate—are some of those beautiful pieces of water which abound in South-Eastern Queensland. This trip affords an opportunity for a lovely drive or ride; indeed, these are here the order of the day, and one cannot find a better spot in South Queensland in which to spend a season of quiet enjoyment. Returning from Killarney to Warwick we pass the celebrated Yangan Cheese Factory. In close proximity to a railway station and creek, the factory seems to have an ideal situation, and many a trophy of the cheese product of this proprietary factory has testified to the support accorded to it by the surrounding cattle owners, as well as to the excellent methods employed in its manufacture.

Just outside Warwick another factory belonging to the same proprietors is seen, this time for the manufacture of "Silverwood" butter

—so named from the nearest railway station—a brand which not only has earned the highest reputation in this Colony, but is even now making a name for itself in other lands. A trial shipment of 1,000 lbs. was dispatched to Hongkong, under the bonus system, and this has been followed by others of the highest quality, intended for the British and other markets. The adaptability of the deep rich soil to the growth of green feed, and the abundance of water and shelter for stock, make this essentially a dairy-farming district.

STANTHORPE.

Fare from Brisbane, 22s. 8d.; distance, 207 miles. Quite a change of scenery awaits the visitor on his arrival at this tin-mining centre. Although—owing to a lull in the main industry—Stanthorpe has little of its former bustle, it still retains evidences of prosperity. Between 900 and 1,200 persons support a fairly large number of stores and other places of business. The local School of Arts contains something under 1,000 volumes, several churches minister to the religious wants of the people, and the proverbial "camaraderie" of the latter offers great inducements to those who would avail themselves of the salubrity of the climate. A considerable trade is carried on with TEXAS, seventy miles distant, famed—so far—for the excellence of its tobacco, and its mining industry. The passenger traffic is catered for by a weekly coach, by which the fare is 20s. Great as the above resources undoubtedly are— and silver mining, at least, never showed better prospects—there is a great agricultural future before this border town. Wheat is successfully raised here, as much as £1 per bag having been realized by Texas growers, and it seems likely that mills will shortly be erected to grind the grain on the spot. As regards silver, some splendid properties have been acquired at the "Silver Spur" and elsewhere, and on Pikedale Station (not far from Texas) so satisfactory has been the quality of the galena ore that steps have been taken to erect machinery, at a heavy cost. The matte obtained from some of the ore assayed roughly: Gold, 5 dwts. per ton; silver, 290½ ozs.; copper, 28 to 38 per cent.

Deep sinking for tin, owing to low prices, is not practised here, but recent advances in the market should encourage the search for the lodes. The resources of this district are not, however, of the mineral kingdom only; as is evidenced by the fact that, recently, Stanthorpe-grown cabbage realized as high as 9s. per dozen in a Western town, at a time when similar vegetables were only realizing 1s. 6d. to 2s. per bag in Brisbane; a fact which speaks volumes for the quality of the former.

GOONDIWINDI.

143 miles from Warwick by coach; fare £2 10s. On this mail route the visitor will pass the township of INGLEWOOD, which is prettily situated on the Macintyre Brook (on which—under the name of the Macintyre River—Goondiwindi is likewise situated). Inglewood is essentially an agricultural district, and tobacco growing holds an important place amongst its industries. The larger town of the two (Goondiwindi), with a population under the thousand, can boast of several Churches, a Hospital, State school, Bank, a School of Arts (about 700 volumes), and a private school, and may lay claim to some importance as the proposed terminus of a branch line of railway to be constructed from Warwick, Dalby, or Pittsworth—as may be sanctioned by Parliament.

Sporting interests are looked after by the Racing Club, and various Athletic, Football, Tennis, and Cricket clubs. Art and literature are catered for by the local photographer, the stationers, and the *M'Intyre Herald*, an excellent newspaper (published Tuesday afternoons). The legal, medical, and accountants' professions are ably represented. In addition to the usual complement of general stores, butchers, bakers, saddlers and blacksmiths, Goondiwindi has a number of builders, cabinet makers, milliners, bootmakers and tailors, a couple of undertakers, a jeweller, chemist, and auctioneer; constituting probably the most important border town of Queensland. The district is said to be well adapted to the cultivation of grapes and oranges, and when connected by rail with the larger markets of Australia may be expected to come greatly into prominence in agricultural matters.

ST. GEORGE.

130 miles coaching from Yeulba; 140 miles from Mitchell. Fare from £2 to £3.

From an agricultural standpoint the township is yet in its infancy. Cereals have been successfully grown for many years, but on a very small scale, and grapes thrive well in the somewhat sandy soil. Black-soil plains of great depth and exceptional fertility are found in the neighbourhood, however, and although at present the importance of this township is mainly due to its position on the great stock routes, there is little doubt that at no distant time agriculture will be largely in evidence. St. George has communication with Goondiwindi by a stock route *via* Well-town. It possesses, amongst other public buildings, a School of Arts containing over 500 volumes of books. The *Standard* is a progressive representative of the Press.

CUNNAMULLA.

140 miles by coach from Charleville, fare £2 10s. This rapidly rising town is of special interest as the terminus of the railway extension from Charleville. A population of some hundreds support five or six stores, besides a brewery, a brickyard, several saddlers, land and station agents, hotels, bakers, butchers, coach works, blacksmiths, and builders; a plumber, surgeon, chemist, solicitor, hairdresser, an auctioneer, an accountant, and a newspaper. There are also two Banks, a Hospital, Divisional Board Office, Public Library (over 800 volumes), State school, and private school for girls. The interests of the town are well looked after by a "Progress Association," and there is some probability that their efforts will result in the establishment of a local fire brigade, and also in the installation of the electric light—for which the power will be derived from the Cunnamulla bore. The town is situated on the Great Bourke Route to New South Wales, and consequently enjoys an important stock and general traffic with that Colony, from which it is about 70 miles distant. Some idea of the volume of the trade may be gathered from the fact that in November alone of 1896 the Customs collections from the two local bonds amounted to £356.

CHARLEVILLE.

Fare from Brisbane, 47s. 1d.; 483 miles. A very important pastoral township, and commercial centre for that portion of the Colony comprised in the Warrego and South Gregory districts. The business establishments include those of the storekeepers (some of them carrying on business on a large scale), bootmakers, auctioneers, butchers, bakers, watchmakers, hairdressers, fruiterers and cordial makers, saddlers, blacksmiths and wheelwrights, Messrs. Cobb & Co.'s coach factory, a soap works, two newspaper and job printing offices, two or more saw-mills, a builder, an upholsterer, and a plumber. In a professional way there are a surgeon, with the usual accompaniment of chemist, one or more solicitors, a barrister, and a surveyor. The wants of the district in the way of clothing are supplied by a tailor and a dressmaker. There are both a private and a State school for boys and girls; other public buildings are the Hospital and School of Arts (over 500 vols.). One of the most promising industries of the place is that of meat preserving, for which purpose extensive works have been erected capable of slaughtering and chilling 400 head of cattle and 7,000 sheep per week. Another feature of this western town is the bore—one of the best known in the Colony for its curative properties. The following is given as an instance:—" Mr.

Leadbetter, of Morven, met with a fall from his horse and came up to Charleville to avail himself of baths at the bore. Mr. Leadbetter tells us that the effect of the water on his injuries was astonishing. In a few days he felt as sound as ever, while before using the water he could scarcely move. The water also cured Mr. Leadbetter, some time previously, of a severe attack of rheumatism; for the alleviation of which complaint, however, its properties are well known." Racing, it may be said, is carried on with vigour in these western towns, and Charleville is no exception to the rule. The Charleville Racing Club is a most popular institution. This is a great coaching centre; routes going from here to Augathella (56 miles), Tambo (136), Adavale (136), Cunnamulla (140), Eulo (180), Barringun (220), Blackall (216), Thargomindah (280), Windorah (306), and Hungerford (380).

ROMA.

Fare from Brisbane, 33s. 4d.; 318 miles. This town has been called the "Queen City of the West," and certainly in some respects the title is not unmerited. For healthfulness the Maranoa district is unsurpassed, and although Roma itself does not exhibit the bustle which it once did—especially at the time it was a railway terminus—still there are evidences on all hands of a commercial solidity and agricultural prosperity which promise well for its future. Here is the chief centre of the grape-growing industry; Maranoa wheat bids fair to hold an important position amongst Queensland breadstuffs; whilst not only grapes, but oranges and other fruits thrive in the district. Mr. Benson—Government fruit expert—considers the district eminently suited to the apricot, prune, fig, peach, olive, pear, &c. The municipality of Roma covers an area of 15 square miles, has an estimated population of 1,400 (December, 1895), and contains 400 dwellings. The numerous well-appointed stores do a considerable trade with the outlying stations, of which there are many fine examples in the district. A School of Arts, musical societies, churches, and solicitors minister to the intellectual, spiritual, and litigious needs of the residents, whilst the Press is ably represented by the *Western Star* and the *Maranoa Advocate*. Several large manufacturing industries are carried on here, the most noticeable being flour-milling. Besides this there are a soap and cordial manufactory, and numbers of wine-making establishments; about 25 miles to the north there is also a large saw-mill. The town enjoys the advantage of having two resident medical men, and so highly adapted is the climate considered for the cure of phthisis, &c., that a suggestion was formerly made to establish here a hospital for consumptives—a proposition which, however, did not find favour at the hands of residents, and appears now to have been abandoned. The present hospital occupies a delightful position. Whilst dry, the climate is not arid, the average yearly rainfall over a term of years having been about 35 inches. The soil in the neighbourhood comprises red and chocolate volcanic, black alluvial (all highly productive), and sandy ridges. The latter are stated, on the authority of Mr. Tardent, to be specially suited to light wines, particularly white; the first-mentioned soils, having a marly or calcareous sub-soil, give—when planted with the right sort of vines—full-bodied and highly flavoured liquorous wines; whilst the alluvial loams (with a fair proportion of lime) yield very palatable white and red wines. Close by is the Village Settlement of Wallumbilla, a prosperous individualistic settlement, from which some splendid samples of the "fruit of the vine" have already found their way to the metropolis.

Reverting to Roma, it should be mentioned that juvenile instruction is by no means neglected, both State and private schools being available for the purpose. The public buildings not already mentioned are the Masonic Hall, Court House, Police Barracks, and Gaol.

The water supply of the town has been hitherto obtained from a large dam on the outskirts of the town, but with a view to obtaining a better supply a movement is on foot—if steps have not already been taken—to test the artesian possibilities of the ground on which the town itself is built.

As the town extends, the high land promises to become the favourite site for both public and private buildings. The streets show great uniformity, and are very roomy, with a width of 99 ft. each. Each of the leading thoroughfares is pleasantly shaded with pepperine and white cedar trees, most of which were planted about eleven years ago, and during that short period have attained a wonderful growth. On almost every hand beautiful shade trees are observed. They are particularly noticeable in Queen's Park, comprising an area of 11½ acres, and situated almost in the centre of the town. The grounds are under the control of the municipality, who have erected a grand stand and lavatory, so that the park is now a favourite resort of local cricketers and athletes generally. There are also two recreation reserves of 63 and 50 acres respectively, which will no doubt prove of incalculable value to the inhabitants of Roma at no distant date.

GYMPIE.

Fare from Brisbane, 12s.; 107 miles. This is an important town of 12,000 inhabitants (Dec., 1895). Although rich deposits of reef gold, in the very heart of the town, have undoubtedly contributed mainly to its support, evidences of agricultural activity are not wanting at the annual agricultural shows which are held here, and there is no doubt that in the near future Gympie will find an important source of wealth in the splendid agricultural lands by which it is surrounded. The estimated number of dwellings within the municipality at the close of 1895 was 2,119 (the fourth greatest in the Colony). Besides these there are a number of churches, schools (State, private, and denominational), an extensive hospital, banks, hotels, a theatre, numerous public buildings, amongst which may be mentioned the Post Office and Town Hall, both substantial buildings, and a School of Arts. The sporting interests of residents are looked after by various racing, football, tennis, &c., clubs; besides which there are a number of musical and literary societies, and lodges. The Press is represented by two high-class papers—the *Gympie Times* and the *Gympie Miner*. Amongst the benevolent institutions are a Ladies' Benevolent Society, a Juvenile Dorcas Society, and an Ambulance Corps—recently supplied with a special ambulance waggon.

Gympie, as will be seen elsewhere, is a most important mining centre. Two of the mines—the "Phœnix Golden Pile" and the "North Smithfield" —paid away £9,800 and £8,354 respectively for one quarter's dividends, the "Columbia Smithfield" and "No. 4 Phœnix" paying £3,000 each during the same quarter, and many others declaring handsome dividends. Towards the close of 1896 several of the above claims, with others, crushed *in one month* 2,169 tons of stone, yielding 6,023 ozs. 8 dwts. of gold, and the dividends paid in that period amounted to *over seventeen thousand pounds sterling!* Although the proprietorship of some of the mines is restricted to a few large shareholders, most of the "scrip" is very well apportioned over the district, and the beneficial effect upon the town of the distribution of these large dividends, in addition to the thousands which are paid away in weekly wages, is apparent.

As regards methods of working, Gympie managers and directors have shown a considerable amount of enterprise. Examples of this may be found in the inauguration on the field of the "cyanide" process for saving the very fine gold; and in the cross-cut—1,200 feet in length— on the property of the No. 4 North Phœnix Co., which resulted in the cutting of a solid reef, yielding over 5 ozs. to the ton. Signs of progress are not wanting in the town itself. Steps have been taken to increase the water supply, a matter of great importance where a numerous population and a quantity of steam power need a large supply.

Some big finds were made in the "seventies" at Monkland, the extreme end of the field. In 1872, for instance, "Nos. 7 and 8 Monkland" reduced 1,514 tons of stone for a return of 10,105 ozs., and in the following year 1,480 tons from "Nos. 2 and 3 South Monkland" gave the handsome return of 11,269 ozs.; the "North Glanmire"—on the same line—in 1881 crushed 6,541 tons for 12,528 ozs.; while its immediate neighbours, the "No. 1 North" and the "Nos. 2 and 3 North Glanmire," turned out some splendid stone a year or two later. The last-mentioned mine in 1885-6 gave nearly 37,000 ozs.

MARYBOROUGH.

Fare from Brisbane by rail, 18s. 5d. (167 miles); by steamer, 20s. saloon (180 miles). This is a very important shipping and manufacturing centre. The estimated population of the municipality at the close of 1895 was 10,000 persons, and the number of dwellings was 2,245. Education, music, literature, and art all receive an unusual amount of attention at the hands of the residents. The School of Arts—an imposing structure erected at a cost of nearly £4,000—contains a museum and over 8,000 volumes, and in this respect is the third in the Colony in point of importance; the curriculum of the establishment, however, yields to none. Elementary and technical education are splendidly catered for, and by a judicious system of penny readings, &c., much useful information has been popularized during certain seasons of the year. Maryborough can also boast of two of the finest Grammar Schools in the Colony (that for boys having cost some £10,000, and that for girls £7,000). These are beautifully situated in extensive and well-kept grounds, and nothing is spared by the management which can minister to the comfort and success of scholars. In addition to spacious show grounds and a beautifully appointed cemetery of 60 acres—constituting one of the sights of the town—there are picturesquely situated Public Gardens on the river banks, within a stone's throw of the Post Office. These are under the care of a resident curator and staff, and contain many rare and interesting plants not commonly found in Botanical Gardens. Access to the "bush-house" may be obtained on application at the curator's lodge. The Maryborough foundries are attaining great prominence for the excellent quality of their work, and many important contracts for sugar-mill machinery and railway locomotives have been successfully carried out. PIALBA—distant 25 miles; fare, 2s. A deservedly popular summer watering-place. From recent indications there seems to be the intention—by encouraging industries along the line of railway—to develope the latent resources of the country, and thus make

H

IRON GATES GORGE

View near Bundaberg.

this an additional source of wealth to Maryborough. At present the chief trade is in sugar, timber, coal, fruit, and iron, the first four being largely produced in the district. Close to the town is the famed Yengarie Sugar Refinery, between which and the distant plantations a large railway traffic in cane and juice is carried on. The latter is conveyed, where practicable, in pipes laid on from the plantations, but that carried by rail is enclosed in enormous cylindrical tanks, each holding some 3,000 gallons of juice. Amongst the notable buildings are the Hospital, situated on the extreme edge of the town, the principal State schools, several of the Hotels and Banks, the Town Hall, and the Catholic, Presbyterian, and Anglican churches—all fine buildings. St. Paul's (of the latter denomination) contains one of the finest peals of bells in the Colony, and the performances of the bellringers upon this peal fully sustain the musical reputation which the place enjoys. In this connection it may be mentioned that there are both a "Liedertafel" and an Operatic Society here. The Press is well and largely represented, the following being the principal publications : *Maryborough Chronicle*, *Wide Bay News*, and *Colonist*.

BUNDABERG.

Fare from Brisbane, by rail, 23s. 7d. (217 miles) ; by steamer, 25s. (saloon), 272 miles. A rising municipality, having an estimated population (December, 1895) of 5,000 persons, exclusive of outlying districts. The prosperity of the town is chiefly due to the large sugar-growing interests with which the residents are identified. In every direction stretch such well-known plantations as Bingera, Fairymead, Mon Repos, Sea View, Waterview, and Windermere, whilst on the east side of the town is situated the far-famed refinery of Messrs. Cran Bros.—until the erection of the Colonial Sugar Company's refinery in Brisbane, the largest in the Colony. The latest machinery has been added by the Messrs. Cran, who at the present time manufacture a large quantity of first-class refined sugar and golden syrup, the juice being conveyed from the plantation to the works. A number of important industries, such as saw-milling, iron foundry work, co-operative dairying, distilling, brewing, ice-making, pottery and brick making, soap-making, and farming, are carried on here to a large extent, so that the future prosperity of the town is assured. Besides the State schools there are a number of public buildings, such as the School of Arts, Theatre (Queen's), Custom House, Court House, the Post Office—a substantial building surmounted by a turret and clock, of which the face is illuminated at night and visible all over the town—and the Hospital. On the bank of the river (Burnett) there is a fine reserve, intended for public gardens, which will be an incalculable boon to residents when the town becomes more crowded; and on the southern boundary of the town is found the Racecourse. A few miles out there is a favourite seaside resort of the residents. The progressive nature of Bundaberg is evident in its Press, the *Mail* and *Star*, and in its social institutions, amongst which the Town Band is not by any means the least, the members of this musical organization having on many occasions gained well-earned honours in competition with those of other towns. Several first-class hotels offer the very best accommodation to visitors. It should be mentioned that Bundaberg has participated to a large extent in the trade with the newly settled ISIS SCRUB (distant about 30 to 33 miles by rail), and has in times past done considerable business with the famed Mt. Perry, from which it is about 67 miles by rail. Another line of railway places this town in direct communication with Rockhampton and Central Districts.

ROCKHAMPTON.

Distance by sea from Brisbane about 420 miles; saloon fare, £3 10s. This is the chief town and port of Central Queensland; indeed, as far as exports are concerned, it holds a higher position than Brisbane. A very important trade is carried on in frozen meat, wool, tallow, sheepskins, gold, precious stones (mostly opals), horses, leather, manure, bones, hoofs, and sugar. In 1898 the value of exports reached £2,434,287, and the imports for the same period were valued at £623,060. The wharfage is commodious, and is being extended. Although the temperature is somewhat high at times, Rockhampton is noted for its healthfulness, the picturesque nature of its suburbs, and the evident prosperity of its inhabitants. Life here in the winter months is all that could be desired—both as regards climatic and social advantages. A School of Arts—one of the finest buildings devoted to that purpose in the Colony—provides ample literary food in its eight or nine thousand volumes; rowing, cricket, tennis, swimming, and rifle clubs afford a variety of out-door sports; whilst numbers of literary, debating, agricultural, pastoral, and musical societies are in operation. Rockhampton enjoys also the distinction of being the seat of two bishoprics, and of having the only cathedral in the Colony which is throughout lighted by electricity. The latter (St. Paul's, Church of England) is an imposing piece of architecture, situated at the corner of William and Alma Streets, but bids fair to be eclipsed by the cathedral lately erected by the Roman Catholic Church. Pleasure seekers will be delighted with the surroundings of the city, and the many pleasure resorts which are within easy access; amongst these may be mentioned the "Bats' Caves," of stalactitic formation. Emu Park, a charming seaside watering-place, is reached by train in less than an hour and a half, at a cost of 5s. 8d. for first-class return ticket; and so popular is the place amongst "Rockhamptonites" that hundreds of residents visit it upon every public holiday. Fishing, yachting, and shooting are to be had in abundance, both here and at the neighbouring township of Yeppoon. Capacious hotels afford every comfort and many of the luxuries of city life; this is especially so at Emu Park. Besides the above, the Botanical Gardens of Rockhampton, in which there is an extensive lagoon whereon numbers of wild fowl disport themselves, afford the means of spending many a pleasant hour. The city is well laid out and lighted—electricity being largely used for this purpose. The progressive spirit of the place is markedly shown in the splendid bridge—illuminated by a chain of powerful "arc" lamps—by which the Fitzroy is spanned, thus connecting North Rockhampton with Rockhampton proper. The public buildings are both numerous and substantial. Besides an imposing Telegraph Office, Supreme Court, Court House, Custom House, Lands Office, Bond Store, Gaol, Lock-up and Police Station, Mines Office, Titles Office and Emigration Depôt, there are a Boys' and Girls' Grammar School, State Schools, and four hospitals, including the capacious General Hospital, which contains 103 beds, and is an exceptionally fine building in point of design, construction, and situation. The city has a State Orphanage and a Denominational Orphanage (Meteor Park), a Benevolent Asylum, and a Lunatic Reception House. There are some fourteen private schools, and one for boys under the direction of the Christian Brothers, a Ladies' Benevolent Society, a couple of daily newspapers—*Morning Bulletin* and *Record*—and three or four important "weeklies"—*Capricornian, People's Newspaper, Church Gazette*, &c. "Prosperity" is stamped upon every feature of this important town, and nowhere is this more apparent than in East Street on a Saturday night, where the turn-out would do credit, both as regards numbers and style, to many an English town. The population of the two boroughs at the end of 1895 was 17,157 persons, the number of dwellings 3,030, and the year's receipts and expenditure each about £24,000, the city of Rockhampton being in this respect second only to Brisbane. Jointly the boroughs cover 54 1-10th square miles, the largest city area in the Colony, in which the streets are remarkably well laid out. Some two and a half miles from the Post Office are the celebrated Lake's Creek Meat Works, which, with the quarters of the employees (of whom

there are many hundreds), constitute an extensive settlement in themselves. The wages sheet is over £200, and the output 300 head of cattle
and 1,000 sheep, per day. A ten-mile ride on the Central Railway (fare
1s. 3d.) brings one to Kabra, whence a coach formerly ran to the far-
famed MOUNT MORGAN. Around the great mine—the richest which
Australia has produced—a flourishing municipality of over 5,000 inhabitants has arisen, containing a number of comfortable hotels, besides 800
or 1,000 dwellings, and more buildings are constantly being erected.
Figures respecting the mining operations will be found elsewhere.
Railway communication with the main line has now been effected by
means of an " Abt " rack railway line, the first of its kind in Australia.

Mount Morgan contains many flourishing public institutions ; possibly
none more so than the Hospital, a well-appointed and beautifully situated
building of substantial dimensions, and especially well supplied with
water. The hotels are numerous and well kept, besides being moderate
in price. There are a School of Arts, a Town Hall, numbers of first-
class business houses, &c.; and the Press is represented by two progressive papers—the *Chronicle* and the *Herald*.

LONGREACH.

424 miles from Rockhampton, fare £2 1s. 7d. This is the most
westerly of our towns having railway communication with the eastern
seaboard, and, as seen for the first time, opens up an entirely new vista
of life. Still, should the visitor expect to find himself beyond the pale
of civilization, he will be most pleasantly disappointed. About a dozen
hotels—many of them offering exceptionally good accommodation—
several churches and banks, a School of Arts (421 vols.), State and
private schools, Court House, Lands Office, Post and Telegraph Office,
and a variety of stores and other places of business constitute the nucleus
of this thriving and progressive pastoral and mining centre. The population of the town and district is over 2,000 persons. Longreach has for
a long time been the starting-point for various coaches : that for Arrilalah
(fare 15s.), Muttaburra (25s.), Winton (58s.), and Vergemont (60s.).
The fact of the Fermoy Opal Fields (Opalton) being reached from here
gives considerable importance to the town, as both miners and buyers
are constantly to and fro. The distance from Longreach is 140 to 150
miles, and from Winton it is 78 miles. The *Winton Herald* stated that
the first discovery of opal there is alleged to have been close on five
years ago, when a Mr. Kerr, then bookkeeper on Warrnambool Downs
station, picked up a nice specimen on the surface. The original pro-

CHARTERS TOWERS FOOTBALLERS

spectors are said to have taken out stone valued at £10,000. The depth of sinking was from 6 ft. to 45 ft., the best specimens being found 14 ft. from the surface. Some beautiful pieces of the precious stone have been bought up by speculators for a mere song, but others have fetched splendid prices. Opalton is on Sandy Creek, a tributary of Vergemont Creek, and the route from Longreach lies over magnificent plains, dotted with spinifex, gidya, &c., being portions of Maneroo, Evesham and Corona runs, &c. A most progressive spirit is evinced by the residents of Opalton township, resulting, amongst other things, in the establish-ment of a ". Progress Association" and "Co-operative Water Supply Society," and in their plucky efforts to lessen crime by wise restrictions on the liquor traffic. Naturally the country about these districts is dry and the climate somewhat hot, but these drawbacks are being greatly mitigated by artesian water supplies; indeed the activity in this direction has never been greater than it is at the present time, and from all appearances it will not be long before the terrors of a drought will be absolutely unknown. Careful attention is also directed to the improve-ment of stock, &c., in furtherance of which an annual show of some merit is held under the auspices of the Marathon Pastoral Society. In speaking of the social aspect, it should be mentioned that the bicycle craze has thoroughly "caught on" in Longreach, where there are some 60 cyclists, and, of course, there is a club for the convenience of devotees. A handsome bridge—completed at a cost of £2,300—spans the Thompson River at Longreach. From Arrilalah (reached by coach) a stock route leads to the Diamantina, and thence to Lake Machatti, Lake Phillipi, and Carcory Hot Springs; thence to Boulia, near which are the famed Elizabeth Hot Springs.

CHARTERS TOWERS.

Fare from Townsville, 9s. 7d.; 82 miles. The centre of the premier goldfield of Queensland, and one of the most progressive towns in the Colony. Many of the mines (as shown elsewhere) are phenomenally rich, but a record was reached when the No. 5 Day Dawn mine had a crushing which *averaged 31 ozs. 12 dwts. of gold per ton of stone.* The dividends paid in one month have amounted to £40,000, and the total for 1898 exceeded £300,000. An electric lighting plant, capable of supplying energy to 1,500 ten-candle power lamps, was installed here at a cost of £7,000, the high-class hotels—of which there is an unlimited choice—as well as many of the business houses being illuminated by the new light. Charters Towers is situated about 1,000 ft. above sea level, and consequently enjoys a most delightful climate; the warmth of the day being almost invariably succeeded by a balmy sea breeze, which seems doubly welcome in these high latitudes. The water supply is of the best; the reservoir capacity is 288,000 gallons, and the cost of construction—including additions—was £76,719 (to end of 1895). The municipality of Charters Towers contains an estimated population of 5,000 persons (December, 1895), and about 1,100 dwellings. Evidences of culture exist in the educational, musical, and social organizations with which the field abounds. Besides Public Schools there are eleven private establishments, and a School of Arts containing some 3,000 volumes. Churches of all denominations are numerous; there are also a Masonic Hall and Hospital, several societies for benevolent purposes, racing clubs, patriotic societies, &c. Business houses and banks are numerous and substantial; the medical and legal professions are also largely represented.

TOWNSVILLE.

Distance by sea from Brisbane about 750 miles; saloon fare (single), £5 10s. A city, on Cleveland Bay, containing 11,000 inhabitants (including census district, 15,000); the seat of the Bishopric of North Queensland, and commercial capital of the North. It is pleasantly situated on the shores of the bay, in full view of Magnetic Island, on the eastern side of which is Horsehoe Bay—a much frequented picnic ground. The Northern Supreme Court is situated here, and amongst other public buildings may be mentioned the Post and Telegraph Offices, a fine solid block of buildings, surmounted by a clock tower; a Lands Office, Town Hall, Divisional Board Hall, Custom House, Court House, Gaol, &c.; a Police Barracks, Titles Office, Hospital, Powder Magazine, Drill Sheds, &c. The Market Buildings are of a substantial nature. Local seaport trade is very extensive, and the buildings of many banking and mercantile houses are very fine. The streets of the city are well laid out and kept, vehicles of every description ply for hire in the streets, whilst regular lines of omnibuses go to and fro between Townsville and the suburbs; and, although the temperature during much of the year is hot in the heart of the town, residence on the sea front (but 100 yards distant) is delightful. Cleveland Bay contributed during the half-year ended on 31st December, 1896, the substantial sum of £107,837 in Customs duties, being second in this respect only to the port of Brisbane. The imports and exports in 1898 were respectively £876,275 and £2,616,511, half of the latter being the product of the goldfields. The port of Townsville is constantly undergoing improvements, and at considerable expense. The jetty has cost nearly £150,000, whilst the total expenditure on the harbour amounts to nearly double that sum —an outlay, however, which seems fully justified by the importance of its maritime trade. Townsville is practically the sole outlet for an enormous area of mineral, pastoral, and agricultural country. Under the first head may be mentioned the rich goldfields of Charters Towers, Ravenswood, and Cape River; agricultural land is to be found in patches all over the district, but pre-eminently the district is suited to grazing— some of the frozen meat shipped from Townsville having given the greatest satisfaction on arrival in London, where it realized ⅛d. to ¼d. per lb. above ordinary prices. The educational standard amongst the residents is high, there being a fine Grammar School, erected at a cost of over £8,000, several private and State Schools, a School of Arts, possessing 3,000 volumes odd, and three newspapers of considerable literary ability, the *Bulletin*, *Star*, and *Herald*. Of benevolent institutions there are a State Orphanage and the Benevolent Society, besides which there is a Reception House for Lunatics. The most luxurious accommodation is found at several of the residential hotels, gas is used throughout the town, and public gardens have been laid out or planned in every direction, over 150 acres being reserved for this and recreation purposes within the city area; whilst Castle Hill towers proudly over the whole to a height of nearly 1,000 ft.

MACKAY.

500 to 540 miles north-west of Brisbane; saloon steamship fare, £4 10s. single. This may be called the " home of sugar," and as such has an able champion in the *Sugar Journal*, which certainly ranks amongst our leading papers and is the best of its kind, in the Colony. Several references have already been made to the sugar-growing industry as carried on here, but it should be added that the district is eminently suited for many other crops—maize, potatoes, tobacco, spices, grapes, and oranges having been grown successfully. The cultivation of mangoes is quite a speciality of the place. The municipality of Mackay had, on the 31st December, 1895, an estimated population of 4,500 persons, with 879 dwellings, but, of course, the population of the *district* would be more than double the above figures. The town itself (on the Pioneer River) is well supplied with a number of good stores, drapers, &c. There are also several branch banks for the transacting of general banking business, a School of Arts (containing some 3,555 vols.), a Hospital, a Custom House, Court House, Post and Telegraph Office, Police Station and

other police quarters. Amongst other institutions, there is a Chamber of
Commerce for the safeguarding of trade, and also a Benevolent Society.
Literature is abundantly supplied by the *Mercury*, *Standard*, and *Chronicle*
—newspapers which have all contributed to the present prosperity of the
town—as well as by other publications supplied by the numerous book-
sellers. The medical and legal professions are both represented; there
are also a couple of chemists in the town. Considerable attention has
always been paid to cattle raising, and meat works have been established
here upon a sound commercial basis. Another industry which promises
to take an important position is Coffee growing. The exports from this
port during 1898 were valued at £382,873 (being £275,359 above the
imports for that period), of which £296,805 was attributed to sugar, and
£52,595 to meat products. Several of the large central, and some of the
"guarantee" sugar mills are situated on the outskirts of Mackay, there
being also a number of smaller private concerns. About 100 miles to
the north is the rapidly rising Proserpine district, which has elsewhere
been alluded to as possessing a large mill, erected with the assistance
of the Government. The soil is most exceptionally fertile, yielding
something like 30 tons of cane to the acre. Most of the institutions of
civilization are found here, viz., two storekeepers, a butcher's shop, a
baker, two sawmills, a blacksmith, an hotel, a school, a Post Office, and a
Police Station, not forgetting telephonic communication with the neighbouring Bloomsbury Telegraph Office. About 8 miles west of the
Proserpine lies the Conway village settlement, whilst small alluvial
miners' camps exist at Kelsey Creek (6 miles from the mill) and Happy
Valley (about 17 miles distant). Of pleasure resorts there are many near
Mackay. Amongst these may be mentioned Eimeo, and most of the
eminences which are found here. Perhaps one of the finest—though not
well-known—places for a day's enjoyment is Mount Oscar, which,
although a private property, is accessible to visitors requesting
permission to avail themselves of the panoramic views which are obtainable from this height.

The stability of Mackay is demonstrated by the fact that, in face of
the most disheartening circumstances, the cane farmers have been able to
hold their own, and a most progressive spirit has been apparent all
through. As an instance of the latter it may be mentioned that steps
were long since taken by the town residents to establish a Telephone
Exchange, and already a large number of subscribers have been secured.
Turf, bicycle, and rifle clubs afford many opportunities for recreation;
Masonic and other lodges are numerous; whilst industrial interests are

Barron Falls.—"The Niagara of Queensland."

Barron Falls.—"The Niagara of Queensland."

looked after by the Agricultural, Pastoral, and Mining Association, and by the Pioneer River Farmers' Association. Of scholastic establishments there is sufficient variety for the most fastidious, these comprising three or four State and five private Schools, besides a High School.

CAIRNS.

Distance from Brisbane, 908 miles; saloon steamer fare, £6 10s. An important shipping centre for the sugar and fruit growing industries, as well as for the extensive gold product of the Hodgkinson, Mulgrave, and Russell River districts, and for Herberton tin. The population of the municipality on Dec. 31st, 1895, was estimated at 2,000 persons, and the dwellings numbered 500. The wide streets, planted with trees, in which are found representatives of all the principal trades and professions, afford a pleasing surprise to the travellers on our coast. The chief of the many points of interest round and about Cairns are, however, the Barron Falls, reached by train in an hour and a quarter, at a cost of 2s. 5d. Here, but 19 miles from town, is some of the grandest scenery in the Southern Hemisphere, and if viewed during the rainy season the sight of the main falls is truly awe-inspiring. The rainfall being heavy in this portion of Queensland, the vegetation is most luxuriant, and many a pretty spot is met with in the "scrubs" which stretch out on every hand. In some of this country—between 18 and 25 miles from the coast—are a group of beautiful pieces of water of which the chief is Lake Eacham, and a visit to Cairns would not be complete without seeing something of these charming places. As has been said, the trade of the port is considerable. The imports during 1898 were valued at £91,333, whilst the exports exceeded £193,000, of which sugar contributed £90,000 and green fruit £44,000. The Press champions of Cairns are the *Argus* and the *Post*. At the present time the Cairns-Herberton railway extends to Mareeba (46 miles), from which point a railway is being constructed by private enterprise to the rich mining district of Chillagoe, and a large accession of traffic and trade may be looked for at the port of this productive region.

Herberton, as has already been remarked, is an extensive table-land, of which the climate is superb and the mineral and agricultural wealth stupendous. The 35 miles between the terminus of the railway line and this mining centre are now traversed twice a week by coach, by which the fare is 20s. Herberton is duly represented by the *Wild River Times*, and much information which has of necessity been omitted in these pages may be obtained from that valuable periodical. Too much could scarcely be said of the productiveness of the district, but the following description of a giant tree of the "Ficus" tribe must suffice : The girth, about 5 ft. from the ground, is 158 ft., and inside of the tree is a hollow *15 ft. in diameter.* Travellers who desire to see this remarkable specimen of tropical growth will find it on Mr. Albert S. Aplin's selection, 12 miles north of Herberton, and close to the townships of Atherton and Carrington.

NORMANTON.

Distance from Brisbane, 1,948 miles; saloon fare, £12. Geographically considered, this is a most important port, and, as has been repeatedly stated, there is little doubt that in this town of 800 inhabitants and about 166 dwellings there are the makings of a large commercial centre. When it is borne in mind that Normanton is virtually the only outlet for the Croydon, Etheridge, Gilbert, Woolgar, and Cloncurry goldfields, and that in addition to these the country which will eventually be tapped by railway systems contains practically unlimited pastoral and mineral wealth, there would seem to be every justification for the early construction of more lines of railway. Notwithstanding present drawbacks, the exports for 1898 reached close on £154,000, in which gold figured conspicuously, the other items of importance being wool and other pastoral products. Normanton, although somewhat depleted of its former population in favour of the rich gold mines of CROYDON, is not without its attractions. The town is well situated, and besides the Government buildings, stores, &c., there is a School of Arts, which contains 1,057 volumes, and was erected at a cost of £2,000. CROYDON—94 miles distant—is reached by rail in five and a half hours, at a cost of 10s. 10d. The population of the latter municipality in 1895 was 1,767 persons, and the number of dwellings was 700, but recent developments of the mines have had the effect of largely increasing the population. Both Normanton and Croydon have their own Press, the latter town, as its size demands, supporting two vigorous papers—the *Golden Age* and *Mining News*. Normanton can only boast of one newspaper—the *Chronicle*— a publication, however, which has always worked faithfully for its constituents.

COOKTOWN.

Distance from Brisbane, 1,008 miles ; fare, £7 10s. Although containing a population of only 2,000 or 3,000 persons (within the municipality), this port has occupied no mean place in the history of the Colony. The value of the exports in 1898 was £85,534, of which £62,000 worth of gold formed the most important item. Next to this is the export of tin from the Annan River and Mount Windsor, which was valued at £5,927, an industry which would be far more largely engaged in were the price to offer greater inducements. The town occupies a prominent position at the mouth of the Endeavour River, and is surrounded by many beautiful stretches of country and places of interest. The buildings number under 1,000, but the position of the town as the port of the Palmer, Limestone, and Coen goldfields, and the rich agricultural lands around it, combine to make it a place of present commercial importance and of great promise in the future. Besides three excellent newspapers —the *Independent*, the *Courier*, and the *Endeavour Beacon*—Cooktown possesses the advantage of a fine School of Arts, containing some 1,834 volumes (December, 1895); State and denominational (R.C.) schools; several societies for the advancement of commercial, agricultural, and social objects; a Fire Brigade, Hospital, churches of the Roman Catholic, Church of England, and other denominations, Banks, &c. All the trades are numerously represented, as are also the medical and legal professions. Besides the gold and tin fields alluded to, much trade finds its way here from the Mitchell River antimony fields and the Chillagoe and Ashtonville silver and lead mines. The local *béche-de-mer* and pearl-shell fisheries are also a source of wealth to the district, which has lately come greatly into prominence owing to the rush of miners to the goldfields of New Guinea, for which this is the port of departure.

PART V.

Commercial and Social Conditions, &c.

SHIPPING in Queensland holds no mean place, and indeed we may be said to be a close competitor with the Southern Colonies and New Zealand. Age being taken into consideration, the extension of these interests is marvellous, a result mainly due to the wide scope offered by a very large number of ports. It will thus be seen that as a colony we have both the natural wealth and facilities for the shipment of that wealth which go to make great nations, and although the direct tonnage entered and cleared at our ports is not very great at present, it needs no special gift of prophecy to foretell an enormous oversea traffic in the near future. The 1896 returns gave the shipping trade of Brisbane as £5,198,644; Rockhampton, £2,975,524; and Townsville, £2,620,493. Five other ports had a trade of over £200,000, five exceeded £100,000, and two exceeded £20,000 per annum. Two of the most noteworthy—although not the busiest—ports of Queensland are those of Gladstone and Bowen. The former is a natural harbour of extreme beauty and exceptional capacity, likely in the near future to become one of great importance. Already a large meat works has been established at this port, which is now in direct communication with the old world by means of a frequent service of magnificent meat-carrying steamers. Bowen is similarly capable of berthing vessels of 9,000 and 10,000 tons register, although not possessing quite so many natural advantages as the first-mentioned port. According to Captain Williams, of the "Denton Grange," when speaking on this subject, it was then only requisite that about 200 yards of dredging be effected to make the port of Bowen "second to none in Australia." In his case he stated that he had had no difficulty whatever in bringing his capacious vessel alongside the wharf. It may be mentioned that a comparison of the total trade in 1895 shows that the value per ton of total shipping in Queensland was more than double that of New South Wales and Victoria, three times that of South Australia, and from four to six times that of Western Australia.

The HISTORY OF QUEENSLAND has been written and re-written, and therefore does not find a place in these pages. Law and order prevail over the length and breadth of the land; the DEFENCE of the Colony on land is entrusted to a fine body of Police, and to a Defence Force, numbering (in 1895) 2,769 officers and men, besides mounted infantry and a large force of volunteers. At sea, the Colony enjoys the protection of a Pan-Colonial squadron, and for active service a marine force of 300 to 400 men is available. The vulnerable points on our coast and strategic positions have been fortified at heavy expense, and are considered to be fairly impregnable. FINANCE, ACCUMU-LATION, and the CONSTITUTION have been so ably dealt with by competent writers, notably by Thornhill Weedon, Esq., of the Statistical Department of Queensland, and by other authorities, that it is unnecessary to touch on these subjects in a work of so limited a size as the present.

The RAILWAYS of this Colony constitute a most important factor in her past and future growth. At the present time about 2,500 miles of railway are completed, some 200 miles of new lines are authorized or under construction, and the building of others is under consideration. Although of no great length in comparison with the large area to be served, our railway system is far more extensive in relation to population than are those of New South Wales, Victoria, Tasmania, South Australia, and New Zealand. The Railway policy of the various Ministries has generally been of a most liberal nature, a course of action which proves to have been fully justified in view of the fact that even at this early stage of our history several of our lines are able to pay the interest on capital without difficulty, whilst others contribute the bulk of that interest. On the whole it may be said that our railways, as at present managed, are in a very satisfactory condition, it being always necessary to bear in mind that the primary object with which State railways are constructed is the development of otherwise inaccessible resources, not the payment of dividends on capital expenditure. A noticeable feature in Queensland railways has been the adoption of a narrow gauge (3 ft. 6 in.), thus materially reducing the cost of construction and maintenance and giving a promise of earlier return for the outlay. From the report of the Commissioner for Railways (1896) it is seen that the cost per mile of railway open in Queensland is £7,024, being lower than that of South Australia, New Zealand, or Victoria, less than half that of the New South Wales system, and somewhat over one-seventh of the cost in the United Kingdom. Further, it is remarkable that whilst Queensland has little more than one-tenth of the population per mile of railway, one-eightieth of the train miles run, and a higher percentage of working expenses to earnings than the United Kingdom, the earnings *per head of population* for the year ending June 30, 1896, were better than those for the United Kingdom, and second—amongst the colonies—only to South Australia. Reviewing the history of our railways since 1865, we find that during the financial year ending June 30, 1896, the tonnage of goods and minerals carried was 1,026,889, the highest on record—having nearly doubled in the decade. The number of train miles run was 4,744,733—also an advance on all previous records, and nearly double that of 1885. The reduction effected in cost per train mile is very satisfactory, the cost having been 4s. 1¾d. in 1876 (earliest recorded), and only 2s. 8½d. in 1895–6 (the lowest on record), or a percentage of working expenses to gross earnings of 59·36—a lower percentage than either Victoria or New Zealand, although higher by 3·37 per cent. than the figures for the United Kingdom on December 31, 1894. As the present working expenses per train mile are already lower than those incurred in the United Kingdom, it is apparent that a comparatively slight increase in gross earnings will make our railway system one of the most cheaply worked—and consequently best paying—systems in the world. The railway traffic earnings for March, 1897, compared with those of March, 1896, showed a net increase of £5,758. Another pleasing feature of our railways is the encouragement afforded by the Administration to local engineers in the acceptance given to tenders for the construction in Queensland of 30 heavy goods locomotives (at £2,390 each), in addition to numbers of hopper waggons, insulated waggons, firewood waggons, open goods waggons, &c., all of which are the means of providing a good deal of work for the iron and timber trades.

THE POSTAL AND TELEGRAPHIC business of Queensland is efficiently conducted by means of some 391 Post Offices, 642 Receiving Offices, 112 Money-Order Offices, 1,139 Private Lock-boxes, 178 Letter Receivers 366 Telegraph Stations, and Telephone Exchanges at Brisbane, Charters Towers and Townsville, with others in course of construction. The length of mail routes on December 31, 1895, was 29,507 miles, and the length of telegraph wires in July, 1896, 17,797¼ miles. The whole is controlled from the General Post Office, Brisbane, at which there is a considerable staff under the direction of the Postmaster-General. The latter gentleman is also charged with the oversight of the Meteorological Department, ably managed by one of the foremost scientists of the day, Clement L. Wragge, Esq., F.R.G.S., F.R.Met.Soc., &c. The staff of the entire department comprises some 92 letter-carriers, and about 1,000 other officials, and the total combined revenue for 1895 was £234,693, an increase on 1894 of £19,079, that derived from postal sources only being the largest ever obtained in this Colony. Some interesting calculations are made in ' Queensland Past and Present ' as to the relative letter-writing capacities of the various colonies and Great Britain, together with a mass of other information to which the enquirer is referred.

SOCIAL CONDITIONS are similar to those obtaining in other English-speaking lands. State Schools are liberally provided for the free education of the young, and new " provisional " schools can be obtained at any place where there are 30 or 40 children with which to form a nucleus. Grammar Schools for both sexes and a large number of private schools are found in all the larger towns. Ninety scholarships for boys, and thirty for girls, are annually competed for by State School children, entitling the successful candidates to three years' free education in a Grammar School. There are also three exhibitions—each of the value of £100 per annum—annually offered to students under 19 years of age who desire a University education. The numerous religious bodies have equal rights—there being no established Church in the Colony. Incidentally, many of the districts over which ministers of religion have charge are very large—notably some of the Western Roman Catholic Dioceses, and that of the Anglican Bishop of Brisbane, whose jurisdiction extends over 209,278 square miles, having a population of 304,072 persons! The latter denomination predominates by a large number.

In addition to the educational advantages provided by the schools, nineteen Technical Colleges—either separate institutions or in conjunction with Schools of Art—are devoted to providing instruction in Trades, Art, and Commerce, and with this object have received State endowments, varying from £100 (as at Zillmere) to £1,000 in the case of the Brisbane College. Over £5,000 has thus been spent in endowments besides annual grants, which amounted to some £2,404 during the two financial years 1895-6.

Museums have also been founded in Brisbane by the Government for the enlightenment of those who wish to become acquainted with the Geology and other branches of the Natural History of the Colony, or with the associations connected with its past and present history. There are numerous scientific, musical, and literary societies, many of these being affiliated with the parent societies in Europe. Amongst these may be mentioned the Royal Society of Queensland, the Royal Geographical Society of Australasia (Queensland branch), the Literary Circle, various Chess Clubs, the Brisbane Draughts Club, the Brisbane Musical Union,

the Brisbane Liedertafel, the Cambrian Choir, Choral Union, Queensland
Shorthand Writers' Association, Amateur Photographic Society, several
Amateur Theatrical and Parliamentary Debating Societies, &c. In
connection with these and kindred associations many most delightful
gatherings take place, while social life has all the amenities—if it does
not always possess the "haut ton"—of the older countries of the world.
"At homes" and "Cinderellas," musical evenings, and garden parties
are as often brought into requisition to promote sociability as is the case
in other lands. Other organizations existing for this end are the clubs,
of which there are several in the Capital, some of them magnificently
appointed. Foremost amongst these may be mentioned the Queensland
Club, having a membership of close on 300 ; the Commercial Travellers'
Club, in Queen Street, is also a well-appointed and convenient rendezvous
for members and their business friends. Besides these there are the
Johnsonian Club, Londoners' Club, Burns and Caledonian Club, &c.
The aged, the infirm, and those of unsound mind are amply cared for by
Government and private benevolence. An Industrial Home is open
to the Blind and Deaf and Dumb; Reformatories and Industrial
Homes are provided for the neglected youth of both sexes, in addition
to some eight asylums for orphan children. Friendly Societies minister
to the wants of sick members and their families, and so popular are
these institutions that in 1895 the figures were, members 19,636, lodges
282, as compared with a membership of 12,301, with 163 lodges and
districts, in 1887. Prominent amongst the Charitable Institutions of
Queensland are the Masonic Lodges, of which there are over one
hundred situated in various parts of the Colony. The Grand Lodge
under each of the three constitutions is in Brisbane.

In the interests of breeders, farmers, and fanciers we have the
Queensland Stockbreeders and Graziers' Association, the National Agricultural and Industrial Association, the Dog and Poultry Society, the
Fruitgrowers' Association, Royal Agricultural Society (Toowoomba), and
a number of other metropolitan and provincial farmers' associations,
agricultural societies, &c. All these have lately been centred in a
Parliamentary Committee styled the "Farmers' Union," and some good
work has been accomplished. One of the most notable developments in
connection with agricultural matters has been the establishment of the
first of our colleges for training young men in farm practice and science.
This has been called the Queensland Agricultural College. The time of
the student is here equally divided between labour in the field and in the
class-room. Every student participates in all the operations of a well-

conducted farm, while competent teachers instruct the pupils in the "why and the wherefore" of farm practices. The present equipment of the College embraces, amongst other items, a farm of 1,692 acres; three dormitories and dining-hall for 56 students; the main College building, 70 ft. by 112 ft., containing lecture-rooms, library, and rooms for study; and a very full assortment of the most modern tools and implements. To these, new farm buildings, books, apparatus, stock and implements are being constantly added. The College opened on July 1, 1897. The inclusive terms charged are £25 per College year for board, washing, lights, and rooms partially furnished, besides instruction. It may be mentioned that the foundation of an excellent herd of cattle has been laid at this College by the importation of several of the best pedigree beasts obtainable in Victoria.

PHYSICAL RECREATION is abundantly provided by clubs for Lawn Tennis, Cricket, Football, Golf, Rowing, Sailing, Rifle practice, Cycling, Bowling, Lacrosse, Polo, Gymnastics, &c., and regular "meets" of the hounds. Race meetings constitute another form of sport, which is, perhaps, more largely engaged in than any other, and numbers of these are held in almost every town and township throughout the Colony, under the auspices of the various racing associations.

GENERAL HOLIDAYS.

In addition to the following General Holidays, many towns throughout the Colony observe weekly half-holidays, of which a list is added for the convenience of the travelling public :—

New Year's Day.
Anniversary Day—January 26th.
St. Patrick's Day—March 17th.
Good Friday.
Easter Eve.
Easter Monday.
St. George's Day—April 23rd.
Eight Hour Day—May 1st.

Queen's Birthday—May 24th.
Lammas Day—August 1st.
Prince of Wales' Birthday—November 9th.
St. Andrew's Day—November 30th.
Separation Day—December 10th.
Christmas Day—December 25th.
Boxing Day—December 26th.
And specially proclaimed holidays.

HALF HOLIDAYS.

Allora—Wednesday.
Barcaldine—Thursday.
Blackall—Saturday.
Bowen—Wednesday.
Bundaberg—Thursday.
Cairns—Thursday.
Charleville—Thursday.
Charters Towers—Thursday.
Clifton—Wednesday.
Cooktown—Wednesday.
Croydon—Thursday.
Dalby—Wednesday.
Gladstone—Thursday.

Gympie—Thursday.
Hughenden—Thursday.
Laidley—Thursday.
Mackay—Wednesday.
Longreach—Thursday.
Maryborough—Friday.
Mt. Morgan—Thursday.
Roma—Wednesday.
Stanthorpe—Wednesday.
Toowoomba—Wednesday.
Townsville—Thursday.
Warwick—Wednesday.

THE LABOUR MARKET.

Compared with the "Old Country," and especially with the continental countries of Europe, the conditions of the worker (more especially in manual labour) in Queensland is exceptionally good. Cases of distress, of course, do and will occur, but as these result from a congestion in some particular quarter, and not from over-population, the remedy is not far to seek.

The item "Shearers," in the wages-table below, may be somewhat vague to those unacquainted with shearing. When it is stated that a man can dispose of 100 to 200 sheep per diem, it will be seen that, notwithstanding the intermittent nature of the shearer's occupation, good wages can be earned. Many sheds employ one or two hundred men for several weeks, at the end of which time they receive their cheque of £40 to £80, and probably move on to a neighbouring shed, where the shearing is just commencing, thus earning sufficient in seven to nine months to support themselves and their families on a snug little homestead, where they can augment their income by some secondary occupation, if so disposed. A record tally was that of a man who recently shore an aggregate of 33,825 sheep (seven sheds), for which he received the substantial sum of £338 odd.

Miners also receive fairly good wages. A good deal of piece work is done; but where day work obtains the earnings of these vary from £2 10s. per week, in the temperate portions of the Colony, to £3 10s., or even £4 on some of the northern fields. Engineers earn £4 to £5 per week Labourers employed by local governing bodies (Divisional Boards, Shire Councils, &c.) receive 5s. to 5s. 6d. per day, gangers receive 6s. to 7s., horse and dray (with driver) 9s. to 10s. 6d., two-horse drays (with driver) 12s. to 12s. 6d., and bullock teams 15s. to 18s. Railway labourers receive similar rates of pay, but have certain advantages over the above.

The following table of present wages (approximate) will give fuller information :—

ARTISAN AND MISCELLANEOUS LABOUR—

Tailors	per diem	5s. to 9s.
Masons (no demand)	,,	10s. to 12s.
Plasterers	,,	6s. to 10s.
Bricklayers	,,	10s. to 14s.
Carpenters	,,	9s. to 11s.
Painters	,,	8s. to 10s.
Blacksmiths	,,	7s. to 9s.
Coachsmiths	,,	7s. to 10s.

Wheelwrights	. . .	per diem	7s. to 10s.
Brickmakers (no demand)		,,	10s.
Butchers	. . .		6s. to 8s.
Bookbinders	. . .	,,	6s. to 9s.
Bakers	. . .		6s. to 9s.
Coopers	. . .	,,	6s. to 8s.
Watchmakers	. . .	,,	6s. 8d. to 10s.
Whitesmiths	.		7s. 6d. to 10s.
Shoemakers	.	,,	4s. 6d. to 7s. 6d.
Engineers	. . .	,,	10s. to 12s.
Cabinetmakers	.		5s. to 10s.
Brassfounders	. . .	,,	7s. to 10s.
Plumbers	. . .		9s.
Quarrymen	.	,,	9s.
General Labourers	. . .	,,	6s. to 9s.
Seamen	. . .	per month	£3 to £5

AGRICULTURAL LABOUR, &c.—

Farm Labourers	. .	Weekly, and found	15s. to 20s.
Ploughmen	. . .	,,	20s. to 22s. 6d.
Reapers	. . .	per annum	£40 to £45
Mowers	. . .	,,	£40 to £45
Threshers	. . .	,,	£40 to £45
Bush Carpenters	. .	Weekly, and found	15s. to 25s.
Bullock Drivers	. .	,,	20s.
Carters	. .		12s.

PASTORAL LABOUR—

Shepherds	. .	per annum	£30 to £45
Stock Keepers	. .	,,	£40 to £60
Hut Keepers	. . .	,,	£30 to £40
Generally Useful Men on Stations		,,	£30 to £52
Sheepwashers	. . .	per diem	6s. to 7s.
Shearers	. .	per 100 sheep sheared	17s. to 20s.

SERVANTS—MALES AND MARRIED COUPLES.

Married Couples without family	.	per annum	£52 to £75
Married Couples with family (no demand)		,,	£40 to £50
Married Couples with family of working boys		,,	£60 to £100
Men Cooks for Hotels	. .	,,	£52 to £100
Grooms	. .	,,	£35 to £60
Gardeners	. .	,,	£40 to £60
Ditto	. .	per diem	6s.

FEMALES—

Barmaids	. . .	per annum	£35 to £65
Cooks	.	,,	£30 to £78
Laundresses	. . .	,,	£30 to £52
General Servants			£20 to £40
Housemaids	. . .	,,	£20 to £40
Nursemaids	.		£20 to £40
Farm House Servants	. .	,,	£20 to £35
Dairy Women	. . .	,,	£26 to £35

OUR ANIMAL WORLD.

Australia has long been recognized as the home of the Kangaroo, and many of its genera are found in Queensland, such as the Great Kangaroo, Wallaby, Pademelon, Rock and Tree Wallaby, Nail-Tail, and Hare Kangaroo, and a couple of rabbit-like animals termed respectively Bettongs and Kangaroo Rats. Although, owing to an abundance of cattle suitable for food, as also to a greatly exaggerated idea of the "strong flavour" of the meat, none of these animals are eaten by colonists (unless it be by a well-seasoned "bushman"), to the aborigines no greater treat can be offered than the prospect of a feast of young wallaby or "possum." Another branch of the Marsupial order are the Phalangers, as represented by the "Flying Squirrel" (varying from the size of a large rabbit down to that of a mouse), the Opossum, the Cuzcos, the Ring-tailed 'Possum, and the "Native Bear," a somewhat strange and misleading name to the new-comer, since this tailless denizen never greatly exceeds the size of an ordinary organ-grinder's monkey, and is one of the most retiring of animals. The Bandicoot also belongs to the same natural order. Allied to these are the Carnivorous Marsupials, of which the Dasyurus, commonly called "Native Cat," is the only Queensland representative. Except for its destructive tendencies in the poultry yard, there is nothing to fear from this small although somewhat fierce animal. Many other members of the class Mammalia are found in our forests and scrubs—such as the Flying-Fox, Beaver-Rat, Bat, and Dingo—and in our seas, of which the Seals, Dugongs, and Porpoises are examples. Special reference must here be made to the Dingo, or Native Dog. As the name implies, the appearance of this animal is similar to that of a dog; a difference is, however, noticeable in the wild look of the eyes, in the characteristic "howl" of these animals when in search of food, and to the peculiar habit which they have of hunting in single file. Although great enemies to sheep and other small domestic animals, which they steal if opportunity offers, these animals are extremely afraid of man and have never been known to attack even children. In many parts of the Colony an animal is found which, although approaching the reptiles, is still a Marsupial, viz., the Spiny Ant-eater, dubbed "Porcupine" by Queenslanders, and a source of great amusement to the young in country districts on account of its ability to roll up in the form of a ball, when its numerous spines make it a nasty customer for dogs or men to meddle with. But possibly the most remarkable of all the lower animals is the "Duckbill," or Platypus. This interesting and harmless creature has the body of a mole, and a head terminating in the "bill" which has given it its popular name. Being amphibious, it is provided with webbed feet. A most peculiar fact in connexion with these creatures is that reproduction is effected by the laying of eggs, whilst the young, when hatched, are nourished by the mother's milk, thus identifying them with the Mammalia.

The BIRDS are too numerous to describe at length. For beauty, many of these—such as the Lyre Bird, Bower Bird, and Regent Bird—are unsurpassed in the world. In size, they vary from the tiny little "Diamond," of many hues, to the Brown Hawk, which soars proudly in search of its prey. Although a few of these are repulsive-looking, and others are destructive to poultry and lambs, we have none of the fierce birds of prey which in other lands are sometimes a menace even to human life. Amongst our avi-fauna is also found that one-time "rara avis," the black swan. A fair specimen of this essentially Australian bird may be seen in the Botanical Gardens of the capital. Another bird peculiar to our land is the "Laughing Jackass," a bird which cannot fail to attract the notice of any visitor who goes beyond the boundaries of the city. Even in the very midst of civilization its indescribable, gurgling, crescendo note may sometimes be heard, generally at sunrise or sunset; a half-weird, half-ludicrous intrusion on the haunts of men. Others of the Kingfisher family are beautifully clothed in the brightest of plumage, and frequent the neighbourhood of water, which the Laughing Jackass does not. Fowl of all sizes abound on our water holes, lakes, and at the mouths of our tidal streams; one of the most noticeable of these is the Pelican, and of course many more might be named. Altogether it is computed by authorities that we have some six or seven hundred different birds in the colony, presenting every variety of form, colour, and note. These have been ably dealt with in a work entitled 'Birds of Australia,' and also in the 'Aldine History of Queensland,' to which the inquirer is referred.

The Native Birds' Protection Association of Queensland issue in a convenient form particulars of the proclamation *re* native birds, dated July 18th, 1894 :—

NATIVE BIRDS ENTIRELY PROTECTED.

From January 1st to December 31st in each year, inclusive.

Black cockatoos
Cassowaries
Cranes
Cuckoos
Dollar birds
Doves
Dragoon birds (Pittas)
Emus
Finches
Grass parrots

Great kingfishers (laughing jackasses)
Herons
Honeyeaters
Ibis
Kingfishers
Kites
Larks
Land Curlews
Magpies (organ birds)
Magpie larks

Martens
Minah birds
Moreporks, or owls
Nankeen kestrels
Nightjars
Pheasants
Robins
Spoonbills
Wagtails
Woodpeckers
Wrens

NATIVE BIRDS' CLOSE SEASON.

From November 1st to April 30th following, inclusive.

Bitterns
Black swans
Bronzewing and wild pigeons
Brown hawks
Bustards or plain turkeys
Curlews
Dottrels

All insectivorous birds
Landrails (all species)
Lyre birds
Native companions
Plover (all species)
Quails
Regent birds
Rifle birds

Satin birds and all bower birds
Tallegallas or scrub turkeys
All waders
Water rails
Wild ducks of any species
Wild geese

Snakes have been briefly referred to, but I would like to remark on the really extraordinary immunity from serious cases of snake-bite which is here enjoyed. Fairly often as I have come into contact with and destroyed these creatures, it has always been apparent that their fear of man has been great, and if this fact were only now widely recognized we should no longer be able to dub any incredulous tale a "snake yarn," since the exaggerated reports of encounters with snakes, &c., which find such ready credence at the hands of some, would die a natural death. That there are a few venomous snakes no one will deny; but so there are in Southern and Central Europe, and even in Great Britain. The Carpet Snake, the largest of our snakes, is entirely non-venomous, and subsists on the smaller marsupials, birds, and poultry, but—in common with several other of these reptiles—when at bay they will bite severely, and may even cause a dangerous wound under certain conditions. The death adder, as its name implies, the black snake, and the large variety of brown snake (not the copper-coloured tree snake) are among the most venomous we have. To any one, however, who is provided with a stick (or switch in preference) even these need give no uneasiness, as one good blow across the back will disable the snake, and render his despatch an easy matter.

Fish, Shell-fish, and Sponges abound in our waters; these will be found described in Mr. D. O'Connor's paper on page 106.

INDEX.

I

Queensland

LAND SELECTION

IN

QUEENSLAND.

"THE LAND ACT, 1897."

The Colony is, as far as necessary, divided into Land Agents' Districts, in each of which there is a Public Land Office and a Government Land Agent, to whom all inquiries respecting the situation, quality, rents. and prices of lands available for selection in his district should be addressed, and from whom plans can be obtained. Connected with the Survey Department, in Brisbane, there is an office for the exhibition and sale of maps, and there full information respecting lands open for selection throughout the Colony may be had.

The several modes in which land may be acquired are (1) by Agricultural Selection, *i.e*, Agricultural Farms and Agricultural Homesteads; (2) Grazing Selections, *i.e.,* Grazing Farms and Grazing Homesteads; (3) Scrub Selections; and (4) Unconditional Selections. The more accessible lands near lines of railway, centres of population, and navigable waters, are set apart for agricultural selection in areas up to 1,280 acres, while opportunities of acquiring grazing selections in areas up to 20,000 acres are given over a great extent of Queensland territory within accessible distance of the seaboard and the various lines of railway.

Except in the case of Scrub Selections and Unconditional Selections, no person who is not a British subject by birth or naturalization, or who is under the age of sixteen years, or who seeks to acquire the land as the agent or servant or trustee of another, will be allowed to select. A married woman is not competent to select an Agricultural Homestead or a Grazing Homestead, unless the disqualification is removed by the Land Court in the case of a married woman who has obtained an order for judicial separation or an order protecting her separate property, or who is living apart from her husband.

Applications for selections must be made in the prescribed form, in triplicate, and be lodged with the Land Agent for the district within which the land is situated. They must be signed by the applicant, but may be lodged in the Land Office by his duly constituted attorney, and must be accompanied by a deposit of a year's rent and one-fifth of the survey fee. Applications lodged prior to the time proclaimed as that at which land is to be open for selection are regarded as simultaneous with those lodged at the time of opening.

Where land is open for different modes of selection alternately, priority among simultaneous applications for the same land is given to an application for it as an Agricultural Homestead as against an application for it as an Agricultural Farm; to an application for it as an Agricultural Farm as against an application for it as an Unconditional Selection: and if the land is open for Grazing Selection, to an application for it as a Grazing Homestead as against an application for it as a Grazing Farm.

Priority among simultaneous applications for the same land by the same mode of selection is determined by lot. unless in the case of simultaneous applications for the same land as a Grazing Selection or an Unconditional Selection a higher rental is tendered than that proclaimed. In that event the highest tender secures priority.

When an application has been accepted by the Land Commissioner and approved by the Court, and the applicant has paid for any improvements that may be on the land, he becomes entitled to receive a licence to occupy the land in the case of an Agricultural Selection or a Grazing Selection, or a lease in the case of a Scrub Selection or an Unconditional Selection. Within six months after the issue of a licence the selector must commence to occupy the land, and must thereafter continue to occupy it in the manner prescribed.

AGRICULTURAL SELECTIONS.

AGRICULTURAL FARMS.

The largest area that may be acquired by any one person as an Agricultural Farm is 1,280 acres. If the same person is the selector of both an Agricultural Farm and an Agricultural Homestead, the joint area must not exceed 1,280 acres. The purchasing price may range from 10s. an acre upwards, as may be declared by proclamation. The term is twenty years. The annual rent is one-fortieth of the purchasing price, and the payments are credited as part of the price.

The land must be continuously occupied by the selector residing personally on it or by his manager or agent doing so. Within five years from the issue of the licence to occupy, or such extended time, not exceeding two years, as the Court may allow, the selector must enclose the land with a good and substantial fence, or make substantial and permanent improvements on it equal in value to such a fence. On the completion of the improvements the selector becomes entitled to a lease of the farm, and may thereafter mortgage it; or, with the permission of the Minister, may subdivide or transfer it; or, with the approval of the Court, may underlet it.

After the improvements have been effected, any lessee (whether he acquired by selection or transfer) who has held the farm for five years and has duly fulfilled the condition of occupation, may pay the part of the purchasing price then remaining unpaid and obtain a deed of grant in fee-simple. After ten years of the term have elapsed the purchase may be completed by the then registered lessee irrespective of the time he has held it.

AGRICULTURAL HOMESTEADS.

Land open to selection as Agricultural Farms is not available for Agricultural Homesteads unless so proclaimed. The area allowed to be selected as an Agricultural Homestead varies with the quality of the land. If the price at which any land (open to both modes of selection) is available to Agricultural Farm selection is not less than £1 an acre, 160 acres is allowed for a Homestead; if its price as a Farm would be less than £1 but not less than 15s., then 320 acres can be taken as a Homestead; and if its price as a Farm would be less than 15s. an acre, then 640 acres is allowed for a Homestead. The price for a Homestead is 2s. 6d. an acre, the annual rent 3d. an acre, and the term ten years.

The land must be continuously occupied by the selector residing personally thereon.

Within five years from the issue of the licence to occupy, or such extended time, not exceeding two years, as the Court may allow, the selector must enclose the land with a good and substantial fence, or make substantial and permanent improvements on it equal in value to such a fence. On the completion of the improvements the selector becomes entitled to a lease.

At any time after five years from the commencement of the term, on the selector proving that the conditions have been duly performed and that the sum expended in improvements on the land has been at the rate of 10s., 5s., or 2s. 6d. an acre respectively, according to the quality of the land, he may pay up the remaining rents, so as to make his total payments equal to 2s. 6d. an acre, and obtain a deed of grant of the land in fee-simple.

The selectors of a group of two or more Agricultural Homesteads may associate together for mutual assistance, and on making proof of *bona fides* to the Commissioner, may receive from him a Special Licence enabling not less than one-half of the whole number to perform the conditions of occupation and improvement for the group. The residence may be upon any one or more of the Homesteads, and if more than 10s. has been expended in improvements on any Homestead while the Special Licence is in force with respect to it, the surplus may be attributed to the others.

GRAZING SELECTIONS.

GRAZING FARMS.

The maximum area allowed to be acquired by any one person as a Grazing Farm is 20,000 acres. The term may be 14, 21, or 28 years, as the proclamation opening the land to selection may declare. The annual rent for the first period of seven years may range from ½d. per acre upwards, as may be proclaimed or tendered. The rent for each subsequent period of seven years will be determined by the Court, but it cannot be decreased at any re-assessment, nor can it be increased by more than one-half of the rent for the period immediately preceding.

A Grazing Farm must be continuously occupied by the selector residing personally on it, or by his manager or agent doing so.

Within three years from the issue of the licence to occupy, or such extended time, not exceeding two years, as the Court may allow, the selector must enclose the land with a good and substantial fence, and must keep it so fenced during the whole of the term. In the case of two or more contiguous farms not exceeding in the aggregate 20,000 acres, the Court may by Special Licence permit the selectors to fence only the outside boundaries of the whole area. If the Proclamation declaring the land open for selection so prescribed, the enclosing fence must be of such character as to prevent the passage of rabbits.

In the case of a group of contiguous Grazing Farms not exceeding eight in number, or 200 square miles in total area, and which are subject to the condition of special fencing just mentioned, the Court may by Special Licence permit the enclosure of the whole area with a fence of such character as to prevent the passage of rabbits, instead of requiring each farm to be separately enclosed.

The selectors of a group of two or more Grazing Farms, the area of none of which exceeds 2,560 acres, may associate together for mutual assistance, and on making proof of *bona fides* to the Commissioner, may receive from him a Special Licence enabling not less than one-half of the whole number, by their personal residence on some one or more of the farms, to perform the condition of occupation in respect of all the farms.

When a Grazing Farm is enclosed in the manner required, the selector becomes entitled to a lease of it, and may thereafter mortgage it; or, with the permission of the Minister, may subdivide or transfer it; or, with the approval of the Court, may underlet it.

GRAZING HOMESTEADS.

Lands open for selection as Grazing Farms must also be open for selection as Grazing Homesteads, and at the same rental and for the same term of lease. As already stated, an application to select as a Grazing Homestead takes precedence of a simultaneous application to select the same land as a Grazing Farm. The conditions and other provisions above mentioned in respect of Grazing Farms are applicable also to Grazing Homesteads, with the following exceptions :—

(1.) During the first five years of the term of a Grazing Homestead the condition of occupation must be performed by the continuous personal residence of the selector on the land.

(2.) Before the expiration of five years from the commencement of the term, or the death of the original lessee, whichever first happens, a Grazing Homestead is not capable of being mortgaged, assigned, or transferred.

SCRUB SELECTIONS.

Lands entirely or extensively overgrown by scrub may be opened for selection as Scrub Selections up to 10,000 acres in area and with a term of thirty years. These are classed according to the proportion covered by scrub, and for periods varying from five to twenty years, according to the classification; no rent is chargeable. During this first period the selector must clear the whole of the scrub in equal proportions each year, and must keep it cleared, and must enclose the selection with a good and substantial fence. The annual rent payable for the subsequent periods ranges from ½d. to 1d. per acre. A negotiable lease is issued to the selector when his application has been approved by the Court.

UNCONDITIONAL SELECTIONS.

The greatest area allowed to be acquired by any one person as an Unconditional Selection in the same District is 1,280 acres; the price per acre ranges from 13s. 4d. upwards, and is payable in twenty annual instalments. As the term implies, no other conditions than the payment of the purchase-money are attached to this mode of selection, the personal disqualifications imposed in connection with other modes being also removed. A negotiable lease for the term of twenty years is issued to the selector when his application to select has been approved by the Court. A deed of grant may be obtained at any time on payment of the balance of the purchasing price.

OCCUPATION LICENCES.

In addition to the several modes of acquiring land by selection above described, provision is made for granting Occupation Licences without conditions other than the payment of rent in respect of lands not held under any other tenure. The tenancy of an Occupation Licen   year to year, and expires on December 31, but may be

renewed by payment on or before September 30 of another year's rent. A licence in determinable at the end of any year by six months' notice previously given to the licence by the Minister. Land held under Occupation Licence may be opened for selection at any time without notice to the licensee, who may, however, continue to occupy it until it is selected. Upon the latter event his interest in the land ceases.

SPECIAL RIGHT OF PRIORITY IN CERTAIN CASES.

Before land becomes available for acquisition under any tenure, it must be so proclaimed in the *Government Gazette*. Right of priority is given in cases of Agricultural Homesteads and Occupation Licences, where it results from a special request that the land is opened to application. In every instance the request must be made through the Land Commissioner of the district in which the land is situated. If for an Agricultural Homestead, it must be accompanied by a deposit equal to 3*d.* an acre. In on the day when the land is declared to be open to selection or licence, and at the time appointed for the receipt of applications, the person at whose request it was so opened lodges an application in proper form, he has a prior claim to the land over other simultaneous applicants. His right of priority does not, however, extend beyond the earliest time when the land thus becomes available. When priority is not secured at

50m.-1,'69 (J56463 8) 2878—8A,1

Lightning Source UK Ltd.
Milton Keynes UK
UKHW04f1414250818
327788UK00016B/1539/P